The Bay of Pigs
and the CIA

The Bay of Pigs and the CIA

by Juan Carlos Rodríguez

State Security Historical Research Center (CIHSE) Cuba

Translated by Mary Todd

OCEAN PRESS

Melbourne • New York

Cover design by David Spratt

ISBN 1-875284-98-2

First printed 1999

Printed in Australia

Published by Ocean Press
Australia: GPO Box 3279, Melbourne, Victoria 3001, Australia
   • Fax: (61-3) 9372 1765 • E-mail: ocean_press@msn.com.au
USA: PO Box 834, Hoboken, NJ 07030 • Fax: 201-617 0203

Library of Congress Catalog Card No: 99-070344

OCEAN PRESS DISTRIBUTORS
United States: LPC/InBook,
      1436 West Randolph St, Chicago, IL 60607, USA
Canada: Login Brothers,
      324 Salteaux Cres, Winnipeg, Manitoba R3J 3T2, Canada
Britain and Europe: Global Book Marketing,
      38 King Street, London, WC2E 8JT, UK
Australia and New Zealand: Astam Books,
      57-61 John Street, Leichhardt, NSW 2040, Australia
Cuba and Latin America: Ocean Press,
      Calle 21 #406, Vedado, Havana, Cuba
Southern Africa: Phambili Agencies,
      PO Box 28680, Kensington 2101, Johannesburg, South Africa

Contents

Publisher's note

The manuscript of *The Bay of Pigs and the CIA* was completed in 1994. The publisher would like to acknowledge the contribution of both Mary Todd, the translator of this English-language edition, and Mirta Muñiz, of the Havana office of Ocean Press.

Introduction

by José Ramón Fernández

The Bay of Pigs and the CIA is an account which explores the origins, development and climax of an era when the United States sought to wipe out the Cuban Revolution. This offensive resulted in the defeat of Attack Brigade 2506 on the sands of the Bay of Pigs (Girón Beach).

The work is based on meticulous investigation in which unpublished, little-known sources are utilized. The most impressive aspect of this book may well be its portrayal of the magnitude of the CIA project. This CIA project encompassed every detail — military, economic and political — of the preparations for and waging of an insurgent war in the mountains; subversive destabilization and terrorism; the psychological climate; the recruiting and training centers and preparation of those forces for a limited conventional confrontation, which included such sophisticated details as mosquito-net hats to protect the invaders' faces; the technical means, composition and structure of the forces; and the ideological preparation of the invading forces.

The enemies of the Cuban Revolution — more concerned with blaming their defeat on mistakes and deficiencies of the U.S. Administrations which were involved than in seeking the true causes of the disaster — have hidden the magnitude of the project.

The author delves extensively into what the Cuban Revolution did in order to confront and defeat the enemy's plans. He pays particular attention to its actions in fighting the counterrevolutionary bands in the Escambray Mountains; countering the CIA's penetration of counterrevolutionary organizations, both those in Cuba and in exile in the United States; countering the acts of sabotage, which included the burning down of some of the largest stores and several factories; and frustrating the assassination attempts aimed against Fidel Castro, which reached a peak in the period leading up to the Bay of Pigs attack. Juan Carlos Rodríguez also examines, in detail, the outstanding effort of Fidel Castro in countering the enemy's psychological operations that were aimed at intimidating the Cuban people. In those operations, all the means, methods and techniques of the propaganda arsenal of psychological warfare were employed, including Radio Swan and unethical rumors — unprecedentedly vicious — such as those behind the "legal custody" operation, which sought to destroy Cuban family ties.

From the strategic and tactical point of view, the operation was not the error it is frequently portrayed. The place selected for the invaders' landing had an airstrip and several buildings and was separated from terra firma by a swamp crossed by only three roads; they dropped paratroopers there to guard those access points. The invaders were well organized and well armed and had good support — but they weren't fighting for a just cause. They lacked the ardor, courage, staunchness, boldness and will to win which inspired the revolutionary forces.

This explains the scope of the victory of the Cuban people, which surely surprised the U.S. Government. That victory was explained only by the courage of a people which saw the revolution of January 1, 1959, as a real possibility for determining its own destiny and, as a result, donned militia uniforms of blue shirts and olive green pants and berets and set out to halt the invaders.

The people who acclaimed Fidel Castro on his triumphant tour of nearly all the island in the first few days of January 1959 were convinced of the validity of their cause and took up arms on April 17, 1961, determined to confront and beat back the aggressors. In that short period of time, the Cuban Revolution's achievements — especially the leading role of Fidel Castro — had put down deep roots in the Cuban people. They identified with the concepts of national sovereignty, social justice, equality and dignity. The Cuban Revolution had solved the problem of agrarian reform; taken sure, tangible steps toward ending racial discrimination and discrimination against women; and guaranteed that the vast masses of the people had access to jobs, education, public health, sports and culture. The people rejected all vestiges of corruption.

The author's account of the changes wrought in the Zapata Swamp (future theater of operations of the Bay of Pigs attack) starting in 1959, not only brings out their aesthetic and political value but also shows the socioeconomic achievements attained in that short time.

"The Cuban people were at the peak of their patriotism and revolutionary fervor, and their support for the Revolution and its leader, Fidel Castro, had reached heights never before attained in the hemisphere," as the author points out. That was the main cause for the mercenaries' defeat. "Get up; the invasion's started! The Americans are attacking! They're in the swamp!" Word flew from house to house in the town of Jagüey Grande, the nearest to the scene of the landing. The people thought U.S. Marines had invaded, and they gathered at militia headquarters, the town hall and the Rebel Army's garrison, asking for weapons and instructions.

The millions of Cubans who, like those in Jagüey Grande, were preparing to fight, had good reason for what they were doing. In addition, unlike the people in other countries, our people were both armed and organized when the attack took place. Moreover, not even the need to defend the Revolution against that great danger led Fidel to make concessions. It wasn't easy to be a militia. You had to earn that right.

I was at the Managua School of Cadets, at the mouth of the La Magdalena River, on the southern slope of the Sierra Maestra Mountains. From there, we climbed Turquino Peak. We had been ordered to climb it 20 times. When we were half way through our task, I was ordered to go to Havana and see Fidel Castro. He told me to look for a place at which to set up a school that would train a large group of workers, union leaders and students selected to lead the militia battalions. When I got in contact with that first group, its members had already, on Fidel's instructions, climbed Turquino Peak five times.

A few weeks after the course was set up in the Militia Leaders' School in Matanzas, militia battalions began to be organized. Fidel sent for me to take charge of directing the training of the battalions in the capital. He asked me how I was going to test their staunchness and determination to be incorporated into the militia. I remember that Fidel proposed that they walk from Managua to Santa Cruz del Norte and back. We checked on the map and measured the distance. The round trip would be over 100 kilometers. You needed to be in excellent shape and well trained to make such a journey. It was almost impossible. Finally, we chose the route from Managua to San Antonio de las Vegas along the Batabanó highway and from there to La Ruda, to the Central Highway, San José, Cuatro Caminos and back to Managua. That was the origin of the famous 64-kilometer test.

The 111th Battalion was the first to pass the test and graduate from the school. Each militia was given a brochure listing the various points along the route, to be stamped at each one. There was a terrible downpour that night. Fidel joined the militia for a part of their trek in the rain. The next morning, nobody returned at the estimated time. We had supposed that they would begin to come in shortly after dawn, but dawn came — and nobody arrived. The first ones arrived at around 10:00 a.m., and then a small trickle came in at 11:00, noon and

1:00 — all exhausted. Later on, those who couldn't pass the test were brought in by a motley collection of vehicles.

At around 4:00 p.m., I called the command cadres together in a classroom, and we analyzed and criticized the trek. Suddenly the door opened, and Fidel came in. I explained what we were doing. He told me to order the battalion to form ranks, and I did so with those who had returned. Some had more energy than others. Fidel spoke to them. He told those who hadn't passed the 64-kilometer test that they would have to pass it to join the battalion but that, if they didn't, they could be volunteers. He asked those who had come in first to stand to one side and told them that they were the "light combat company," a shock force whose members would have a different purpose and different weapons than the others. In closing, he told those who hadn't passed the test that they could leave if they wished to and that, if they stayed, they would have to repeat the trek. Nobody left. "When will we do it?" he asked. Every group has extremists, and that group was no exception. "Today!" many of them replied excitedly. It was finally decided to do it two days later. And all of them passed.

While taking the course, the militia didn't live or sleep in buildings. They had hammocks slung between trees; cooked over camp fires; used rudimentary latrines dug in the ground; had no running water — and, therefore, no showers — and had no light other than the moon and stars. When it rained, everything was wet and muddy. They did military exercises all day and guard duty at night. It wasn't easy. And every battalion had 995 members.

At the end of the course, which lasted two weeks, each militia was given a green beret, and these became symbols. The beret presentation ceremony was a time of celebration. The militias became a huge school of revolutionaries, and the command cadres came from the anonymity of their ranks, not castes. They were industrial workers, farmers, intellectuals and students.

The soldiers and officers of the Rebel Army and of the Revolutionary National Police also had to pass very difficult tests. Skilled in guerrilla warfare, they had barely begun to master the new weapons and the art of conventional warfare when the landing took place. The tank troops learned how to load their guns while on the way to the combat area. Those few pilots we had took off in planes which they themselves described as "homeland or death" affairs, hovering between just good enough and too bad to fly, which were kept aloft thanks to the inventiveness of the mechanics and courage of the pilots. The soldiers in the main columns were mobilized constantly.

All of those tests, that concept of Fidel's — which came from the Sierra Maestra — contributed greatly to the high morale in the militias and the Revolutionary Armed Forces (which had emerged from the Rebel Army). This was especially so for those from the city who had never lived in such difficult, rustic conditions — out in the open, in the rain and dew, day and night. That morale was of decisive importance in the defeat of the bands of armed counterrevolutionaries and of the mercenaries who came on the Bay of Pigs invasion. It was also important during the October 1962 Missile Crisis. It has been repeated over and over again and has become one of our people's traditions.

It is a passion like that which has been demonstrated recently, like that which is especially seen in the face of a real, imminent danger — like the one at the Bay of Pigs, where the people's victory amazed the world and preserved the Cuban Revolution. That spirit is the only explanation for how the Cuban people managed to defeat the enormous plan of aggression described in this book.

J. R. Fernández
Havana

H Hour

The rubber raft left the speedboat, and its occupants — four frogmen and their commanding officer, Grayston Lynch ("Gray") — silently headed toward the coast. They wore black swimsuits, undershirts and rubber sandals; their faces, too, were blackened.

They paddled far to the right, where a flimsy wall would hide them from sight, even though intelligence reports stated that the area was practically uninhabited and that the few Cubans on shore were construction workers who were putting up a tourist center — and, since it was Sunday, would be far away, in their own homes.

The information was correct.

Soon afterwards, when they had seen that the bottom was around two fathoms down, the four swimmers submerged. Grayston Lynch remained lying on the raft, with the muzzle of his Browning automatic rifle sticking out over the front.

The frogmen spread out and began swimming toward the beach, observing the bottom, looking for obstructions. Those obstacles which rose to within eight feet of the surface were marked with buoys, and the best places for beaching the LCU and LCVP landing craft which would carry the armored equipment, the heavy weapons and the troops were marked with position lights that were visible only from the sea, where the fleet waited.

It was H Hour of D Day. Attack Brigade 2506 was preparing to make an amphibious and air landing to establish a beachhead on an inhospitable strip of terra firma with lush vegetation that was cut off from the rest of the island of Cuba by a vast swamp. They would set up a base there from which to carry out land and air operations against Fidel Castro's government. Between D+3 and D+5 Days (three and five days after D Day), they would set up a provisional government and ask the Western nations, particularly in Latin America, for official recognition and military support. For that purpose, they had publicly announced the formation of the Cuban Revolutionary Council (CRC) a month earlier.

José Miró Cardona, a political figure who had not been involved with the Batista dictatorship and had held the post of Prime Minister in the January 1959 revolutionary government, was President of the CRC. Half a dozen other figures from the Cuban political scene were included in the executive, which was considered the nucleus of the provisional government.

Even though the U.S. Government was in charge of the entire operation, measures had been taken to make it seem an action of Cuban exiles who were opposed to Fidel Castro. That was the basic stipulation.

Before approving the plan, President John F. Kennedy had insisted that there should be no overt participation by the Armed Forces of the United States. His decision was determined by the balance of forces between East and West at that time. The U.S. President knew that if he authorized intervention by the Marines or Air Force, he couldn't consider defeat. It would probably mean a massive attack on Cuba, which could lead the United States into a war with the Soviet Union or perhaps the loss of Berlin — and all this without ruling out action by the Soviet Union anywhere else in the world. Moreover, no less important, an attack on Cuba would imply bitter resistance by the supporters of the Cuban Revolution, who, according to U.S. intelligence estimates, constituted the overwhelming majority of the Cuban population.

Keeping Kennedy's directive in mind, Operation Pluto had been drawn up and approved with the expectation that it could be carried out successfully without massive U.S. assistance. The landing was inspired by the attack on Iwo Jima, the most complex amphibious operation in the entire war in the Pacific, and by that on Inchon, in North Korea. There, the U.S. troops had encountered a coast without ports, where they had landed on beaches. It wasn't by chance, therefore, that Brigade 2506 was commanded by U.S. Marine Corps Colonel Jack Hawkins ("Frank"), one of the heroes of that battle.

Unlike the beaches of Iwo Jima, which had been infested with machine-gun nests, those of the Bay of Pigs were practically unprotected. The Cubans knew that an invasion was in the works. It isn't possible to keep the preparations for a conventional, frontal, massive attack completely hidden. But the leaders of the Cuban Government didn't know where, when or how the invasion would take place. Because of this, they had to spread their forces out along the borders of an island with 5,746 kilometers of coastline. Moreover, the Attack Brigade had had another piece of luck when, several days earlier, Commander Fidel Castro had ordered a battalion of militia to go to the place that had been chosen for the landing, but difficulties and lack of military organization had kept the order from being carried out. Girón Beach, the main beachhead, was defended only by half a dozen charcoal makers who were members of the local militia. The closest military forces of any consequence were at the Australia Sugar Mill, 30 kilometers from Larga Beach and 70 kilometers from Girón Beach. The Brigade's staff were informed of this during the final briefing. On the decks of the ships which had brought them from the Atlantic coast of Nicaragua to southern Cuba, the military chiefs kept an eye on the luminous markers near the obstacles and landing points. They formed a straight line parallel to the coast, bright as shining stars.

The invaders felt confident and safe. Their ships were neither fragile nor poorly armed. The flotilla which had brought them consisted of five merchant ships carrying 36 aluminum outboard motorboats 18 feet long, two LCI infantry landing craft that had been reconditioned as heavily armed escorts, three landing craft utilities and four LCVPs which had been taken in close to the coast by the *San Marcos*, a transport-landing ship dock belonging to the U.S. Navy. The transport ship had carried out the maneuver two hours earlier in excellent style.

It was the landing ship dock (LSD) *San Marcos* moving up the column of invasion ships rapidly, exactly on time. By the time the ships stopped, the LSD already had "ballast down": its crew had pumped in water to flood the well deck where all the three landing craft utility (LCU's) and the four landing craft vehicles and personnel (LCVP's) with their tanks, trucks and other equipment were waiting. As soon as the water was up to the level of the sea outside, the LSD opened its rear doors and the seven small vessels steamed out, manned by the CIA instructors who had trained its Cuban crews in Vieques.

An eighth craft appeared on Gray's radar, also according to plan. It was a landing craft mechanized (LCM) with an American Navy crew. It headed for the *Caribe*, picked up Silvio Pérez and his 43 Brigade men and then moved along the next column of LCU's and LCVP's. At each landing craft, the CIA crew got off and the Cuban crew and vehicle drivers got on...

Again the Cubans were impressed by the precision of American seamanship and the LSD's further visible demonstration of close Navy support. Most of the men had seen the *San Marcos* only as an enormous blacked-out shadow, but its size and distinctive sounds told them that it was an American mother ship... Captain Tirado of the *Río Escondido*, who had been in radio contact with the LSD, felt good when an American voice wished him good luck.[1]

After receiving the order from Grayston Lynch (the U.S. officer who remained on the coast), Commander José Pérez San Román, a Cuban exile, instructed his men to jump into the vessels that would take them to Girón Beach. He was excited. "It's just like in war movies," he thought.

The first men began to go down the ropes. In the next few hours, they would be followed by five M-42 Walker tanks; 11 two-and-a-half-ton trucks armed with 12.7-mm machine guns; 30 81-mm and 106.7-mm mortars; 28 recoilless 57- and 75-mm cannon; 50 88.9-mm rocket launchers; 47 bazookas; 46 .50- and .30- caliber machine guns; 9,000 M-1, Garand, Browning automatic and M-3 rifles and submachine guns; eight tons of high explosives; communications equipment, including field telephones and switchboards; 38,000 gallons of fuel for vehicles and 17,000 gallons of aviation fuel; 150 tons of ammunition; 24,000 pounds of food, together with plenty of drinking water; 1.5 tons of white phosphorus; 700 air-to-ground missiles; 500 fragmentation bombs; 300 gallons of aviation oil; 20 tons of .50-caliber ammunition; 10 quarter-ton jeeps; a five-ton tank truck; a tractor; a tractor crane; and 13 tows. Each soldier carried enough ammunition to last him three days.

The paratroopers carried a supplementary load. Later, when analyzing the causes of the defeat, General Maxwell Taylor said that the invaders carried a lot of supplies. At the urging of Lieutenant Colonel Hawkins, the plan's organizers had seen to it that there would be three days' worth of supplies of all kinds at the beachhead before the general unloading began.

In six hours, when dawn broke on April 17, 1961, the battalion of paratroopers would be dropped on the northern border of the swamp, and the roads which crossed it would be cut to keep Cuban troops from using them. It would be equivalent to establishing two more beachheads on the other side of the swamp. The paratroopers would establish immediate contact with the troops that had landed.

The operations plan called for three squadrons of B-26 light bombers to attack three Cuban airfields on D-2 Day, two days before H Hour, to destroy the planes while they were still on the ground. However, just in case there were any surprises, the *Blagar* and *Barbara J.* escort ships were armed with 75-mm recoilless cannon, and every

---

[1] Peter Wyden, *Bay of Pigs: The Untold Story*, 216-7.

ship in the fleet had .50-caliber machine guns mounted in its bow and stern and on its port and starboard sides.

Between 1500 and 1700 hours on the first day of the landing, two B-26s would arrive at the occupied airport to provide air support. Since they would be operating from the beachhead, they wouldn't need stores of additional fuel and would have tail guns for fighting enemy interceptor-fighter planes.

Beginning on D+1 Day, daily reconnaissance flights would be made along the Cienfuegos-Aguada de Pasajeros-Jagüey Grande line (the towns closest to the landing area) to harass and destroy military targets.

The planes would also patrol the area between Havana and Jagüey Grande, along the Havana-Santa Clara-Cienfuegos line, along the Cienfuegos-Manicaragua-Topes de Collantes line, between Havana and Pinar del Río and between Holguín and Cienfuegos, to keep military forces from being brought into the landing area.

To carry out its missions, Brigade 2506's Tactical Air Force had 16 B-26 light bombers. In addition to being a kind of plane which private citizens could buy — helping to provide some cover for the air force being assembled — they were the same kind of bomber used in Cuba. Each plane had a crew of two. The tail gunner position had been eliminated to leave space for extra fuel, to increase the planes' radius of action. Their main base, Happy Valley, was in Puerto Cabezas, Nicaragua, some 580 miles (two hours and 50 minutes flying time) from the Bay of Pigs. Each plane would be able to remain over Cuban territory for an hour to an hour and a half.

The Tactical Air Force also had six C-54 — a military version of the Douglas DC-4 — paramilitary special planes without any ident-ification (no serial numbers on their engines and no manufacturer's markings), equipped with state-of-the-art electronic devices, and six C-46s.

Those transport planes would drop the paratroopers in position. The Tactical Air Force had 61 pilots of Cuban origin, plus navigators, radio operators and maintenance crews. Half a dozen mechanics were on board the landing craft; they would work on the planes which landed at the Girón Beach airport.

Six U.S. advisers had stayed with the pilots throughout all the months of training; others had passed through, on rotation. Colonel Stanley W. Berli, of the U.S. Air Force, was in charge of the force's operations.

The previous afternoon, at the strong urging of Secretary of State Dean Rusk, President Kennedy had cancelled the second attack on Cuban airfields, which had been planned for dawn of that day.

Photos taken by U-2 spy planes showed that only eight planes — a T-33, two B-26s, a DC-3, an F-47, a C-47, an AT-6 and a Catalina — had been destroyed or damaged during the attack on Saturday, April 15. The Revolutionary Air Force still had some operational capability.

The second air attack — now called off — was to have destroyed the remaining enemy planes on the ground.

The mission was really extremely difficult. Those in charge of the operation knew that the first attack was the main one and that there was no reason for thinking that, once the airfields' defenses had been reinforced, the revolutionary planes could be destroyed during the second attack. On Saturday, April 15, and Sunday, April 16, three new batteries of antiaircraft guns had been installed at San Antonio, the most important airport. The planes were camouflaged and scattered. Their pilots remained under the plane's wings in a state of maximum alert.

Since the first attack, which had the benefit of the surprise factor, had proved ineffective, it was too much to suppose that the second would be entirely successful.

The Plans Department of the U.S. Central Intelligence Agency had assured them that between 2,500 and 3,000 activists on the island were organized in opposition to the Cuban Government. Since mid-February, 35 of the CIA's best agents of Cuban origin, who had been trained in the jungles of Panama and Guatemala, had been infiltrated into Cuba to train those activists in the use of the most modern explosives and other weapons, to organize the airlifting in of war matériel and to advise on the most important acts of sabotage to be carried out in support of the invasion.

Members of the underground organizations knew that the United States was preparing an invasion of Cuba, and they had the means needed to support it. To guarantee the people's collaboration, or at least get them to reject revolutionary ideas, a campaign of psychological warfare had been drawn up to be broadcast over radio stations dedicated to that purpose. One of them, Radio Swan — Radio Free Cuba — had gone on the air clearly, powerfully and confidently 11 months earlier. David A. Phillips, one of the CIA's top propaganda experts, headed the project.

The radio station broadcast false reports about legions of insurgents who didn't exist and battles which had never taken place.

In addition, it exhorted the people to carry out acts of sabotage and spread all kinds of rumors.

For the underground organizations as well as for the leaders of the Cuban Revolution, the bombings of the airfields 48 hours earlier had unmistakably indicated that an invasion was imminent. A message soon to be broadcast over Radio Swan would be the signal for the uprising, which had been prepared for so long. The message would say:

Alert! Alert! Look well at the rainbow. The fish will rise very soon. Chico is in the house. Visit him. The sky is blue. Place a notice in the tree. The tree is green and brown. The letters arrived well. The letters are white. The fish will not take much time to rise.

The fish is red.[2]

Another message would be broadcast at 3:44 a.m., directed at the Cuban Revolutionary Armed Forces:

Take up strategic positions that control roads and railroads! Make prisoners of or shoot those who refuse to obey orders!... All planes must stay on the ground. See that no Fidelist plane takes off. Destroy its radios; destroy its tail; break its instruments; and puncture its fuel tanks! Refuse to give service! Inform your friends that freedom and honor await those who join us, as death will overtake the traitors who do not![3]

That was the last effort to neutralize the Cuban Rebel Army.

An estimated 300 insurgents still remained in the Escambray Mountains, though their possibilities were limited — only recently, the Cuban Government had launched an offensive against them from which they hadn't recovered. Other groups of insurgents were still active, waiting for the invasion, in Oriente, Camagüey, Matanzas and Pinar del Río provinces. According to reports, a group of 80 men operated near Jagüey Grande, 30 kilometers from the landing area, and there were others in Cárdenas and Colón. In the coastal cities of Cienfuegos and Trinidad, forces hostile to the government were expected to cooperate with the Brigade as soon as the opportunity arose. They were to destroy the main railway and highway bridges in

---

[2] John Bartlow Martin, *Adlai Stevenson and the World.*
[3] David Wise and Thomas Ross, *The Invisible Government,* 64; Jon Elliston, *On U.S. Propaganda and the Bay of Pigs Invasion: A Chronology,* Cuba Documentation Project, National Security Archives.

and around Havana, Matanzas, Jovellanos, Colón, Santa Clara and Cienfuegos, to cut off the landing area.

In spite of its efforts to keep the people from supporting the Revolution, the CIA acknowledged in its directives that Fidel Castro had the broad support of the Cuban people. On March 10, Sherman Kent, Director of the CIA's National Estimates Board, had sent Director Allen Dulles a secret memorandum in which, commenting that Fidel Castro seemed to be growing steadily stronger, not weaker, he warned that they shouldn't count on much support for the invasion inside Cuba.

The assassination of Fidel Castro was given top priority. Mafia contacts had smuggled several capsules containing synthetic botulin into Cuba in March (an effective poison that would act on any food and would prove fatal 12 hours after being consumed). Now, to administer the capsules, they waited for the leader of the Cuban Revolution to visit one of his favorite restaurants in the capital. The capsules were in the hands of determined people, who had been given the go-ahead some days earlier. The idea was that if the landing coincided with Fidel's death, the Army's and militia's shock over the loss of their charismatic leader would considerably lessen their response capability.

Once the beachhead was established, the invaders were to engage in clean-up and consolidation work in the towns that were taken. A force of 62 men who had been assigned that task waited aboard the *Atlantic*, the last ship in the convoy, for orders to land. They had been rigorously selected, especially for their trustworthiness. They were to carry out Operation 40. Their mission: to arrest, interrogate, and, at their discretion, kill the main military and civilian leaders of the Revolutionary Government and to seize the files of the intelligence bodies, public buildings, banks, communications centers and factories. They were also prepared to carry out missions in the enemy's rear guard. To do so, they had been equipped with sophisticated weapons: M-3 submachine guns and pistols with silencers; live phosphorus detonators which could be hidden in pockets; and miniature flame throwers which fit comfortably in the hand and could throw columns of white phosphorus for a distance of 50 feet. The members of Operation 40 would place trusted civilians in the key posts in the cities. As soon as the hostilities were over, the members of Operation 40 would become part of the civilian intelligence which would be created in Cuba.

According to the plan of operations, a force of 168 men would land at Baracoa, in the easternmost part of Cuba, the night before D Day, the day of the landing. This would confuse the revolutionary leaders, making them think that that was the main direction of the invasion, and would lead them to move considerable forces and matériel to that region. After landing, that invading force would move toward the U.S. Naval Base at Guantánamo, against which it would simulate an attack, so as to make it appear that the Cuban Government was the aggressor.

Laying the groundwork for the pro-U.S. provisional government that was to be set up on or around D+5 Day, the State Department had obtained agreement from at least six Latin American governments that they would immediately recognize it. The Cuban Revolutionary Council's appointment of a press secretary several days earlier had been the final touch in covering up the United States's participation in the invasion. Several people had been brought in and isolated on the Opa-Locka military base; they were to keep the press informed on the progress of the battle that was about to begin.

The CIA had contracted the services of Lem Jones and Associates, a New York advertising firm. At midnight on April 17, H Hour, it was preparing to turn in its first communiqué, to be issued just after dawn. It read as follows:

Cuban Revolutionary Council
Via: Lem Jones and Associates Agency
280 Madison Avenue, New York
For immediate publication
April 17, 1961

Bulletin 1
This morning, Dr. José Miró Cardona, Chairman of the Revolutionary Council, made the following statement:

Before dawn, Cuban patriots in the cities and in the hills began the battle to liberate our homeland of Fidel Castro and rid the Cubans of international communism's cruel oppression.[4]

A U.S. naval group would remain in the waters of the Cayman Islands, south of the landing area, ready to go to the aid of the provisional government as soon as the U.S. Government recognized it. That group included the LPH-4 *Boxer*, an amphibious helicopter carrier from which a battalion of the 2nd Division of Marines would be transported to the beachhead once the provisional government had been recognized and assistance had been approved; the CVS-0 *Essex*, an

---

4 Wyden, *Bay of Pigs*, 207; CRC, *Bulletin No. 1*, 4/17/61.

aircraft carrier with several squadrons of fighter planes on board; the DD-507 *Conway*, DD-756 *Murray* and *USS Percy*, all destroyers; the *Eaton*, which had headed the invasion flotilla from Puerto Cabezas to the Bay of Pigs; and the CVA *Shangri La*, an aircraft carrier with a capacity for 70 planes.

The GCI *Northampton*, the flagship with the commanding officers of the Atlantic Second Fleet on board, was riding at anchor in the Florida seas just off the island of Bimini. The orders for the destroyers and submarines used to protect and escort the invading fleet on its way from Nicaragua to the landing area had come from it.

Richard Bissell, CIA Special Plans Director and the brains behind the operation; Tracy Barnes, Bissell's aide; General Charles P. Cabell, Deputy Director of the CIA; Howard Hunt and Frank Droller, in charge of the Cuban politicians and the cover operations; David A. Phillips, in charge of propaganda; Jack Esterline, in charge of the task force against Cuba; and several dozen more CIA and U.S. Army, Navy and Air Force officers were at their posts. They remained in permanent contact with Generals Shoup, Wheeler and Gray (General Gray headed the supervisory group from the Pentagon); Admiral Arleigh Burke, Commandant of the Marines; and Admiral Lyman Lemnitzer, Chief of the Joint Chiefs of Staff.

David A. Phillips was the CIA officer in charge of press relations. He had already prepared rough drafts describing the key moments: the beginning of the patriots' struggle, the seizure and consolidation of the beachhead, the uprisings in the cities, the CRC's arrival in Cuban territory, the course of the battles, the constitution of the provisional government, the first governments to recognize the new Cuban government, the U.S. Government's recognition of it, approval of the aid requested by the provisional government and the sending of the first U.S. troops to the liberated areas.

Operation Pluto was under way, the largest-scale project ever organized by the U.S. Central Intelligence Agency in close collaboration and with the approval of the Joint Chiefs of Staff.

Thirty-nine kilometers west of Girón Beach, at Larga Beach, another landing point, William Rip Robertson (the officer whom the Cubans called "Crocodile," because of his scaly skin) and a group of frogmen had just marked the best approaches for the vessels. Then he put up a luminous yellow sign reading "WELCOME, LIBERATORS. COURTESY OF THE *BARBARA J*." where the invaders would be sure to see it.

That euphemistic phrase was used confidently, because of the careful planning of the military operation, the enormous amount of war matériel employed and the limited objective of the mission. This is worth repeating. The only thing that Attack Brigade 2506 had to do was establish a beachhead and hold it for 72 hours.

An important psychological factor boosted the invaders' morale that dawn. It had been repeated over and over again since they had been recruited: "The Americans are with us, and the Americans can't lose!"

Thirteen months had gone by since President Dwight D. Eisenhower had signed the memorandum ordering the creation of a fighting force of Cuban exiles. Battle was inevitable.

A purely Cuban affair

Former U.S. President Dwight D. Eisenhower described the steps taken in preparation for the April 17, 1961, attack as follows:

> On March 17 1960 I ordered the Agency to commence the training of Cuban exiles, principally in Guatemala, for the possible future day when they could return to their country. Another idea was that we commence to construct an anti-Castro force in Cuba itself. Some thought that we should quarantine the island, arguing that if the economy quickly collapsed, the Cubans themselves would over-throw Castro.[5]

The euphemisms in this excerpt don't really hide the reality from its readers. Eisenhower is talking about invasion ("return to their country"), subversion and internal destabilization ("construct an anti-Castro force in Cuba itself") and a total — naval and air — blockade ("quarantine the island").

Such language was being used in the White House just 15 months after the triumph of the Cuban Revolution, long before Cuba had any commitments with the Soviet Union and before any laws were adopted that gave Cuba's political process a nationalist character with a program of social justice that had broad, unquestionable support from the people.

In that relatively short period of time, the Agrarian Reform Law was approved and went into effect. More than 100,000 tenant farmers, sharecroppers and squatters were given title to the land they worked, thus wiping out those inhuman forms of exploitation. The deeds were signed by Fidel Castro. Since there wasn't enough cash to pay the former owners for it outright, they were given bonds which guaranteed that they would receive compensation in the near future. In addition, rents were cut by 50 percent, and the rates for electricity and telephone service were also reduced. Those measures had a great social impact. The National Savings and Housing Institute (INAV) was

---

[5] Dwight D. Eisenhower, *The White House Years: Waging Peace 1956-1961*, 401.

created and began a vast program of housing construction throughout the country. The budget for the Presidential Palace's upkeep was reduced from nearly 5 million pesos to 1 million pesos a year. The recently created Council of Ministers approved a budget for the immediate construction of 200 schools, with 5,000 classrooms, mainly in the rural areas, and reduced the cost of the textbooks used in general education by 25 to 35 percent. The prices of medicine were cut by 15 to 20 percent. On July 17, 1959, the Revolutionary Government approved a budget for a children's protection program. Tens of thousands of needy children, shoeshine boys, street vendors and beggars began going to school. The spiraling increase in begging, prostitution, gambling and drugs came to an abrupt halt during the first year after the triumph of the Revolution, and analysts saw clearly that those scourges of society would soon be completely eliminated.

Going throughout the country, Fidel Castro gave instructions for the construction of roads and highways in isolated areas and for the first steps to be taken in creating the Rural Medical Service. The National Printshop (IN), the National Institute of Agrarian Reform (INRA), the Cuban Institute of Cinematography (ICAIC) and the National Institute of the Tourist Industry (INIT) were founded.

Months before President Eisenhower gave his order, *Bohemia*, the largest-circulation magazine in Cuba, took a poll whose results left no doubts: 90.2 percent of the Cuban people supported the government's actions.

The CIA began to act against Cuba prior to March 17, the date on which Eisenhower said the order was given. Eisenhower himself stated, "In a matter of weeks, after Castro had entered Havana, we in the government began to examine the methods that could be effective in curbing Castro."[6]

On January 14, 1960, the National Security Council made a review of U.S.-Cuban relations since January 1959. Roy Rubottom, Assistant Secretary of State for Inter-American Affairs, commented that:

> The period from January to March [1959] might be characterized as the honeymoon period of the Castro government. In April a downward trend in U.S.-Cuban relations had been evident... In June we had reached the decision that it was not possible to achieve our objectives with Castro in power and had agreed to undertake the program referred to by [U.S. Undersecretary of State for Political Affairs] Mr. Merchant. In July and August we had been busy drawing up a program to replace Castro. However some U.S.

---

6 Ibid, 404.

companies reported to us during this time that they were making some progress in negotiations, a factor that caused us to slow the implementation of our program. The hope expressed by these companies did not materialize. October was a period of clarification... On October 31, in agreement with the CIA, the Department had recommended to the President approval of a program along the lines referred to by Mr. Merchant. The approved program authorized us to support elements in Cuba opposed to the Castro government while making Castro's downfall seem to be the result of his own mistakes.[7]

President Eisenhower's March 17 memo included one aspect that would be upheld by both his and the Kennedy Administrations: the United States didn't want anyone to know what it was doing. The CIA immediately gave top priority to planning how to comply with the Presidential order. Richard Bissell,[8] the CIA's number-two man, was personally in charge of the strategy for overthrowing the Cuban Government. He ordered that there should be no pale faces on the beach. The image that would be shown to the world would be that of a conflict among Cubans: an effort by the exiles, financed by contributions from Cubans and U.S. citizens who had been hurt by the revolutionary laws. The affair would be kept perfectly secret, and, when the time came, even though others might suppose that the attack came from high levels of the U.S. Government, they wouldn't be able to prove it. That was the "plausible denial" theory then in vogue. Bissell was euphoric. After the expected outcome, everybody would view him as the logical successor to CIA Director Allen Dulles.

---

[7] Piero Gleijeses, "Ships in the Night: The CIA, the White House and the Bay of Pigs", *Journal of Latin American Studies* 27, 3.

[8] Richard Mervin Bissell was born in New England into a well-off family; studied at Yale and taught there during the 1930s. During World War II, he was named Executive Director of Naval Supplies, supplying the U.S. forces and their allies all over the world. In 1946, he became a professor of economics at MIT. He was called to Washington at the beginning of the Cold War and in April 1948 began to work in the Marshall Plan. In 1953, his friend Allen Dulles, who had just been named Director of the CIA, invited him to join the Agency. Five years later, Bissell was named Plans Director. He directed the plans for the *Corona*, the first spy satellite, and became known as a pioneer of air reconnaissance, which made a considerable contribution to improving technical intelligence during the Cold War. Paradoxically, he is remembered not for any of his successes but rather for his worst failure: the Bay of Pigs. An Agency summary made months after the disaster assigned much of the responsibility for the failure to Bissell, and he was forced to resign on February 28, 1962. Two months later, a year after the Bay of Pigs defeat, President Kennedy awarded him the National Security Medal.

The program of undercover actions which Bissell had supervised and approved had been drawn up by the WH/4 (Branch 4 of the Western Hemisphere Division) task force, created two months earlier, on January 18, and headed by Jack Esterline, the former CIA station chief in Caracas.

Esterline was the person immediately responsible for developing the plan. He would be one of Bissell's three key subordinates on the Cuban project. The other two would be Jack Hawkins, who took charge of the military project some months later, when it was decided to use a conventional shock force to invade the island, and Colonel Stanley Beerli, who was in charge of air operations. This preference for the military aspect wasn't coincidental. It would characterize the operation from start to finish. Military aggression, not the political aspect, would be the main factor that would determine the outcome of the Cuban problem. Howard Hunt and Frank Bender would use the Cuban exile leaders to make a lot of noise. Bissell gave top priority to only one project outside the military sphere: the propaganda program for the psychological softening up of the Cuban people.

The program which Eisenhower approved contained four main themes:

a. the creation of a unified political force of opposition to Castro outside Cuba,
b. the development of a propaganda program,
c. the creation of an underground force on the island and the promotion of insurgency in the country's mountains and
d. the creation of a paramilitary force outside Cuba.

The plan centered around subversion from within; infiltration of the island; generous supplies of weapons, explosives and means of communication; and psychological warfare. These actions would be complemented with a program of economic and diplomatic pressure aimed at isolating Cuba and getting the OAS to impose sanctions on Cuba, not ruling out the possibility of the OAS itself taking action, backed up by the Resolution of Caracas.

The Minutes of that March 17, 1960 meeting stated:

The President said that he knows of no better plan for dealing with this situation. The great problem is leakage and breach of security. Everyone must be prepared to swear that he has not heard of it.[9]

---

[9] Gleijeses, "Ships in the Night: The CIA, the White House and the Bay of Pigs", 5.

A command post for the project, Quarters Eye, was set up in Washington, equipped with the best resources of the era. The building had a roomful of electronic maps and a communications room containing sophisticated equipment. The maps, at a scale of one to 50,000, had been made fairly recently (in 1957) and were based on aerial photographs taken at great heights by the U.S. Navy. They were constantly updated with new photos taken by cameras on U-2 spy planes and with reports from agents working inside Cuba. The walls of the map room were made of glass, to make it easy to see them. Red lights indicated insurgency areas in the mountains and large-scale acts of sabotage and terrorism in the cities. Orange and purple lights marked less important actions of the same kind. Thus, each light stood for a column of insurgents, an economic target which had been destroyed, an assassination attempt, a radio operator, a team that had been infiltrated, the point from which an agent was sending messages or an area for parachuting in arms and explosives.

In the communications room, many telephones, radio units and teletype machines that worked in code linked Quarters Eye with the safe houses assigned to the project and with the training bases in Guatemala, Panama and Florida. The propaganda plans aimed at softening up the Cuban people psychologically were drawn up in other offices, then put into effect through radio stations, the press, television, movies and publications of all kinds. That's where the pamphlets that were dropped over Cuba were written, where the flights for airlifting in supplies for the groups of insurgents were drawn up and where the plans for dropping incendiary bombs on fields of sugarcane were made.

Quarters Eye was the center of the web of an enormous conspiracy aimed at crushing a revolution which was beginning to defy the most powerful country on earth. One of the first actions taken there was to organize the political opposition to Fidel Castro; it would serve as a mask behind which Quarters Eye would hide.

Recommendations made by CIA experts on Cuban affairs and by State Department officials were kept in mind when selecting the members of the unified political front outside Cuba, which was to include a wide spectrum of Fidel Castro's political opponents. Participating in the selection were William D. Pawley, former U.S. Ambassador to Brazil and a friend of dictator Fulgencio Batista; William Wieland, head of the Caribbean Bureau of the State Department; Roy Rubottom, Assistant Secretary of State for Inter-American Affairs; and James Noel, chief of the CIA station in Havana.

The so-called Democratic Revolutionary Front (FRD) was created, whose founding members (all of Cuban origin) had established and represented five different counterrevolutionary and/or underground organizations.

1. Revolutionary Rescue Movement (Rescate)

Manuel Antonio de Varona Loredo, 52, was a traditional politician who had been President of the Senate and Prime Minister in the administration of Dr. Carlos Prío Socarrás. He had been one of the few political leaders who had remained in Cuba during the Batista dictatorship, working in the government-tolerated opposition. As repression was stepped up, the fact that he was still in Cuba led to his rising in the ranks of his party. He opposed Fidel Castro's insurrectional line and thought that the military would solve Cuba's problems with a traditional coup. Everything he did was with a view to his becoming President of the Republic. Varona was a rightist in the aristocratic mold. He owned an insurance company with a branch in Puerto Rico. While holding high-ranking positions in the Prío Administration and during the 1950s, Varona forged links with the U.S. Mafia capos who controlled Havana's gambling casinos. Those relations ensured that his fortune increased but also made him dependent on them after January 1, 1959. He was the one who, having been contacted by the Mafia in 1961, sent the poison capsules of synthetic botulin from Miami to Cuba as part of the plan to assassinate Fidel Castro just before the landing.

After the triumph of the Revolution, he had stayed in Cuba, working in the legal opposition to the government. He opposed the promulgation of laws which benefited the people as a whole and presented himself as a champion of the owners adversely affected by those laws. On June 12, 1959, during a television appearance, he attacked the Agrarian Reform Law, claiming that it went counter to the 1940 Constitution, then still in effect. Moreover, he criticized the National Institute of Agrarian Reform, "because it is more powerful than the President of the Republic and the entire Government... We object to INRA because it is governed by just two people... "[10] Fidel Castro was one of them. Varona went even farther that night, stating, "I think that, since the Revolutionary Government has been in power for over five months, it should set a limit to its mandate."[11]

His corrupt past (which was shared by most of those on the political scene during the years of the Republic) and his attacks on the

---

[10] Antonio Núñez Jiménez, *En marcha con Fidel*, 190.
[11] Ibid.

Revolution completely discredited him in Cuba — but it won him supporters in the State Department and the CIA. With the help of CIA officers working in Havana under diplomatic cover, he created the Revolutionary Rescue Movement (Rescate), whose few but fanatical members would use underground methods. He began conspiring against the Cuban Government. Soon afterwards, the Agency asked him to leave Cuba and go to the United States. It was early 1960. Varona recalled, "An Embassy official called me in and proposed that I leave the country to head up a movement against Castro... "[12]

2. Movement of Revolutionary Recovery (MRR)
Manuel Artime Bueza, 28, a former officer in the Rebel Army who had a solid religious background, was selected for very different reasons. Artime was the nephew of José Angel Bueza, a popular poet at the time, whose already outmoded modernism may have contributed to the slightly syrupy oratory of the improvised political leader.

Artime had become a member of the Radical Liberation Party (PLR), a Christian Democratic group, in 1957. When he joined the Rebel Army in December 1958, he had graduated as a doctor and hoped to become a psychiatrist. In the first few weeks of 1959, Artime was appointed second in command of Zone 0-22, in the Manzanillo region. From that post, carrying out the instructions of Major Humberto Sorí Marín, Minister of Agriculture, and Rogelio González Corzo, Director of Agriculture, Artime promoted the work of the so-called Rural Commandos, a kind of Peace Corps composed of young people, most of whom belonged to the University Catholic Group (ACU) in Havana. Working in pairs, they stayed in the homes of farmers in the area, helped them in their agricultural work and instilled religious beliefs. Meanwhile, on La Sierra, a 77,550-acre farm, they taught a variety of the Agrarian Reform that wouldn't hurt the interests of the large landowners — especially U.S. landowners. Unknown to them, a draft Agrarian Reform Law would soon be presented to the Cuban Council of Ministers.

Artime maintained close relations with Major Hubert Matos. After Matos's conspiracy in Camagüey was crushed in October 1959, the Rural Commandos were dissolved. In the months that followed, many of their members joined the counterrevolutionary organizations that the CIA was creating and fomenting throughout the country. Humberto Sorí Marín contacted the CIA, and Rogelio González Corzo became the Agency's main agent in the country.

---

[12] *Girón, ¿derrota o traición?*, television documentary, 1991. Copy in the State Security Historical Research Center (Havana).

With help from the U.S. Embassy, Manuel Artime managed to leave Cuba clandestinely and go to the United States. Evidently, his actions in Oriente Province had been linked to the efforts of the CIA to counter the work of the Revolutionary Government. In the United States, Artime organized the Movement of Revolutionary Recovery (MRR). At the beginning, the MRR drew its members from the July 26 Movement, the Rebel Army and the Revolutionary National Police — individuals who had opposed the dictator Fulgencio Batista but had political ambitions or felt pushed aside. Others were opportunists who had hopped on the revolutionary bandwagon when it became clear that Fidel Castro's strategy would triumph. Many of them wanted revolution — just not so much of it — and all, to one degree or another, were dogmatically anti-communist.

In a few months, working under the direction of the CIA, which had sponsored its creation, the MRR was established throughout the country. It received large amounts of war matériel and became the most belligerent counterrevolutionary organization, even though, like the others, it never constituted a serious threat to the Revolution.

In the latter half of 1960, the CIA began supplying the organization by air and sea. It used diverse means, such as the ferry that ran between Key West and Havana, stashing M-1 rifles, grenades, ammunition and explosives in the cars. In addition, arms were sent in at various points along the coast and were dropped on farms belonging to members of or collaborators with the organization.

Its members carried out many acts of sabotage and fostered and supported several insurgent groups in the mountain areas. Dozens of them left Cuba clandestinely to go to CIA training camps in Guatemala and Panama, and they planned several assassination attempts against the main leaders of the Revolution.

The reactionary clergy — especially those of Spanish origin — in whose classrooms many of them had been taught, supported them in their actions.

The MRR used methods of underground struggle which it inherited from the battles against the Batista dictatorship. Its members — organized in small cells with a pyramidal structure — contacted each other only in public places, and its coordinators travelled from one place to another by means of public transportation.

3. Christian Democratic Movement (MDC)

José Ignacio Rasco, a history professor who represented the Christian Democratic Movement (MDC), was another of the politicians "acceptable" to the Washington-sponsored project. Rasco had been a leader of the Catholic Youth (JC) and, like almost all of the traditional politicians, had supported the Revolutionary Government during the first few weeks after the triumph of the Revolution. His hostility toward Fidel Castro's government had a stamp of its own: he wanted the Catholic Church to oppose the Revolution. Therefore, he promoted activities by the Catholic organizations in the country: Young Catholic Students (JCE), the University Catholic Group (ACU) and Young Catholic Workers (JOC). One of the main organizers of the Catholic Congress which was held in late 1959, he drew up its program, papers and conclusions. He is attributed with having created the slogan "Charity, charity, charity" during the Congress to counter the people's demands that proven war criminals be shot.

One of the Congress's resolutions led to the creation of the Christian Democratic Movement, which Rasco headed. It engaged in organizational work, especially in the exclusive private Catholic schools in the capital, with the support of the Church hierarchy. In a grandstanding ploy (he wasn't being persecuted at all and carried out his political work publicly), Rasco sought asylum in April 1960. The CIA, with which he had maintained contact through the U.S. Embassy, had also asked him to leave the country and join the Democratic Revolutionary Front.

The specialists in the CIA's Cuban program had thought that if they managed to convince believers that Fidel Castro was the Antichrist, the Revolution would lose its popular support.

At the triumph of the Revolution, most of the clergy in Cuba consisted of Spanish prelates with reactionary, Falangist political positions. Religious schools, universities and other educational institutions were concentrated in the exclusive neighborhoods in the capital. The Catholic University of Santo Tomás de Villanueva, run by U.S. Augustinian priests, was the most important Catholic educational institution. It soon clashed with the Revolution. Pastorals and editorials proliferated in those first two years, enlarging on the "Rome or Moscow" thesis, which was reduced to "Revolution or counter-revolution." Those pastorals were published in the hostile press, especially in the *Diario de la Marina*, and commented upon by its editor, José Ignacio Rivero, in the "Vulcano y Relámpagos" (Vulcan and Lightning) section.

The counterrevolutionary harangues were largely echoed by the students in those schools, most of whom were members of the wealthy classes. One former student of the Belén School — the same school in which Fidel Castro had studied — recalled an activity attended by

Bishop Eduardo Boza Masvidal, one of the prelates who fought against the Cuban Government with the greatest vigor:

> The students from the Lestonac, El Verbo Encarnado, La Salle, Los Maristas, Nuestra Señora del Rosario and Nuestra Señora de los Angeles religious schools were called together to attend the activity. I remember that the most vehement nuns were those from Nuestra Señora de los Angeles and Nuestra Señora del Rosario, who jumped up and down and shouted, "Long live Boza, down with Fidel!" Then the students began to do it, too. When the Bishop arrived, they welcomed him with applause and shouts of "Long live Boza, long live Boza"; "Boza, yes; communism, no"; and "Boza, Boza, bash the reds before the evil monster spreads." During his speech, the Bishop pointed out that we should carry out the Revolution of Christ, which was the only true one, since it was a revolution of love and equality for all men. I very clearly remember that he said that the rich had abused the poor greatly, that communism had arisen because of their selfishness and that we had to help the poor. Most of the students who were there were the sons and daughters of the rich, and they didn't like this last bit very much. There was very little applause at the end.

The clergy who acknowledged the Revolution's humanitarian work created a patriotic-religious organization called With the Cross and With the Homeland (Con la Cruz y Con la Patria). Those grassroots priests and laymen justified their action by considering that it was possible to be both Catholic and revolutionary and advocated that the Church free itself of its alliances with the interests which were fighting against the Revolution. The high-ranking Church hierarchy repressed and punished them for their attitude. Students in the private Catholic schools who identified with the revolutionary process were expelled from their schools.

The Cuban Government didn't rise to the acts of provocation. Rather, it handled the religious question very wisely, maintaining strict respect for religious work and parishioners, which was in complete accord with its policy. More than once, Fidel Castro pointed out that the process of social justice which was being carried out in the country was identical to Christian postulates. Hundreds of thousands of believers continued to support the Revolution.

4. Triple A

Dr. Aureliano Sánchez Arango, a traditional politician and head of the Triple A party, was another of the leaders who was selected. Sánchez Arango, who had been Secretary of State in the Prío Administration, left Cuba in mid-1960. After his departure, Triple A went underground. Its members engaged in terrorist actions, such as burning down factories and clothing stores, damaging electricity towers and scattering tacks during Carnivals. In late 1960, several members of the organization began following the recently appointed Ambassador of the Soviet Union, seeking to assassinate him.

In June, July and August 1960, Triple A and the Revolutionary Rescue Movement fomented the first uprisings in the Escambray Mountains. Cuban State Security had penetrated Triple A from the time of its formation and had an agent on its national leadership before the Bay of Pigs invasion. As a result, its main leaders were captured in several operations that were carried out between March 19 and 29, 1961, just two weeks before D Day.

5. Montecristi

Montecristi, headed by Justo Carrillo, was also contacted by the CIA. It is said that this organization never had more than one hundred members, including Carrillo's family. All were middle class. Publicly, however, he pretended that he led a large group. During the period of the Batista dictatorship, Montecristi used all its energy in fundraising. After the 1959 revolution, Carrillo was appointed President of the Agricultural and Industrial Development Bank of Cuba (BANFAIC). As such, he placed his friends in government posts and was unscrupulous with the funds for which he was responsible. After some clashes with the revolutionary leadership, he went to the United States.

Other organizations in the FRD

Later on, other counterrevolutionary organizations joined the FRD. Among them, the November 30 Movement (M-30-11), the Student Revolutionary Directorate (DRE) and the People's Revolutionary Movement (MRP) acquired some notoriety. This last became one of the worst terrorist underground organizations inside Cuba. Manuel Ray Rivero, an engineer who had headed the July 26 Movement's Civic Resistance movement at the national level during the Batista dictatorship, created it in mid-1960. When the Revolution triumphed, he was appointed Minister of Public Works. From that position, he began to conspire against the revolutionary aspects of the process. He was an attractive prospect for the CIA. He hadn't been involved with the Batista regime and had supported the Revolution at the beginning. His Social Democratic politics would inevitably lead him to a head-on clash with the Revolution. An expert in underground conspiracy, he created a very tight organization. In addition, he had prestige, for he argued that the real leaders opposing Fidel Castro should remain in Cuba and face the risks which stemmed from such a difficult struggle. From every point of view, it seemed that the CIA had found someone who embodied the same qualities Fidel Castro had demonstrated in the struggle, though many in the Agency rejected him, considering that his political line of "Fidelism without Fidel" was a dangerous one.

However, Ray's closest collaborators began to note strange things in his behavior. He made his moves with such extreme caution that the suspicious began to consider him ridiculous, if not cowardly.

He was hard to find, and some of the people in the organization started to think that, after he had gotten things going and was known to have done so, he had decided to play it safe. Then, one day in November 1960, just five months after the MRP had been founded, he left the country with the help of CIA officers in Havana but without a word to the other leaders of the movement. He left a message saying that he was going to the United States to establish contacts, but none of us believed that.[13]

Even so, he appointed himself the MRP's delegate to the FRD and, from the comfort of exile during which he received a considerable amount of money each month, several times tried to take over the leadership of the Front.

Meanwhile, in Cuba, the MRP stepped up its actions as the CIA managed to supply it with weapons and explosives. On the eve of the invasion, advised by Jorge Comellas ("Cawy"), an agent whom the CIA had specially trained for terrorist actions, the MRP was responsible for the worst act of sabotage carried out anywhere in the country: two incendiary devices reduced El Encanto, the largest department store in Cuba, to a heap of rubble. Members of the organization also carried out acts of sabotage in tobacco warehouses, the national paper factory, several port installations, two of Woolworth's large branches in the capital and other places. At its peak, the MRP had cells of conspirators in the telephone, electric power, insurance, medical, transportation, liquor, banking, graphic arts, shoe, leather, restaurant, construction and civil aviation sectors.

---

[13] Statement by Reynold González, National Coordinator of the MRP. Archives of the Ministry of the Interior, Cuba.

As Howard Hunt, the CIA officer assigned to work with the five founding members of the Democratic Revolutionary Front, recalled in his memoirs, it was easy to get them to meet; what was exhausting was their haggling over the money the CIA was to give them. They asked for a monthly budget of $435,000 for activities abroad; $200,000 to increase operations in Cuba; and around $105,000 for a contingency fund, salaries and the Front's office expenses — a total of around $740,000.

It was finally agreed that the money assigned to the Front would be used to set up FRD offices in the main cities in the western hemisphere, including the United States. In addition, the CIA would pick up the tab for its propaganda; the trips that FRD teams made throughout the world for propaganda purposes; the weapons, vessels and communications equipment supplied to teams of infiltrators; recruiting; and other paramilitary operations.

On June 20, 1960, the Democratic Revolutionary Front and its five leaders were presented to the press. During the ceremony, the CIA officers who had organized the FRD and would manipulate its leaders from then on remained in their rooms. Moments earlier, they had authorized a press release and a political manifesto calling for the overthrow of Fidel Castro.

Using a theory that the CIA specialists had drawn up, the FRD manifesto "justified" its activities by claiming that the Revolution had been betrayed. In one of its paragraphs, it referred to "Commander Fidel Castro's regime's Sovietizing betrayal of the original, noble aims of the Cuban Revolution." It also stated, "It isn't possible to remain indifferent, in view of the most coercive legal, physical and psychological terror recorded in our history." The document went on at length about unimportant matters, largely anti-communist ranting.

The 12-point political program, which was to be put into effect as soon as the Revolutionary Government was overthrown, was presented at the end of the meeting. Three of those points unequivocally showed the true intentions of those "freedom fighters." They were as follows:

• the elimination of the Communist Party;
• a review of the sanctions imposed by the ordinary courts for infractions committed prior to January 1, 1959 (this meant a review of the sentences given the dictatorship's war criminals and torturers); and
• the retention of the Agrarian Reform, but as established in the 1940 Constitution, without dispossessions or abuses.

How can you carry out an agrarian reform without dispossessing the land of the large (mainly U.S.) landowners? It was simply an effort to retain the name while divesting it of any real effectiveness, because the farmers in Cuba were strongly in favor of the Agrarian Reform which the Revolutionary Government had implemented.

To make it even less likely that the project against the Cuban Revolution might be linked to the U.S. Government, it was decided to establish the Front's main office in Mexico City. Soon after that was done, branch offices were opened in other Latin American countries. Even though the Front had some independence, the CIA paid the piper and called the tune.

> Through Tony I convened the FRD Mexico City delegation and introduced Sam to them as their guide, mentor, paymaster and contact with me, the representative of the Bender group. Having set up fronts for me before, Sam went to work immediately. The delegation opened a downtown office and began producing a weekly newspaper named *Mambí*.[14]

From then on, the Democratic Revolutionary Front would serve as a cover for the U.S. aggression. President Eisenhower had demanded precisely this.

The Mexican Government wasn't fooled, however. Even though the CIA officers in Mexico tried to cover up the real nature of their relations with the FRD (Hunt resumed his old cover as a writer of detective novels), the Mexican authorities quickly became suspicious. They began to put pressure on the CIA officers in charge of the office. As a result, the members of the Front's executive decided to leave Mexico City and return to Miami. President Eisenhower endorsed the decision, and the FRD moved back on October 3, 1960.

The leaders of the Front traveled extensively, promoting their crusade against Castro. Their propaganda groups went all over the world.

Some Cuban exiles actually believed that they were responsible for the program of struggle. Such was the case of former Colonel Martín Elena, a man in the confidence of Antonio de Varona, who headed the FRD's illusory staff in Miami. He set about drawing up a strategy for the landing in Cuba. In fact, he drew up several invasion plans, all of which ended up in the waste basket at Quarters Eye.

---

14 Howard Hunt, *Give Us This Day*, 52.

I regarded the colonel as a figurehead who ought to be kept busy in Miami with military plans. Cuban plans, in any case, were not the ones that would be used on D-Day, but plans that were being developed by CIA and the Pentagon through the Joint Chiefs of Staff. Cuban military planning, therefore, was a harmless exercise and might prove tangentially useful if they became known to Castro's agents and served as deception material — disinformation. To paraphrase a homily: this was too important to be left to Cuban generals.[15]

Farther on, Hunt cited Martín Elena as saying, "I don't see how I can pretend to command when in reality I do not."[16] As for the activities and organizational ability of the FRD leaders, Howard Hunt — who should know — described them as follows:

Rasco, Varona and Carrillo were seldom available until after midday. Artime, who had been up half the night attending to his growing flock, would appear red-eyed and unshaven, and Roberto de Varona would usually open the meetings by reporting how many new recruits for the camps his brother had gained the previous day. This usually provoked an outcry from Carrillo (whose Montecristi movement seemed to be limited to blood relatives). Next, Rasco would inquire wearily about arms and boats for his adherents in Florida. Finally, Artime, the junior member, would launch into an impassioned statement of why it was necessary to defeat Castro, and how this could not be done unless petty jealousies were put aside.[17]

The exiles repeated over and over again that the struggle against Castro was a purely Cuban affair, and they finally came to believe it. In fact, even though the CIA allowed them to make a lot of noise, it excluded them from all the decision making.

At the Trax Base, for example, which was commanded by U.S. officers, some Cuban recruits were stopped dead when they demanded that they be given greater participation in planning. As José Pérez San Román himself stated:

Is it or is it not true that Captain Oscar Alfonso Carol, the top Cuban leader at the Trax Base, in Guatemala, was removed from

---

[15] Ibid, 61.
[16] Ibid, 158.
[17] Ibid, 53-4.

participation because he demanded that we Cuban leaders have something to say about how operations would be conducted and the future of the struggle in our country? The answer is yes. I know; I was there.[18]

Others who protested were treated even worse. Machine guns were aimed at them, and they were disarmed and sent to a prison in the Guatemalan jungle. Years later, a journalist asked Tony Varona what he thought about the U.S. officers. His reply was, "They were neither friends nor enemies; they were Americans."[19]

While those "political leaders" were being kept busy playing at war against Fidel Castro, no time was lost in Quarters Eye. The military experts of the Pentagon and the Agency were drawing up and implementing military plans. The CIA had begun to project the actions of a subversive war even before the Front was established. On May 19, working in the utmost secrecy on Usseppa, a semidesert island near Fort Myers, Florida, a group of exiles chosen by the counter-revolutionary organizations themselves had begun rigorous training for a war of insurgency and clandestine actions.

[18] José Pérez San Román, *Respuesta*, 23.
[19] *Girón, ¿derrota o traición?*, documentary, 1991.

A paramilitary force

The first recruiting was done in Miami in April and May 1960. For this purpose, the CIA used the leaders of the organizations which would later constitute the Democratic Revolutionary Front.

Manuel Artime came to see me at the beginning of May 1960 — or, rather, one of the San Románs (the one named José, who later commanded the force that attacked Girón Beach) invited me to a meeting with the men who had been officers in the army which had been broken up... Manuel Artime presided over the meeting. Artime told us that he was in contact with the U.S. Government and that we had been called together to organize a force with which to fight the Cuban Government.[20]

The counterrevolutionary organizations operating inside Cuba sent other future recruits from there. Manuel H. Reyes García some time later told Cuba's Department of State Security:

I began to work actively in the MRR in 1960, beginning as a liaison between Rogelio González Corzo ("Francisco"), the coordinator in Oriente, and an individual named Enrique Ross... In March 1960, Rogelio González told me that I had to go to the United States as part of a group that would receive military training... I left for the United States in April 1960 and, following "Francisco's" instructions, immediately went to the Hispanic Center to make contact with a nun... She and somebody named Quintero came to see me, and we went to a house... There was a bed for Artime, too... The first group of 10 left for training on Usseppa Island on around May 20, and another group of 10 left two days later.[21]

---

[20] Statement by Miguel Angel Orozco Crespo, member of an infiltration team. Archives of the Cuban Ministry of the Interior.

[21] Statement by Manuel H. Reyes García, member of an infiltration team. Archives of the Cuban Ministry of the Interior.

Manuel H. Reyes would be the radio-telegraph operator of one of the teams which were infiltrated into Cuba on the eve of the Bay of Pigs attack.

The first agents who had been recruited left for Usseppa Island on May 19. A CIA officer who said his name was "Carl" picked them up at the house. The group of Cubans had been instructed not to talk to him, but, during the days of training on the island, some of them learned that he had helped train Castillo Armas's mercenary forces in Guatemala.

After a five-hour trip by road, the members of the group came to a little dock, where they boarded a motorboat that took them to Usseppa.

The island, close to Fort Myers, Florida, looked like a recreation spot. It had a dock, a tennis court and several cabañas, among other installations. The new recruits' fingerprints and photographs were taken, and they were given several tests to measure their skills and intelligence. Other groups kept coming, until there were 61 men in all (some sources say 66). Half of them had been members of Fulgencio Batista's army.

Usseppa was the first phase in the process of selecting and training the future members of the paramilitary groups. It operated as a physical and mental checkup center, and it was also where the men were given their first classes in telegraphy and guerrilla warfare. All of them were given lie detector tests. Questions were repeated over and over again asking if they sympathized with communist ideas, if they had read Marxist literature and if they had ever engaged in homosexual practices.

Around two weeks later, the group was split in two. One of those subgroups consisted of around 30 of the more skilled men (as some put it) or those who hadn't come from the Army (according to others), who were given a course in radio-telegraphy while on the island. The other subgroup consisted exclusively of former Army men; its members left in the latter half of June.

The members of the Army group were flown in an unmarked Douglas C-54 for seven hours to a jungle area where they took an eight-week course in guerrilla warfare. They were transported in absolute secrecy, and nobody told them where they were, but, since the foghorns of ships going through a canal could be heard constantly, they realized they were in Panama.

U.S. officers trained them in the use of infantry weapons and in shooting. They were also given classes in explosives, especially those used in sabotage and demolition; guerrilla tactics; intelligence;

counterintelligence; psychological warfare; evasion and escape; interrogations; how to function underground; and how to receive supplies that were airlifted in or brought by boat.

They learned how to do invisible writing, including a state-of-the-art method for making it visible, using special carbon paper that left no traces.

The men who had remained on Usseppa Island became the radio operators for the teams. They had six hours of classes a day, learning Morse code, the theory of electrical physics and other topics related to telegraphy. On July 5, they, too, left the island. The same procedures as those followed for transporting the former Army men were used in flying them for nearly eight hours to a landing strip in the middle of the jungle, but this time it wasn't in Panama. The more curious among them identified the country from the registration numbers of the military trucks that were waiting for them on the airfield. They were in Guatemala.

They were taken to Helvetia Farm, in Retalhuleu, where they set up the Trax Base and continued their radio operators' course. (They had been instructed not to give their real names to the almost 160 recruits who were already at the farm.) On August 21, those who had taken the guerrilla warfare course in Panama joined them. Called "cadres," they were placed in charge of training the rest of the troops (including the new recruits who kept arriving from Miami), supervised by U.S. instructors.

The recruiting centers in Miami were very active.

> Finally I was picked up — one of three or four people — and we were driven by car to the Homestead area, south of Miami, where we were taken to an empty house out in the middle of the woods. First we were assigned registration numbers. Mine was 2718... We were strip-searched by [exile] Cuban officers to make sure we weren't carrying any forbidden articles, like compasses or weapons... Later the same day our watches were taken away and we were put in an enclosed truck and driven in circles... Soon after, we heard an aircraft pull up to the hangar... And off we went, directly into the plane.[22]

Officially, the training in guerrilla warfare and in promoting urban uprisings began at the Trax Base on September 19, and the recruits were ready to go into action by the end of November. However, it was absolutely necessary to have created insurgent-controlled areas in

---

[22] Félix Rodríguez, *Shadow Warrior*.

Cuba's mountains and a strong underground movement in the cities, and it hadn't been possible to do this.

The few groups operating in the Escambray Mountains were continually harassed, and the supplies which the CIA airlifted in for them kept falling into the hands of the militias and Cuban Rebel Army. In the cities, counterrevolutionary activities were severely limited by the work of State Security and the people's responses to those groups' acts of provocation. This situation led the CIA chiefs to change their plans.

On November 4, 1960, a coded cable was sent from the CIA's headquarters in Langley, Virginia, to the officer in charge of the project in Guatemala, ordering him to cut back on the training in guerrilla warfare and to introduce conventional training for an amphibious and airborne attack force. Thus, Operation Trinidad was born. It consisted of landing a brigade, both by sea and by air, with the support of an air force of its own, to establish a beachhead near the city of Trinidad, seize the airport there and form a provisional government which would ask for international recognition and then request military support for overthrowing Fidel Castro's government. The CIA made this important change on its own, without the approval of Eisenhower's outgoing administration or the consent of the incoming Kennedy Administration.

A new stage began at the Trax Base. The grey and black teams disappeared, and the agents-turned-recruits were formed into companies and battalions. A rigorous selection was made to create a few teams with highly skilled agents whose main missions from then on would be to enter Cuba clandestinely, establish contact with the underground, train its members, arrange for the reception of arms and explosives and take part in acts of sabotage against key targets to support the invasion.

The new plans called for those men to support, not organize, guerrilla groups and subversive actions in the cities. They would serve as reinforcements for the subversive organizations which already operated in Cuba, whose main leaders were making repeated clandestine trips to the United States and were being trained just as rigorously as the agents on Usseppa, in Panama and at the Trax Base.

The paramilitary forces had been divided. Most of them would be in the Attack Brigade; those in the smaller group would form the teams of special agents.

Eighty-three recruits were chosen for this last force. They included some of those who had been on Usseppa Island and in Panama and others who had been outstanding in the training at Trax.

On December 5, they were sent to San José de Buenavista Farm, in Escuintla Department, Guatemala. The base was known as "Garrapatenango," because of the abundance of ticks (*garrapatas*, in Spanish). There, they received very rigorous special training in survival exercises. For weeks, they had to keep constantly on the move without being seen by the local population, carrying weapons, equipment and organizing operations for picking up supplies that were airlifted in — which was, moreover, the only way they could be supplied. When the airlift operation failed, they had nothing to eat; then they had to live off the land.

At the end of the 15-day course, they were taken back to the airfield in closed (canvas-covered) trucks whose windows had been painted black, and were flown to Panama. Once again, it wasn't hard to identify where they were, for they could see a large ship in the distance, moving slowly through a lock. They immediately ruled out the possibility of its being the Suez Canal, because there was tropical vegetation rather than sand. Moreover, packages that had been thrown away bore labels reading "Fort Clayton — Canal Zone."

This time, their training consisted of mastering advanced weapons from socialist countries and learning how to live clandestinely, including following suspects in enemy territory. In addition, they were given more classes in intelligence and propaganda, practiced picking up supplies brought in by sea and by air, and had target practice. They had six instructors: two U.S. citizens and four Europeans.

The men had been organized in six teams, each with 15 members. The training ended in mid-January, and 47 men were finally selected. Those who had been chosen as telegraph operators were given a week of classes in theory at Centenary College of Louisiana. This completed their training. On January 29, they flew to New Orleans and then on to Miami. The other members of the teams left Panama by air for an unidentified destination. This was a testing measure.

The six members of my team (which was called Inca) were loaded into a plane and told that we were going to Cuba. "Carl", the instructor, went with us. Each of us had a .45-caliber pistol, a .38-caliber Bulldog revolver and an M-2, plus a change of civilian clothes and a [Cuban] Rebel Army uniform — they were of different ranks — in addition to the camouflage suits we were wearing. After four and a half hours in the air, the bottom hatch was opened, and we were ordered to jump. We dropped the package of our things first; then Carl jumped, and then we did. When we landed, we picked everything up and went into a small woods that was nearby. We took off our camouflage suits, dressed in civilian clothes and buried everything, together with the parachutes and weapons — all except the .38 revolvers. Then some militia appeared half a kilometer from where we had landed. At first, they scared the life out of us, but then, when they came closer, they congratulated us because we had carried out the operation in less than an hour. Later, we were taken by light truck to the Retalhuleu airport. We had landed in Guatemala.[23]

---

[23] Testimony of Benigno Pérez Vivanco, member of an infiltration team.

Entering Cuba illegally

The day after the practice drop in Guatemala, the teams were taken to Miami, where they joined the radio operators. They stayed in a CIA safe house near Homestead, where they were to remain until they were sent to Cuba. The house was comfortable enough to make it a pleasant stay. The men were given money and permission to visit their wives and other relatives. On or around February 8, the teams led by Benigno Pérez, Manuel Blanco Navarro and Oscar Alfonso Carol — these last two had been officers in Batista's Army — were taken to a dock on Key West and left for Cuba.

The first landing attempt was made along the northern coast of Las Villas Province, where Benigno's team was to go ashore and join the groups of insurgents operating in the Escambray Mountains, against whom a powerful revolutionary offensive known as "cleaning up the Escambray" was being directed. Benigno had been selected for that mission because he had fought against the Batista dictatorship in those same mountains.

There, the Inca team was to quickly arrange for receiving airlifts of arms and explosives and train the insurgents. The team also brought in a load of weapons. The attempt failed, and they had to go back to Miami. Blanco Navarro's team, which had been ordered to Pinar del Río Province, and Oscar Carol's, which had also been sent to Las Villas, did no better. The infiltration operation began under uncertain omens, but it was still several weeks before the invasion.

The agents used several means for entering the country by sea and air, both legal and illegal.

On February 13, 1961, agent Manuel Reyes García walked down the ramp of a commercial plane that had flown from Miami to Havana. He carried false documents. Immediately contacting the chiefs of the internal counterrevolution, he began his work of subversion.

The next day, Valentine's Day, Félix Rodríguez Mendigutía, Segundo Borges, José González Castro, Javier Souto (radio operator) and Edgar Sopo entered Cuba in the Arcos de Canasí area, on the Havana-Matanzas border. They brought two tons of communications equipment, weapons and explosives. Some counterrevolutionaries were waiting on the coast to welcome the team, and they immediately took the load and buried it. A few days later, Cuban State Security seized everything they had brought, for one of the supposed collaborators worked for Cuban Security. The team split in two: Segundo Borges, Javier Souto and José González headed for Las Villas Province, while Edgar Sopo and the chief, Félix Rodríguez, went to Havana, where they met with Rogelio González Corzo, one of the main underground leaders, the next day.

Gustavo Enrique Casuso Pérez was assigned as radio operator for an uprising in the Sierra Maestra Mountains. He and Alberto Muller, the main organizer of the project, entered Cuba clandestinely along the northern coast of Havana. The uprising was to take place a few days before the Bay of Pigs attack. Casuso's main job was to coordinate the weapons and equipment drops for those troops, which had been organized by the Student Revolutionary Directorate (DRE). The mission wasn't successful because the squadrons of Brigade 2506's Tactical Air Force were moving their base from Guatemala to Happy Valley, in Nicaragua, during that first week in April.

Oliverio Tomeu, who headed another team, managed to take his men to Camagüey Province.

At the end of February, Manuel Blanco Navarro made another attempt to reach Pinar del Río Province. His vessel received the signals of another, as agreed upon, but, when they drew closer, they saw that its hull was olive green and, thinking it belonged to the Revolutionary Navy, they turned tail.

Benigno Pérez and his team failed once again, and a message radioed to the yacht ordered them back to Key West. Later, they were sent to New Orleans, where each one was given $200 and a week off, which — as they testified later — they spent bar-hopping.

Oscar Alfonso Carol managed to enter Cuba illegally in early March. At around that same time, Juan Manuel Guillot Castellanos, who had been conspiring in Cuba at the service of the CIA ever since late 1959 and had gone to the United States on Feburary 13, returned clandestinely with three team members who had been instructed to take their orders from him.

Adolfo Mendoza ("Raúl") and Jorge García Rubio ("Tony"), both CIA radio operators for the teams, and CIA agent Emilio Rivero Caro, who was to head a counterrevolutionary organization in Pinar del Río, were parachuted into a farm in Santa Cruz del Sur, Camagüey Province, in early March. The three agents brought a large amount of weapons with them.

Jorge García Rubio was assigned as radio operator for an important underground organization that operated in Havana. It was headed by Alfredo Izaguirre de la Riva and José Pujals Mederos, both of whom had been recruited by the U.S. Embassy in 1959. They hid García Rubio in Izaguirre's apartment in the FOCSA building and the broadcasting transmitter on a farm in Santiago de las Vegas, a town on the outskirts of Havana. Shortly afterwards, following CIA instructions, the group headed by those agents prepared to blow up the Tallapiedra electric power plant.

Jorge Rojas Castellanos, the son of a well-known general under Batista, also entered the country illegally. When he was around 200 meters from the coast, his rubber raft turned over, and he had to swim to shore. Soon after his arrival, a car which had been sent to get him picked him up on the Vía Blanca highway. Among other things, he was to pinpoint areas for air drops of weapons and explosives for the groups of insurgents who were operating near Jaguey Grande, in southern Matanzas Province. Rojas Castellanos didn't know that he would be operating in the area where the invasion would take place, because, at that time in March, the CIA hadn't yet selected the site. With the help of the group headed by the self-styled "Colonel" Juan José Catalá Coste ("Pichi"), he toured his assigned region for close to 20 days. Like all the other members of the teams, before leaving the United States he had been given a .45 Browning pistol, two additional magazines, two boxes of .45 bullets, an M-3 light machine gun which had been adapted for use in cities, a belt with three clips, two MK2 hand grenades, a small knapsack and materials for sending invisible messages.

During that period, in late February and early March 1960, other team members also entered Cuba illegally. They included Manuel Blanco Navarro, who had made an earlier attempt; Miguel Pentón; and Jorge Comellas ("Cawy").

Miguel Angel Orozco Crespo and the other members of his team drew close to the coast in an unmarked boat with all lights doused, but they couldn't land, because they failed to make contact. Hours later, they returned to Key West. When the Bay of Pigs invasion began, Orozco was in the safe house in Homestead.

Loads of weapons and explosives for the fifth column in Cuba continued to be sent in throughout February and March, now with the support of the infiltration teams. Many of those loads entered the country along the Palmarejo section of the coast, which was called Fundora Point in the CIA documents. That area — with dense vegetation and caves, low hills and few inhabitants — is between

Santa Cruz del Norte and Arcos de Canasí, on the northern coast, around 80 kilometers east of the capital. An infiltration team and Marcial Arufe, one of the most active underground chiefs, retrieved the shipments.

Two of the highest-ranking chiefs in the underground — former Major Humberto Sorí Marín, Military Coordinator of the Revolutionary Unity Front (FUR), and Rafael Díaz Hanscom, its National Coordinator — entered Cuba illegally at Fundora Point on March 13. The CIA had chosen them to head the largest operation to be carried out in support of the invasion. Manuel Lorenzo Puig Miyar landed with them, and they brought 14 tons of weapons and explosives, which Marcial Arufe hid.

On March 22, Benigno Pérez Vivanco finally managed to enter Cuba (it was his third attempt). As he described it later:

> On March 22, we drew close to the coast, at Palmarejo. They called it Fundora Point. We went very carefully, on a mother ship, because we were afraid that they were waiting for us. We stayed around five miles from the coast, waiting for the reception team to send us signals. When, at last, we saw the lights — two green and one red — we were told to get into a fiberglass speedboat. Another boat with the 16 tons of weapons came behind us. Marcial Arufe was waiting on the coast with a truck, in which some of the weapons and explosives were loaded. Rafael García Rubio, my radio-telegraph operator, and I were driven to Havana and hidden in a safe house, and we set about training various underground groups.[24]

The infiltrated agents tried to carry out the missions for which they had been trained for nearly eight months: contact the counter-revolutionary organizations on the island; establish and guarantee communication with Quarters Eye; pinpoint areas which would be suitable for receiving air drops of weapons and explosives; organize uprisings of insurgents in the mountain areas, mainly in the Sierra de los Organos Mountains (in Pinar del Río Province), the Escambray Mountains (in Las Villas Province) and the Sierra Maestra Mountains (in Oriente Province); train the various underground groups in weapons handling and the use of explosives; and take part in important actions.

Up until the day of the landing, those who hadn't yet been arrested remained in radio contact with the CIA, which sent them orders and

---

[24] Testimony of Benigno Pérez Vivanco, member of an infiltration team.

warned them about safety measures. José Pujals Mederos, who had a radio operator working for him, told the Cuban Department of State Security after he was arrested:

> The CIA was very happy with the infiltration teams' work in Santa Clara... On or around April 1, before the Bay of Pigs attack, we were warned not to be taken in by a diversionary invasion in the southern part of Camagüey Province... Two days before the bombings, a message came warning us that G-2 [Cuban Security] had stepped up its vigilance in the railroad stations, airports and communications centers and that we should stay away from such places, so as not to be arrested.

The team agents organized air drops of weapons and explosives; trained dozens of underground activists in how to handle those death-dealing weapons; sent intelligence messages containing military, economic and political data and reports on the people's morale and state of mind; and participated directly in acts of sabotage, such as the one which turned the largest department store in the country into a heap of rubble. Others promoted uprisings in the Escambray and Sierra Maestra Mountains. Still others sought asylum in embassies as soon as they set foot in Cuba.

Infiltration teams wiped out before the battle

The strategic defeat dealt to the U.S. Government and its intelligence services testifies to the effectiveness of the incipient bodies of Cuban State Security.

Manuel Reyes García, the first U.S. agent to enter the country clandestinely, though he employed legal means to do so, lay low during the Bay of Pigs invasion — "inactive," as he called it. Later, he sent various kinds of messages until he was arrested.

The team sent to Santa Clara under the command of Félix Rodríguez Mendigutía didn't achieve any of its objectives. It did nothing even when the Cuban airports were bombed as the prelude to the invasion. Félix Rodríguez first hid in a conspirator's home and then went to the residence of a Spanish diplomat. From there, he was taken clandestinely to the Venezuelan Embassy and left Cuba on September 13.

Edgar Sopo did the same, and Javier Souto managed to escape minutes before he was to have been arrested in Santa Clara. Later, he went to Havana and was given asylum in the Embassy of Ecuador. Segundo Borges and José González Castro remained in hiding in Santa Clara together with Miguel Pentón, another team member. The three were arrested on April 21 and were taken to the G-2 office in the city.

They were held in Santa Clara for 25 days and were then sent to Havana. Then an amazing thing happened in the headquarters of Cuban State Security, something which showed the tensions of the moment and the lack of organizational experience there: the papers referring to the three were lost. As a result, they weren't given due importance and weren't interrogated again. On September 10, they were transferred to a place which had very few guards, while efforts were made to clarify their situation.

The cell where they were kept was next to a small garage filled with car parts. For six days, using an iron bar which they took from one of the beds, they dug a hole in the wall, and, at 4:00 a.m. on October 11, they managed to escape. When they jumped into the garage, they found that there was only one guard there, and he was napping. A few days later, they sought asylum.

After helping to carry out several acts of sabotage in Havana in March — especially against electric power lines — Gustavo Enrique Casuso Pérez, the team radio operator who had entered Cuba together with the leader of the Student Revolutionary Directorate (DRE) counterrevolutionary organization, took up arms in the Sierra Maestra on April 4, along with Alberto Muller and 45 other men. His mission was to guarantee communication and organize the reception of air drops of supplies, but the air drops never took place. Seeking to remain unnoticed, the group never engaged in combat. On April 21, a Cuban Rebel Army patrol ran into it and inflicted its first losses. Some days later, the rest of the insurgents were captured.

The team headed by Oliverio Tomeu didn't carry out its orders to cut the Matanzas-Camagüey highway. Learning that other counter-revolutionaries had been arrested, Tomeu fled to Havana and sought asylum in the Embassy of Argentina.

Manuel Blanco Navarro, a former officer in Batista's Army, managed to enter Cuba clandestinely on his third attempt, but was captured shortly thereafter.

Adolfo Mendoza, one of the radio operators who parachuted into southern Camagüey Province, sought asylum three days after setting foot in Cuba.

Jorge García Rubio ("Tony"), who also parachuted in, replaced him. On April 15, the day the airports were bombed, he received a message telling him to turn his receiver on every four hours. The arrests that State Security made with the help of the Committees for the Defense of the Revolution (CDRs) forced him to move and to hide the radio equipment. Three months later, he sought asylum in the Colombian Embassy.

On March 18, just five days after having entered Cuba illegally, Humberto Sorí Marín and Rafael Díaz Hanscom — the main chiefs of the Revolutionary Unity Front, whom the CIA had chosen to unleash a vast plan of acts of sabotage and terrorism in support of the invasion — were arrested in a Security operation, as were Manuel Lorenzo Puig Miyar, a radio operator and team member, and Rogelio González Corzo, an underground chief and CIA liaison who had been working for the CIA for two years under the pseudonym "Francisco."

At 6:00 a.m. on April 21, Benigno Pérez Vivanco, chief of the Inca team, and Rafael Ernesto García Rubio, his second-in-command, headed back to the apartment — considered one of the safest in Havana — where they had been hiding ever since their illegal entry in

Cuba on March 23. They had just spent the night with two women at a pay-by-the-hour motel. Since arriving in Cuba, they had trained several groups in weapons and explosives handling and had also sent information back to headquarters, in the United States.

As soon as they entered the apartment, a group of uniformed men knocked on the door. Marcial Arufe shot at the Security agents, wounding three of them, but they returned his fire and shot him dead. Benigno and Rafael were arrested. Soon afterwards, the 16 tons of weapons and explosives they had brought were seized.

In time, Miguel Angel Orozco Crespo, one of the best students in the training camps, headed up the Special Missions Groups in the CIA's operations against Cuba. On November 5, 1962, near the end of the October Missile Crisis, he was arrested after landing in Pinar del Río Province with the mission of sabotaging the cable cars that were used to take copper out of the Matahambre Mines.

Cuban Security captured 23 of the 35 agents who had entered Cuba illegally in the weeks prior to the Bay of Pigs invasion. Thus, two thirds of the agents who had been trained with the greatest care by excellent instructors, provided with the most advanced means of communication of their era and backed up by the best CIA agents in the country, were discovered and captured by the youngest State Security body in the world less than 18 months after the first of them had entered the country.

The psychological climate

I [told the CIA's Richard Bissell that I] intended to organize exile groups of women, workers, professionals, and students to act as propaganda fronts. I would support a number of exile publications. Radio broadcasts and, eventually, leaflet drops would be the vital operations. I would need my own airplane for the leaflet drops just before and on the day of the invasion, and a large medium-wave radio station...

I told Bissell that I would need a powerful transmitter, perhaps 50 kilowatts, to broadcast on medium-wave. Cuban listeners, unlike Guatemalans [in 1954], were not accustomed to short-wave. Further, we would be competing with Fidel Castro...

"Do the necessary," Bissell said. "...How long will it take to create the proper psychological climate?"

— *David A. Phillips*[25]

This conversation took place on April 17, 1960, in the office of Richard Bissell, Plans Director in the CIA. Bissell was in charge of the operation for wiping out the Cuban Revolution. Phillips replied that, although it had taken only six weeks in Guatemala, it would require close to six months in Cuba. In fact, Phillips had a whole year in which to psychologically soften up the Cuban people, because the invasion took place exactly a year after that meeting — on April 17, 1961.

Bissell considered the creation of a radio station whose broadcasts would be beamed at the Cuban people to be the most important part of the anti-Cuban operation. He entrusted the project to actor-journalist David A. Phillips, who was one of the Agency's best propaganda experts. Phillips had organized the radio war against Jacobo Arbenz in 1954; he was up to date on Cuba, since he had been posted to Havana in the final years of Fulgencio Batista's dictatorial rule; and, after the

---

25 David A. Phillips, *The Night Watch*, 88-9.

triumph of the Revolution, he had taken part in several plans against the government, including at least one plot to assassinate Fidel Castro.

After his first meeting with Bissell, Phillips threw himself into the task. The first thing he did was select the place from which to broadcast to Cuba. He chose Swan Island, a speck of land in the Gulf of Honduras, 97 miles north of Patuca Point, Honduras, south of the westernmost tip of Cuba. The island belonged to the United States, though the Honduran Government also claimed it.

A group of specialists made a study and designed the antenna system. The technical support was fully guaranteed by the Army, Navy and Air Force. Phillips's team set about trying to find a 50-kw. transmitter with antennae so its broadcasts would reach nearly all of Cuban territory and get through in spite of interference.

The only available transmitter was in the Federal Republic of Germany, installed on a train. It was to be sent to the United States, to be used by the Voice of America — one of the stations controlled by the U.S. Government which had been harassing Cuba ever since 1959, though with the limitations imposed by its being a government station. Several telephone calls were made, and ownership of the transmitter passed to the CIA. Since Swan Island didn't have a port or beach where the heavy equipment could be unloaded, a detachment of Navy engineers was sent to the island and quickly built a dock, which was ready before the arrival of the ship bringing the transmitter. Meanwhile, another battalion built an airstrip for cargo planes and prepared around five blocks of land for the installation of the three huge steel towers that would serve as antennae for the project.

Once the work was under way, Phillips went to Boston to give a veneer of legality to the new enterprise. There, he contacted Thomas Dudley Cabot, an old collaborator with the CIA and former President of the United Fruit Company. In 1951, Cabot had also been Director of the State Department's Office of International Security Affairs. Phillips and Cabot reached an agreement, and the Gibraltar Steamship Corporation, whose headquarters were at 437 Fifth Avenue, New York, publicly announced that it had leased land on Swan Island for operating a radio station.

One detail which Phillips apparently let slip caught the attention of journalists: the steamship company, which appeared as the owner of the station, hadn't owned any ships at all for the last 10 years. Its "business manager" stated that the station would broadcast music, sit-coms and news. He told the journalists that it was a strictly commercial company and that it hoped to get advertisers — it didn't have any yet, but it was negotiating.

Certainly, when the station went on the air, it had Coca-Cola, Colgate, Pan American, GoodYear and other ads. Coincidentally, all of those companies had been adversely affected by the laws of the Revolutionary Government.

While legal cover was being created for the projected station, other CIA officers recruited several dozen Cuban exiles in Miami as technicians, journalists and announcers. They included the journalists Sergio Carbó, Humberto Medrano, Ulises Carbó (who later came on the invasion), Francisco Gutiérrez and José Ignacio Rivero and the announcers Arturo Artalejo and Alberto Gandero, whose voices had been heard in Cuba for years; Enrique Huerta; Angel del Cerro; Luis Conte Agüero, a journalist who had had a radio program in Cuba during the struggle against the Batista dictatorship; and Pepita Riera.

Phillips thought that Pepita might become another "Tokyo Rose." (That legendary radio announcer, whose real name was Iva Toguri, had been born in the United States in 1916. During World War II, the U.S. authorities interned her family along with thousands of other Japanese citizens and U.S. citizens of Japanese descent living in the United States. They were put in "camps" simply because the United States was at war with their country of origin. Iva escaped that fate because she happened to be in Tokyo on a visit when the war broke out. Her mastery of English opened the doors of the Japanese Special Services to her, and she began working at a radio station whose programs were beamed at the U.S. forces stationed in the Pacific. Her harangues were so inflamed and impassioned that, when Japan was occupied, her captors treated her as a war criminal.)

The radio war unleashed against Cuba sought to repeat the "Tokyo Rose" legend, but, in fact, "Havana Rose" was nothing but a caricature who failed to convince even her enthusiastic sponsors.

Radio Cuba Libre (Radio Swan) went on the air on the evening of May 17, 1960, just 30 days after Phillips' meeting with Bissell. The 1160-khz broadcast came in loud and clear. Cuban audiences were very familiar with the voices, which were combined in an extensive program of news, commentaries, editorials and special features that sought to undermine confidence in the Revolution. The content consisted of vicious lies that were hard to check and prophecies of bloodbaths. Its boastful tone was impossible to miss.

That initial aim was broadened. As the invasion plan was developed, the radio station also served as liaison with the groups of insurgents who were operating in the Cuban mountains, the counterrevolutionaries in the cities and the scores of underground agents the CIA had recruited.

Phillips' network grew to control not only Radio Swan but also stations WRUL, Miami's WGBS, Key West's WKWF, New Orleans's WWL and WMIE (which still exists as one of the counterrevolutionary stations in Florida, under the call signal WQBA La Cubanísima). These stations were all low-key and weren't recognized as being opposed to Fidel Castro. Their purpose was to influence Cubans of all political shades and encourage them to support the invaders.

Radio Swan still had primary strategic responsibility within this network. It broadcast for a whole year, seeking to carry out the task Bissell had assigned to it: that of confusing ordinary Cubans. The following reports, which it broadcast, testify eloquently to that aim. They were monitored by Cuban counterintelligence between June 1960 and April 1961.

- Napoleon: using channel you know, send report on the Communists, collaborators and their local supporters in the area in which you operate.
- Teodomico: when the first grenades explode, stand next to the wall; if you throw yourself on the ground, don't do so close to the grenade. Get some kerosene lanterns, because the electric power will be cut very soon.
- Teodomico: remember that those who are coming are Cubans, not U.S. citizens. When they land, join them, as they will be given heavy artillery cover.
- Fidel Castro is going to create a church in which the priests and nuns will be mere government employees.
- Cuban mothers! Pay attention: the next law issued by the Government will take your children away from you from the time they are 5 until they are 18.
- The body of a militia was found at kilometer 7 on the Rancho Boyeros highway. The bodies of three militia were found hanged at the corner of 90th Street and 43rd Avenue, in Marianao.
- Militia! Be careful when you go out. Go only in groups of three, as they do in Russia. If you don't want to die, change sides and join the ranks of the true revolution.
- Prisoners' relatives can't visit them any more, because the prisoners are being sent to Russia.
- Che is going to Russia to save his skin, and he won't be in Cuba on the day of the struggle, which is fast approaching.
- The bodies of three militia were found hanged at the corner of 42nd Street and 11th Avenue, in Marianao.

- They're asking for a million clothes hangers. The people won't believe it's because they're needed. They'll be used to make barbed wire fences to protect the rulers.
- The United States has prohibited shipments of all goods to Cuba.
- People of Cuba! The hour of liberation is fast approaching.
- Fidel is trying to find a way to destroy the Church, but this cannot be. Cubans! Go to church and do what the clergy tell you.
- A group of students was arrested in Camagüey for burning buses.
- A priest was arrested in Pinar del Río for having given food to the poor in that territory.
- Our underground services have reported a shoot-out at the Rancho Boyeros airport, which caused flights to be cancelled.
- Attention, Cuba! Attention, Cuba! The butterflies arrived successfully.
- Even the quiet of the grave has ended in Cuba. During the latest militia mobilization, Colón Cemetery was turned into a campsite. Militia are cooking their meals on the tombs and have put up beds in the pantheons. Washing has been hung out in some areas. As yet unconfirmed rumors state that the vandals have desecrated some graves.

One of the reactionary newspapers that still circulated in Cuba published cartoons showing militia taking jewels from the tombs. This lie was relatively easy to check, however; all anyone had to do was go to the cemetery to see for themselves.

After the triumph of the Revolution, the Cuban press, like most of the other mass media, remained untouched. Only those means of communication which belonged to dictator Fulgencio Batista (TV Channel 12 and the Circuito Nacional Cubano radio station) and to other notorious figures linked to the dictatorship (the Cadena Oriental de Radio, Unión Radio and Reloj de Cuba radio stations and the newspapers *Ataja, Alerta, Mañana* and *Tiempo en Cuba*) were taken over.

The large dailies which remained, *Bohemia* magazine, the television channels and the CMQ and Radio Progreso national radio networks all defended the prevailing economic structure in the country, which had caused terrible social ills, and submissively accepted political dependence on the United States. Even the most daring critics considered it a necessary evil.

Shortly after the 1959 Revolution, the U.S. press began a rabid smear campaign against the Cuban Government. The *Time-Life* consortium, *U.S. News and World Report, Visión* and the daily *Miami Herald* were among the most vociferous. That effort, which became an operation for softening up the Cuban people psychologically and molding U.S. and Latin American public opinion, had its beginnings in those first few months. In May 1959, Miami's *Diario de Las Américas* published a UPI article reporting that police forces had made a dawn attack on a convent of nuns. The Bishop of Camagüey promptly declared that the report was completely unfounded, but his statement wasn't published in the United States.

Throughout 1959 and in the first few months of 1960, overtly or covertly, the press harassed, slandered and spewed forth poison against the main figures of the Revolutionary Government, trotting out the spectre of communism for the purpose. The press of the era featured editorials and articles, statements by officials of the U.S. Government, and sensational news items about defections and counterrevolutionary actions.

Their titles speak for themselves: "The Church Persecuted," "Christ Shows the Way to Freedom," "Catholicism, Yes; Communism, No," "Party Plurality," "They Want to Bring the Cold War to America," "Democracy Cannot Exist Where Free Enterprise Is Destroyed," "The Conspiracy against Freedom" and "Democracy Made in Moscow."

In the United States, the press launched daily attacks on Cuba, seeking to discredit what was happening there. The *World Telegram* called Fidel a liar, and another daily compared him with Hitler and Mussolini. *Time* called Díaz Lanz, Urrutia and Huber Matos prominent Cubans. The King Feature Syndicate wrote that, as soon as Castro opened his mouth, you could tell he wasn't rational, for his voice was one of hatred, not compassion, and he was driven by a blood lust, not any desire to provide food and shelter for the poor. The *Philadelphia Bulletin* noted that the important thing, when speaking of Castro, was to ask not where he was going but how long he would stay in power. And an editorial in the New York *Mirror* called openly for U.S. Marines to intervene, saying that the United States should act promptly, for Cuba wasn't just any Caribbean island but could become a base for the enemies of the United States.

In Cuba, the reactionary press competed with its U.S. counterparts. The *Diario de la Marina* and *Avance* became mouthpieces of the counterrevolutionary campaign. In those circumstances, the Provincial Journalists' Association resolved on December 26, 1959, that workers on the newspapers could append clarifying notes to articles containing false or slanderous information against the Revolutionary Government. Thus, the *coletilla*, or workers' commentary, was born. The owners responded by engaging in various maneuvers and wound up by trying to paralyze the press. The workers' reply was overwhelming, for they took over the companies and appointed new editors from among themselves. Between January 18 and July 18, 1960, all of the newspapers, magazines and radio and television stations in the country which had taken part in the campaigns against the government were taken over. Phillips found himself up against a situation that made it extremely difficult for him to do his work in Cuba: his allies in the media had been wiped out. The psychological climate would have to be created and imposed from abroad. However, this didn't mean entirely abandoning propaganda against the Revolutionary Government on its own soil.

Cuba didn't have enough radars of the right kind, so Phillips took advantage of that fact to draw up a program for dropping leaflets, using several small planes based in the Florida Keys. Hundreds of thousands of pamphlets began to be dropped over Cuba, spreading lies and calling on the people to carry out acts of sabotage, burn the fields of sugarcane and try to kill militia and government leaders. Naturally, Radio Swan backed up the pamphlet campaign, which did succeed in confusing some of the population. This was shown during the campaign which said that parents would lose legal custody of their children.

Legal custody of children

Operation Peter Pan began to take shape in Washington in mid-1960. (It was called that because Peter Pan had taken the three darling children away to Never-Never Land.) The name was sadly ironic: for many of those children who were sent out of Cuba, the United States would be a land from which they would never, never return home. The operation formed part of the arsenal used to psychologically soften up the Cuban people. With it, the Propaganda Section in Quarters Eye decided to unleash a propaganda campaign to make ordinary Cubans believe that, under a communist government, children — like the land, industries, stores and housing — would become the property of the state. If that happened, parents would lose legal custody of their children.

The CIA experts were confident that, if they managed to sow that doubt in some of the people, the fear would gather momentum and could lead to the exodus of thousands of children, split up families and thus undermine the families' support of the government. Undoubtedly, it would be a most effective destabilizing measure.

The first phase of the operation consisted of having the radio station carry a "news" bulletin that would alarm the people and be spread by word of mouth. Therefore, one October night in 1960, Radio Swan made its first reference to this subject in its 8:00 news broadcast:

> Cuban mothers, don't let them take your children away! The Revolutionary Government will take them away from you when they turn five and will keep them until they are 18. By that time, they will be materialist monsters.[26]

Several days later, they added a key word — *law* — to that report:

> Attention, Cubans! Remember how, in the past, at this hour of liberation, we told you about many of the laws which the

---

[26] Archives of the State Security Historical Research Center, Havana.

Government put into effect later on. For example, the Urban Reform.

Now, we announce the next law: they will take your children away from you when they turn five years old and keep them until they are 18. And, by the time they are returned to you, they will have become materialist fiends, and Fidel Castro will have become the Mother Superior of Cuba. Don't let them take your children away!

Attention, Cubans! Go to church and follow the instructions given you by the clergy.[27]

During the following months, over and over again, the station would rebroadcast that false "news item" about children being taken away from their parents. In December 1960, the CIA experts felt that the idea had taken root on the island and decided to go on to the next phase, which would split Cuban families and finally cause some of them to oppose the government. That would guarantee solid support for the invaders. Under apparently legal cover, using the services of the Catholic Church, the children's exodus began. Operation Peter Pan was carried out under a religious cloak as "humanitarian assistance" provided by the Catholic Services Bureau in Florida. Its main protagonist, who allowed himself to be used as a figurehead, was Monsignor Bryan O. Walsh.

As he recalled some years later, he entered the State Department by a side door. It seemed very mysterious to him, as if he were working for the FBI or some such thing. He reported that, in the course of a three-hour-long conversation, he was asked to take part in a plan to take children out of Cuba, being assured that visa waivers would be issued.

High-ranking officials in the State Department and in the Attorney General's Office, plus the CIA officer in charge of the program, who said his name was Harold Bishop, took part in those initial meetings. In fact, "Bishop" was David A. Phillips. Naturally, he had to be there. He had created Radio Swan and Operation Peter Pan. Years later, he became notorious when one of the investigators on the U.S. House of Representatives' Special Committee on Assassinations said that he might have been the CIA officer who talked with Lee Harvey Oswald in a building in Dallas two months before President Kennedy was assassinated. Phillips was thus included in the long list of U.S. intelligence agents who were linked in one way or another to that murder.

---

[27] Archives of the State Security Historical Research Center, Havana.

By the time the State Department meetings ended, Monsignor Walsh had the first 500 visa waivers in his briefcase. The CIA had been clear: authorization would be granted only to children and adolescents between five and 18 years old. Not to their parents, who would remain in Cuba to swell the ranks of the opposition to Fidel Castro. At least, they would have a moral pretext for doing so.

Walsh contacted other bishops in Florida to find a reliable collaborator in Havana, to whom he would send the visa waivers secretly. A week later, Ramón Grau Alsina,[28] who was in charge of the Catholic Welfare Bureau in Cuba, accepted the job of promoting the children's exodus from Cuba. "Mongo" Grau had been conspiring against the Cuban Revolution ever since its triumph and was a member of Rescate, one of the subversive organizations that was closely linked to the CIA through the Democratic Revolutionary Front.

The Customs and Immigration Service officials at Havana's José Martí International Airport were surprised to see a dozen children traveling unaccompanied to the United States on December 26, 1960, but their documents were in order, and their parents were seeing them off. Therefore, they stamped their passports.

The first shipment to Never-Never Land was on its way. From then on, the CIA could depend on the complicity of the Church hierarchy in Cuba.

The priest of Santa María del Rosario went all over the island, but never to my house. He sent an intermediary once a week who would sit in the little green reception room in my house; I would give her the package of visa waivers, and she would give me the new list of names.[29]

James Baker, a U.S. citizen who headed Ruston Academy — an American school in Havana — until it was nationalized, brought a large number of visa waivers to Cuba. He became a sort of program secretary.

The first 500 children left by the end of March 1961. Then Monsignor Walsh, following the instructions of the CIA officer in charge of Operation Peter Pan, asked the Immigration Service for 500 more visa waivers. On receiving the request, the Immigration officer asked him if he was trying to take all Cuban children out of the country. The exodus really gathered momentum. Baker recalled that he was in the Miami airport from 9:00 in the morning until late at

---

28 Former Cuban President Ramón Grau San Martín was his uncle.
29 Statement by Ramón Grau Alsina. Archives of the Cuban Ministry of the Interior.

night — sometimes 11:00, midnight or 1:00 a.m. — because the last flight was supposed to arrive at around 8:00, and sometimes there were three or four flights a day.[30]

Some of the people who were conspiring against the Cuban Government used that means to get their children away from the dangerous atmosphere in which they were living; other families, fearing a possible invasion of the island — which was talked about daily — chose to send their children away from such an eventuality. Still others, out of ignorance, really believed that the Government was going to take their children away from them. Many of the farmers who took up arms in the mountains during the final months of 1960 were motivated by the campaign, stating that they feared they would lose legal custody of their children.

Leopoldina Grau Alsina, "Mongo" Grau's sister, was one of the people most closely involved in the program. Many years later, when she was released from prison, she revealed in an interview the essence of that dirty operation:

Q: You were one of the top people promoting the counter-revolutionary campaign concerning legal custody of children.

A: Yes. We spread a rumor saying that the Communist Government owned the children lock, stock and barrel and that parents would lose legal custody of their children. We said the children would be sent to Russia. We even printed a fake "law" of the Revolutionary Government to that effect.

Q: Did you sincerely believe that?

A: No, not really.

Q: Then why did you do it?

A: It was a way to destabilize the government. To make the people begin to lose faith in the Revolution.

Q: That's quite a shameless attitude.

A: Perhaps, but we were at war with the Government, and, in a war, anything goes.

In the days leading up to the invasion, Radio Swan had sent many messages to the counterrevolutionaries who were operating in the underground. It described imaginary battles in the mountains in which entire battalions were defeated and announced new uprisings, acts of sabotage, and conflicts amongst and desertions from the ranks of the revolutionaries.

---

[30] Interview with Mercedes Arce, the author's archives.

Early on the morning of the day of the landing, the station announced the "victorious advance of the invaders, the seizure of cities and the flight of the main leaders of the Revolution." A sample of the "news items" carried by the U.S. media at the time follows below:

- The invading forces have occupied the city of Pinar del Río, capital of the province of the same name. The invasion of Matanzas and Santiago Provinces is progressing favorably. (UPI)
- An invading force has reached Cuba's main east-west highway, advancing from Matanzas Province to cut the island in two. (UPI)
- The Isle of Pines was taken by the insurgents; 10,000 political prisoners were set free and have joined the uprising. (UPI)
- A thousand soldiers of former President Carlos Prío Socarrás landed in Oriente Province. (AP)
- Luis Conte Agüero has landed with his commandos at the port of Bayamo and is marching toward the Escambray to join the victorious invading troops. (Radio Swan)

Eleven million leaflets openly inciting the people to rebel were at Happy Valley, Nicaragua (where Brigade 2506's squadron of planes was based), ready to be dropped over Cuba. In the end, they were burned.

How did the Cuban people — who had been subjected to psychological warfare for a whole year — react? Had they been softened up? The answer is well known, but one typical example of what occurred all over the country was what happened in the small town of Jagüey Grande, the one nearest the area where the landing took place.

At around 1:00 a.m., a militia who was on duty at the police station received a phone call in which he was told that a landing was taking place and that he should advise the battalion which was posted at a nearby sugar mill. He immediately passed on the warning, and the chief of the battalion, without waiting for orders, set out toward the beach with his forces. Meanwhile, the news spread like wildfire through the town. Many of the men there belonged to another battalion and were home on leave. Word spread from house to house, and they used any means they could to get to headquarters to obtain their weapons.

During the early morning hours, rumors were rife: "Get up; the invasion's started! The Americans are attacking! They're in the swamp!" The people gathered at militia headquarters, the Town Hall and the Rebel Army's garrison, asking for weapons and instructions. The Federation of Cuban Women (FMC) mobilized its members and sent them to the Red Cross. Ordinary citizens volunteered to protect the town's key points: the electric power station, the shortwave radio station, the town's water tanks and the gasoline storage tanks.

Boxes of rifles were opened at the Rebel Army's garrison, and they were distributed to a group of citizens who said they knew how to use them. Thirty-two of them were selected, and they set off quickly in two trucks, heading for the landing area.

By 10:00 a.m., members of the Committees for the Defense of the Revolution had arrested the best-known counterrevolutionaries, and they were taken to the city of Matanzas in a truck. People cheered militia on their way to the front lines, shouting, "Watch out for the planes! Give them hell! Homeland or Death!"

Dozens of men and women became first-aid workers and stretcher bearers and went out in search of the wounded, using vehicles which they commandeered from the counterrevolutionaries and painted with a white cross. The old people attended burial services and dug graves. There was one moment when over 60 bodies — of both revolutionaries and invaders — came in together. All were given Christian burials.

None of the inhabitants of Jagüey Grande, soldiers or militia — on any of the battlefronts — went over to Brigade 2506. And this was true throughout Cuba.

Imitating Fidel Castro

The heavy plane was ordered to take off. Up in the control tower, the officer in charge of the operation wished Eduardo Ferrer, the pilot, good luck. He would fly the unmarked plane (which had no emblems on its fuselage by which it could be identified) without any radio contact for four hours from the Rethaluleu air base, in the Guatemalan jungle, to central Cuba.

Eduardo Ferrer had worked as a pilot for Aerovías Q, a Cuban commercial airline which had pulled up stakes and gone to the United States shortly after the 1959 Revolution. Now, he was going to violate Cuban airspace and run the risk of being shot at from the ground. Eduardo Ferrer was a CIA pilot. His mission was to drop a load of weapons and explosives at an insurgent camp.

He drew close to the Cuban coast at around midnight. Then he turned off the lights on board and moved the control stick forward. The four-engine plane began to descend.

When he entered the Guamuhaya Range, he made several turns to avoid hitting the tops of the mountains. Soon afterwards, on coming out of a bank of clouds, he saw the cross of lights like twinkling stars marking the drop area. His altimeter showed 400 feet. It was the right height for making the drop. He pushed the button that turned on the green light and pressed the buzzer. The parachute drop officers connected the static lines and dropped the packages. A few seconds later, half a dozen parachutes opened in the darkness of the night. Ferrer made a sharp turn and headed south to sweep out over the Atlantic Ocean.

After gaining altitude, he turned the lights back on, put the plane on automatic pilot, drank some coffee and lit a cigarette. The drop had been a success. He felt satisfied, even though he knew that the men who had coordinated the operation in the enemy's rear guard deserved most of the credit.

Ferrer was right. The operation had been meticulously synchronized. What Ferrer and his superiors in Quarters Eye didn't know was that Cuban State Security had taken part in it.

Preparations for the air drop had begun a month earlier, when Benigno Balsa, an activist in the Movement of Revolutionary Recovery (MRR) underground organization, was called in to see its coordinator. On arriving at the impressive mansion at 17th and H Streets, in Vedado, Havana, Benigno thought that this man would have plenty of reasons for opposing Castro. By that time in 1960, in the latter half of the second year of the Revolution, the Cuban bourgeoisie had been practically eliminated.

Lino Bernabé, the owner of the house and one of the national coordinators of the underground organization, led him to the library and went straight to the point. "The U.S. Embassy" — that was the somewhat euphemistic manner used by anti-Castro agents in referring to the CIA Station in the Embassy — "asked me to select a farm in the Escambray for dropping a load of weapons for Commander Joaquín Membrive's people. Right now, the only thing the Americans need is a map with the name of the farm and those adjoining it. Obviously, they have already mapped the region."

The next day, Balsa and a man he trusted set out by car for the old colonial city of Trinidad, which — lying on a spur of the Escambray Mountains — was the general headquarters for the insurgent rear guard that had been operating in the mountains for the last three months.

The city was still in a state of euphoria over the Revolution, with signs everywhere bearing revolutionary emblems and platoons of militia marching through its cobblestone streets. But the atmosphere was sultry. In low-voiced conversations and street-corner whisperings, as harbingers of the coming storm, you could hear, "There are insurgents in the Escambray!"

After going to several houses, Balsa found the local head of the MRR, to whom he conveyed the CIA's request. The man told him he needed two days to contact the insurgent chief and select the farm. Balsa agreed. Without any story to explain why he was staying in the city for two days, Balsa would surely have appeared suspect to the members of the Committees for the Defense of the Revolution, an organization which had been created not long before in every block in every city in the country. Therefore, he decided to go on to Cienfuegos, a city 100 kilometers farther to the west, where he had relatives and old friends. He would take advantage of the trip to contact other cells in the organization which supplied men and weapons to the anti-Castro insurgents in the Escambray.

He returned to Trinidad 48 hours later and, a few hours after that, started back to the capital. The map that the Air Operations Section at

Quarters Eye had requested was packed tightly in a small cylindrical box of talcum powder hidden beneath the car's motor.

A week later, Air Force Colonel Stanley W. Beerli located the name of the farm on the military map hanging on the wall of his office: El Lumbre.

Two weeks passed, and MRR coordinator Lino Bernabé asked Balsa to come in again. "Go back to Trinidad. The uprising will take place three days from now," he said, the words bursting out of him even before he had sat down on the sofa. "Tell them that they should dig four pits in the drop area and light bonfires in them that are visible only from the air. The pits should be 100 meters apart, in the form of a square. At midnight, a group of men lined up along the imaginary cross will shine flashlights on their backs. The parachutes will fall on them."

Balsa set off for Trinidad and, on the night the drop was to take place, remained hidden in a safe house belonging to the MRR, where he would be informed of the results of the operation. He couldn't fall asleep. The air operation was the most important one in which he had participated and was considered decisive for supporting the insurgent column that was operating in the region under the leadership of the MRR, the strongest of the organizations that were opposing the Revolutionary Government. Therefore, he was startled when, early in the morning, someone started banging on the door of the house where he was in hiding.

"The first shot rang out when we were about to open the boxes," the recent arrival said. Balsa sat down in front of him and begged him to calm down. "Then there were bursts. They caught us off guard. They were militia who operated in the area, and it seems they heard the plane and saw the parachutes. Most of Membrive's men who took part in the operation were taken prisoner, but he wasn't there. It's a miracle that I managed to escape. The worst thing is, we lost the boxes." Balsa frowned. The man's story was convincing. "Were you the only one who escaped?" he asked doubtfully. "No," the man replied, not understanding everything that was implied by the question. "Four others came down with me."

Balsa started back to Havana to report the failure of the operation to Lino Bernabé, but first he went to a safe house and met with a high-ranking officer of State Security. Benigno Balsa was an undercover agent operating inside MRR, where he held the post of supplies chief for the insurgents in the Escambray Mountains.

Those events, which Benigno Balsa described to me, took place in September 1960.

Three months earlier, the organizations in the Democratic Revolutionary Front had promised the CIA that they would foment insurgency in the mountains of Cuba, especially the Escambray.

Bissell was a firm believer in the possibility of developing a powerful insurgent movement based on guerrilla struggle, a movement as powerful as the one Fidel Castro had headed just two years before. The reasoning in the Quarters Eye office was that, since Castro had defeated Batista with guerrillas, they should be able to oust him from power by using his own methods. It seemed simplistic, but Bissell knew what he was doing. His insurgents wouldn't have to wrest their weapons from the enemy, as Castro had had to do, or to save up pennies to buy them. His insurgents would be supplied by air with hundreds of tons of weapons and explosives and plenty of money and food. The anti-Castro movement would have training camps, a fleet of armed ships and highly skilled command cadres and instructors. That's why the grey and black teams were being trained at the Trax Base, in Guatemala.

Castro had triumphed with very little; how could he, who had so much, fail? All he had to do was imitate him.

The members of the Democratic Revolutionary Front, following CIA instructions, set about instructing their followers on the island in how to organize uprisings. Antonio Varona, Coordinator of the FRD and top leader of Rescate, appointed his brother-in-law, José Ramón Ruisánchez ("Mongo"), a lard dealer who was still in Cuba, to head the subversive project. Ruisánchez would operate under the pseudonym of "Augusto" and, with Varona's support, would rise to the rank of Commander. He would direct the operations from his luxury residence in the exclusive Country Club neighborhood.

The CIA station in Havana supplied Ruisánchez with radio equipment with which to communicate with the insurgent forces in the mountains.

Osvaldo Ramírez, a former lieutenant in the Rebel Army, became an insurgent on August 12, 1960, and rose to become their top leader. (Ramírez had had problems with the revolutionary authorities when, a few weeks after the triumph of the Revolution, he had evicted a group of farmers who had moved onto the land of a rich landowner in the Caracusey area, where Ramírez was chief of the military post, and burned their thatched-roof huts.)

That same day, Sinesio Walsh, a former major in the Rebel Army's Second Front of the Escambray, also headed for the mountains, along with a group of friends and relatives. Three days later, on August 15, Evelio Duque Millar, who had close relations with the clergy, did the same. "Commander Augusto" quickly named him military chief of the Army of Liberation, keeping the title of civilian chief for himself.

Commander Plinio Prieto, a friend of former President Carlos Prío, went secretly to Miami, hidden aboard the *Río Escondido*, a merchant vessel. In the United States, he met with CIA officers and was trained in handling means of communication. On his return, he brought back a radio unit which he installed in the Escambray Mountains. With it, he would fix the coordinates to guide the pilots who would drop the loads of weapons for the camps under his command.

William Alexander Morgan, a former paratrooper and adventurer, had arrived in Cuba in 1958, saying that he came to avenge the death of a friend who had been killed by Batista's soldiers. He established contact with Eloy Gutiérrez Menoyo and, soon afterwards, took up arms in the Escambray. He quickly rose to the rank of major in the Rebel Army's Second Front. After the triumph of the Revolution, he was involved in a conspiracy to overthrow the Government. Its threads spread from the Dominican capital, and it had the discreet and tentative support of the CIA. Morgan and Gutiérrez Menoyo warned Fidel of the conspiracy, but some think that Morgan decided to change sides and wait for another opportunity when he realized that too many people were involved in the plot for it to remain a secret.

It seems that Morgan's opportunity came in mid-1960. One night in September, he called all of his guards together in a room in his house in Havana and told them categorically that he had decided to rebel against the Government and that he was confident that all of them would follow him. He said that those who didn't would be convicting themselves as spies or Communists. Morgan was popular because of his conviviality and had previously expressed public admiration for Fidel Castro. He declared the meeting ended after saying that the U.S. Embassy would give him everything he wanted. His claim was no exaggeration.

A few days later, using his post as head of the Department of Fluvial Restocking in INRA — which meant, among other things, that he was in charge of breeding bullfrogs and planting gardenias in the Guanayara Lagoon, in the Escambray — he began to move supplies into the mountains. He set up a recruiting and training center in the home of Clotilde Pérez, an old friend and collaborator. Once the area was consolidated, the new recruits would be trained by the black teams, which were winding up their training in the Guatemalan jungle. He decided to use his INRA post and to keep on playing a double game while moving weapons and explosives to the Escambray.

Commander Evelio Duque was surprised but not displeased by José Ramón Ruisánchez's orders not to attack but to lie low. The order came from Quarters Eye and was aimed at increasing the number of insurgents, providing them with arms and training them without exposing them. It was thought that by the time the Cuban Government became aware of the situation, it would be too late to reverse it.

The secrecy surrounding the presence of insurgents in the Escambray Mountains didn't last long. Farmers warned the military chiefs in Las Villas Province of movements of men and weapons and even of shooting practice. Some patrols were immediately dispatched.

First, we went to Plinio Prieto's father- and mother-in-law's house, but he had already left. Then we went to Clotilde Pérez's house. We surrounded it and caught two insurgents who were hiding there. The others had gone. We seized a shortwave radio set and several knapsacks, officers' insignia and blankets — but no weapons. We took Clotilde, the Spaniard, prisoner. After that, we went out nearly every day, but we didn't find any of the insurgents. Then confidential information reached us concerning where Plinio and his troops were. While we were preparing to go, an order came from Fidel to suspend the operations.[31]

In September 1960, it seemed that an insurgent force would remain in the Escambray Mountains. For the moment, its members would try to avoid clashes with the few patrols which went out after them. Their combat mission was to begin as soon as the CIA teams arrived. However, the calm in those beautiful surroundings didn't last long. The storm which would hit the insurgents was massing at Hoyo de Manicaragua, a farm on the mountain spurs which was world-famous for the high quality of its tobacco.

On September 8, the first large force which the Revolution had trained to fight the insurgents completed its training and prepared to begin operations. Fidel Castro had been aware of the presence of armed men in the mountains. In July 1960, when the first reports about them came in, he gave instructions that a farmers' militia be organized in that mountain area as a means for meeting the threat. Around 800 farmers gathered at La Campana Farm. There, they were given classes in weapons handling, infantry, tactics and shooting. They were divided up in 25 platoons, each headed by a Rebel Army officer who had distinguished himself in the anti-Batista guerrilla struggle.

---

[31] Testimony of Rebel Army Lieutenant Víctor Cortés, the author's archives.

I was near Guayabal de Yateras, Yateritas, close to Guantánamo, when Fidel ordered Major Feliberto Olivera to choose 25 Rebel Army officers, those who were best at hiking... We were taken to La Campana.[32]

Most of those officers were of farming stock.

Their training ended on September 5, and Fidel Castro paid an unannounced visit to the camp. Standing on a small hill, he spoke to them about the political situation in the Escambray, the U.S. Government's plans and the kind of weapons the insurgents had. He placed special emphasis on how they should behave toward the farmers' families and during combat.

Elio Jorge was one of the Escambray farmers who presented themselves at La Campana in July 1960. He came alone, having walked a long way. He had been plowing when a friend had gone up to him and told him "confidentially" that he should be very careful, because insurgents were in the area, and they had their eye on him because they knew he was a revolutionary and had benefited from the Agrarian Reform. Elio left his plow in the furrow, let the oxen loose and headed for his thatched-roof hut.

"I'm going to La Campana," I told my wife, and I set out. At La Campana, I saw Fidel for the first time. He climbed up on a little hill and talked to us. He told us what we had to do when we met up with the insurgents. Then he ordered a crate of rifles to be opened, and he shot with a Czech rifle. Then with a machine gun with legs, standing. He told us that we had to respect the farmers; that we couldn't take anything without permission; and that, if they gave us food, we should pay in cash. He said we had to respect prisoners. I liked that.[33]

Fidel spoke for around 30 minutes. Beside him, "Boliche" Broche, another of the farmers, held a canteen. Every so often, he passed it to Fidel.

When Fidel left La Campana, he went to Cienfuegos, a city southeast of the Escambray Mountains. There, in a fifth-floor room in the Jagua Hotel, he met with the officers who would take part in the operation. He spread out a map on the bed and explained the strategy they should use. Fidel had decided to break the battalion up into platoons and send them into the mountain area by different access

---

[32] Testimony of Rebel Army Lieutenant Addis Torres, the author's archives.
[33] Testimony of Elio Jorge, farmer.

routes. After their combing operation, the platoons would converge at Topes de Collantes, a massif in the southern part of the range, where a modern sanatorium for tuberculosis patients had been built.

While in Cienfuegos, Fidel was informed that a group of insurgents was in the region. He immediately organized a patrol and prepared to go out after them. "Where are you going?" Juan Milián, the guide, remembers that Major Manuel Fajardo, who had just been named chief of operations, asked him. "What do you mean, where am I going? I'm the one who gives the orders here." The reply allowed for no more liberties. Fidel directed the operation in person, and several insurgents were quickly captured.

On September 8, the 800 farmers, wearing green shirts and blue pants, left La Campana. Elio Jorge recalls that the members of his platoon were taken by train to the point from which they were to climb toward Topes. They began to comb the territory assigned to them along the railroad line where they were left.

The groups of insurgents knew nothing about the offensive which was being launched. José Ramón Ruisánchez was insisting on their being unified (since they belonged to different organizations in the FRD, they had slightly different interests). For that purpose, a unification agreement was promoted, and it took shape on September 10, when the representatives of several counterrevolutionary organizations signed a Provisional Pact. The principles agreed upon included keeping the preparatory activities and organization of the insurgent forces secret and maintaining combat passivity, so as to avoid a military response from the revolutionary leadership. They didn't know that they were practically surrounded at the time.

The idea of operating with farmers from the area was based on the revolutionary leadership's strategic concept of opposing the insurgent forces with the people who lived in the area, allied with the Government, which made it easier to penetrate that intricate world of family and traditional relations which tended to govern the struggle in those mountains.

The idea wasn't new. It had first been used on August 21, 1959, in Pinar del Río Province. Fidel Castro had been exploring the Great Cave of Santo Tomás, and, during a rest, Leandro Malagón, a farmer, told him about the abuses that Corporal Lara and his men — all fugitives from revolutionary justice — were committing. Lara had been a soldier of the Batista dictatorship and, at the triumph of the Revolution, had been condemned to death for the murder of 20 civilians. He managed to escape, however, and fled to the Organos Mountains. He was pursued, but without result. After listening to the farmer, Fidel told him to choose 12 men. They were given weapons and a little training.

"Fidel's ordered me to get 12 farmers from the area together for a job, and you're one of them," Leandro Rodríguez Malagón told me. "Then we learned that the mission was to catch some counter-revolutionaries who had rebelled and were under the comand of the outlaw Lara... When we had been training at the Managua military camp for 26 days, Fidel visited us and, after checking that we were ready, told me, 'Malagón, you have three months to capture the counterrevolutionary band. If you do it, Cuba will have a farmers' militia.'"[34]

Within a matter of weeks, Corporal Lara was captured, and Cuba had a militia.

The Escambray was no exception. The fact that farmers who knew the terrain took part in the operations ensured that pursuit would be successful.

We were camped on the Aguacate, and I had lain down in my hammock to sleep the first quarter of the night and wake up at midnight. I knew that the insurgents moved around at night. The barking of a dog far away woke me. The barks showed where the men were. After a silence, I heard more barking. "Now they're at so-and-so's farm," I thought, and I woke up the troops. We advanced, following the sound of the barks. Two hours later, the dogs stopped barking. "They've camped at such-and-so's farm," I told my platoon, and we went there. We found the trail left by the enemy troops. If you see the grass flattened, they have just gone past. I decided to wait for dawn to go into combat. As soon as the sky started to get light, I positioned my squads and advanced with great caution. When we got near the insurgents' camp, I saw men rocking back and forth in hammocks. Then I remembered what Fidel had said: "Throw yourselves on the ground and open fire. Don't stop firing, and organize the combat." That's what I did. One of the first men we wounded was the second-in-command of the insurgents' column, which demoralized them. From the wilderness, their chief shouted at me, "You shitty Communists, now look what you've done!" I knew Edel Montiel very well, and I replied, "Come out in the open, and let's settle this between us."

---

[34] Testimony published in *Granma*, April 17, 1987, 4.

Montiel had a lot of respect for me from past experience and didn't take up my challenge.[35]

Elio Jorge's words had an immediate effect. The troop was dispersed, and several insurgents were captured. Edel Montiel managed to get away, however, and left the Escambray for the United States in December.

The fiercest battle against the insurgents was waged in the area known as Cariblanca, and former Major Sinesio Walsh, the head of the troops, was captured in the course of it. While he was being taken to La Campana, the driver of the jeep tuned in to Radio Swan and heard a report which stated that Walsh was continuing to inflict serious defeats on the Castro militia.

Former Major Plinio Prieto was captured in the city of Cumanayagua on October 18, 1960, and John Maples Spiritus, a U.S. citizen and CIA agent who was on a secret mission related to the activities of Major William Morgan, was captured soon afterwards. Plinio's and Spiritus's statements led to the arrest of Morgan and Jesús Carreras, another Major at the Rebel Army's Second Front who was involved in counterrevolutionary activities.

On September 30, a new air operation ended in tragicomedy. The parachutes landed inside a recently created cooperative. The farmers immediately took the boxes to the administration building. Major Manuel Fajardo, chief of operations in the Escambray, appeared shortly afterwards. He proceeded to open the boxes and make an initial inventory:

> One bazooka, two 60-mm mortars, two light bipod machine guns, two Browning automatic pistols, 19 Thompson machine guns, six Garand rifles, eight Springfield rifles, two .45 pistols, 108 hand grenades, 16 boxes of TNT and plenty of ammunition.[36]

It was enough to arm a party of around 45 men. Moreover, foreseeing that the militia would try to cut off the insurgents' sources of food, their suppliers included seven sacks of black beans, three sacks of rice and a sack of salt. The Major took the weapons away and gave the food to the poorest farmers in the area.

The reports which began to reach "Commander Augusto," "Mongo" Ruisánchez, couldn't have been more discouraging. The

---

[35] Testimony of Elio Jorge, in the author's archives.
[36] Archives of the Cuban Ministry of the Interior. Bureau of Counterrevolutionary Bands collection.

silence surrounding the insurgents' presence in the Escambray had been broken. Forces composed of farmers' militias led by veteran Rebel Army guerrillas had burst into the Escambray along nearly all of the access routes, and they were combing the territory tree by tree. Several clashes had taken place, and nearly 200 men had been captured. Weapons, radio equipment and campsites had been seized. And, even though several insurgent chiefs — including Osvaldo Ramírez and Evelio Duque — had managed to evade the offensive, it was clear that, in those conditions, they couldn't hold out until the teams arrived from Guatemala.

Ruisánchez wasted no time in informing the U.S. Embassy of the new problems, and messages were radioed from there to Quarters Eye.

In other mountain areas in the country, the CIA hadn't managed to consolidate any insurgent territories.

By the end of October 1960, at the conclusion of the first large-scale operation carried out against the insurgent centers, 177 insurgents and collaborators, including the chiefs Plinio Prieto and Sinesio Walsh, were tried at Santa Clara's Leoncio Vidal Garrison. William Morgan was arraigned.

On November 4, a message in code was sent from Quarters Eye to Colonel Frank J. Egan, commander of the Trax Base. It instructed him to begin training for conventional warfare. The men would be organized in an attack brigade.

The CIA and Richard Bissell, its Special Plans Director, had just abandoned the strategy of destroying the Cuban Revolution by means of guerrilla warfare. It wouldn't be excluded, however; in the future, it would be employed to support the new project. Invasion was on the agenda.

No doubt about it: it was impossible to imitate Fidel Castro.

The Trax Base

Irán was surprised by the deserted aspect of the house. He looked at his watch and realized that it was slow. He walked faster, opened the gate, crossed the front yard, ran up the six steps two at a time and rang the bell. It was the house where he had signed up 10 days before.

In several businesses and factories, the bosses told the Cuban exiles who work for them that they should sign up at the Front's office on N.W. 12th Street, between 9th and 10th Avenues, to leave for Cuba — naturally, this means as part of the invasion army — and that, once they've signed up, they should go by periodically. After about a week, I was called to the office again, but, when I got there at around 7:00 p.m., I couldn't find anybody. Everybody had left, but I was given a telephone number to call — of the place they had gone to. When I called it, they answered, giving me the address and telling me that I could still make it if I hurried.[37]

Colonel Martín Elena, chief of staff of the FRD, opened the door in person. "You're late," he said coldly and made a gesture of disapproval. Irán said nothing. He had never been anything but a civilian before, and he felt ridiculous there, enlisted for a war for which he had simply arrived late. For some seconds, the man's disapproving look crushed him. He was just getting ready to turn around and leave when the colonel broke the silence. "Come in," he said.

The large, two-story white frame house was a human anthill. Around 50 men were preparing to leave. After his passport was checked, Irán was given a bag. In it, he found one khaki-colored uniform, three dark green uniforms, two dark green caps, two pairs of boots, a jacket, six pairs of socks and four sets of underwear, two blue caps and two belts. Then another Cuban filled in a form for him with the information required for his getting paid. He would get $175 a

---

[37] Statement by Irán Gómez Rodríguez, invader. Archives of the Cuban Ministry of the Interior.

month, because he didn't have any children. If he'd had any children, he would have been paid $25 more for each one. When they asked where he wanted the money sent, he said, "To my parents." He thought that this would help his parents get through their economic difficulties. Irán didn't worry about where the money was coming from. Some people had told him that it had been contributed by U.S. citizens whose property had been expropriated by the Revolution; somebody else had said that the U.S. Government had to be behind it all.

Lastly, he was given a dog tag, which Irán hung around his neck. It had a number stamped on it, which would be his identification from then on.

Irán Gómez Rodríguez had left Cuba on June 24, 1959, six months after Fidel Castro's victory, after coming to the conclusion that Cuba had nothing to offer him. During the rule of Fulgencio Batista, Irán had been a grade five administrative head in the Ministry of the Interior, working directly under the Minister, and had run (unsuccessfully) for alderman in the 1954 election.

After January 1, he was marked as a Batista man and had to put up with his neighbors' scorn. Worst of all, his father, who had been a policeman, was being investigated. Then he left for Miami, where around 10,000 Cubans who had left the island during the previous six months were taking over 8th Street, turning it into the nucleus of Little Havana. Irán began working for Delta Air Lines, earning $70 a week, which was enough for living decently but not enough for the ambitions of one who had tasted power and was 31. That's why, when he was told about the recruiting offices at 17th and Biscayne Boulevard; 27 Flager Street, N.W.; 1045 27th Avenue, S.W.; and 3593 12th Street, N.W., among many others, he didn't think twice about it. He was in the United States, and that seemed to be the first step toward going back to Cuba.

He had a medical checkup in the recruiting office, and then they took a blood sample in a laboratory and his lungs were examined. He waited 10 days before somebody called him and told him to go by the 12th Street office again — to be there at 6:00 p.m. and to take along a toothbrush and razor.

Irán looked at the number on his dog tag again and thought about death. Then he shivered. A little while later, he had to strip and was frisked very thoroughly, so they could be sure he wasn't taking along any articles that were prohibited, such as a compass or weapons. It was time to leave. That was when he saw the first U.S. citizen, at the moment of leaving the house. The mission assigned to the Cubans ended there, with the recruiting centers. When the more important part began, the Americans took over.

Through an interpreter, the man told them how many men would go in each truck. Irán settled himself in a truck with Hertz markings, along with 15 others. The American closed the door and locked it. Irán realized that he was already a recruit. And he sighed with relief. During the last few days, while waiting for a telegram, he had almost believed the propaganda which said the Front was a force composed exclusively of Cuban exiles who wanted to liberate their homeland. He had lost sleep over that. He couldn't imagine himself in a pleasure yacht landing in Cuba armed with a rifle. This wouldn't be anything like the attack on the Moncada Garrison or the landing of the *Granma*. Therefore, even though the American treated him in a distant manner and had shut him in that light truck without telling him where he was going or even saying good-bye or good luck, Irán felt relieved.

"It looks like the Americans are involved," he commented to Alberto Julio Bolet Suárez, the young man sitting next to him, who agreed with a smile. Bolet, too, felt relieved. At 21, he didn't want to lose his life on an enterprise whose outcome was doubtful. He was willing to risk his life — it was a dangerous undertaking — but, if the Americans were in it, it would be a cinch to remove Fidel Castro from power. Then he would recover what belonged to him.

> I left Cuba with my family to live in Miami on July 22, 1959. We left for economic reasons: when my father's 25-acre (10-hectare) chicken farm was placed under government control, he was out of work... I signed up in the Front's office... because I felt the Revolution had hurt me. All the propaganda in the Cuban and American newspapers, on the radio and in the TV news made me believe that Cuba had a communist dictatorship run by Russians, Chinese and Czechs. Several of my friends had signed up, too, and were prisoners.[38]

Unlike many of them, Albertico hadn't had to go to the United States after the triumph of the Revolution, for he had been studying civil engineering at the University of Miami at the time.

"Do you think the Americans are going to land with us?" another passenger in the truck asked timidly. It was Manuel Menéndez Pou, 21 years old. He had left Cuba because his father, who had been President of Aspuru y Cía., S.A., had lost his job when the company was nationalized. Later, Manuel's father had been offered a job in

---

[38] Statement by Alberto Julio Bolet Suárez, invader.

Miami as the export representative of several companies doing business with South America, so the family had moved to the United States.[39]

"I think we'll land first. They'll come behind us," Néstor Pino, another of the passengers, said. After graduating from the university in 1957, he had entered the Military Academy of the National Army. He had decided to follow in the footsteps of his father, a retired lieutenant colonel, but Néstor Pino's dreams of a military career were never realized. On January 21, 1959, a bearded officer had given him his discharge. After the Rebels had occupied the Military Academy, Néstor hadn't disguised his scorn for those shabby guerrillas, who didn't snap into a brace in front of their superiors and who were so popular with the girls. Shortly afterwards, Néstor was arrested and sent to La Cabaña Prison, accused of being involved in the conspiracy against Fidel Castro that Dominican dictator Rafael Leónidas Trujillo had organized. Four months later, the case against him was dismissed for lack of evidence, and he was released. In August 1960, after conspiring for several months, he heard that exiles were being recruited for an army against Fidel Castro, so he went to Miami. That same month, Néstor got back into military uniform — this time, as a recruit for the future expeditionaries.

"The Americans are invading Cuba because they won't let them take away their property," José Ramón Pérez Peña added from the other bench while lighting up a cigarette — so what if the American had said there should be no smoking inside the truck? "And we're going along for the ride." José Ramón, 25, had been born in Sagua la Grande and had worked for the Woolworth's chain in the city of Camagüey. When the Revolutionary Government nationalized Woolworth's, he went to New York with 20 other employees, accepting the company's offer of jobs for all of them who wanted to go to the United States. He had begun working for $90 a week but had quit when two of his friends urged him to sign up at the Front's office.

Arturo Menéndez Rodil didn't seem to be paying any attention to the conversation in the truck. His thoughts were in the cafeteria on 8th Street where his girlfriend was working. He was so head over heels in love that he had followed her to the United States. Now, she had dropped him, and Arturito — disappointed and terribly depressed — had enlisted, even though he couldn't care less about politics. He thought that she would come looking for him when she learned of his decision to go on this crazy military adventure, and everything would

---

[39] Statement by Manuel Menéndez Pou, invader.

be alright. But there he was in that truck with that bag on his lap, headed for who knew what.

The trip lasted for two hours. Then the truck stopped inside a hangar on an air base they didn't recognize. They thought they were a long way from Miami. In fact, the Opa-Locka base was only 30 minutes northwest of downtown Miami and less than an hour from Homestead. The driver of the truck, a CIA officer in the paramilitary group that operated in Miami and was commanded by a Colonel Rodrick, had been ordered to drive around in circles on the outskirts of the city before heading for the airport. The long trip was part of a plan to keep the recruits in the dark, to avoid possible infiltration by pro-Castro agents.

For the same reason, the first order given them by the American who opened the door of the truck inside the hangar was for them to put their watches and all other personal belongings they had in their pockets into an envelope. This was to keep them from measuring the flight time from the training base. The officer in charge then ordered them to strip. Soon afterwards, four Americans examined their bodies, clothing and bundles carefully. From then on, it would be impossible for any agent of Castro's to send out information about the operation. They would only be able to do so if they managed to escape from the camps, which was almost impossible, or if they waited patiently until after the landing on the island. And, then, it would be too late.

An hour after the back door of the truck had been opened, dividing the word *Hertz*, which covered it, in two, another American closed it again. The recruits remained inside, in silence. They felt unhappy about having been searched. After all, none of them had any reason to help Fidel Castro. After going a short distance, the truck turned, stopped, backed up slowly and then stopped again. Then the door was opened once more. "Come on, get out! Get a move on! Eyes front!" another American standing by the door shouted in broken Spanish. The recruits tumbled out of the truck and got into a plane. Inside, they couldn't see anything of where they were, because the curtains had been drawn. The captain of the plane told them where to sit. He didn't seem to be American or Cuban. Later, in the camp, they decided he was a European, perhaps a White Russian or a Pole. They were right. The pilots who had been contracted to take the recruits from Miami to the training base were veterans of the Cold War in Europe.

Thirty minutes later, the four-engine Douglas C-54 (military version) rolled down the runway and took off. In its belly, it carried 50 new recruits, none of whom could see out. The windows had been painted over. But Arturo Menéndez Rodil wasn't even aware of that;

unlucky in love, he settled himself in his seat, not caring about anything. His thoughts were elsewhere, with his girlfriend. But he shivered when he felt the plane touch down again. "They've taken us to Cuba!" he exclaimed. The faces of the men who heard him contracted. It couldn't be possible. None of them, except for those who had been in the army, even knew how to shoot.

When the door of the plane was opened, the surprised recruits saw the same man who had closed it. "Get a move on! Move it!" the American shouted again, and the recruits went back to the truck. It took them to a hangar that had 100 cots in it. "There was a problem with the plane, so the flight's postponed till tomorrow night," one of the Americans said. "Until then, nobody will leave here. You'll have a good breakfast, lunch and dinner tomorrow. Rest, and don't think a lot. Good night."

The doors of the hangar were padlocked.

The recruits left again the next night. This time, they had better luck. After almost seven hours of flying, the C-54 landed on a runway in the middle of a jungle. When the door of the plane was opened and the sunlight poured in, the men who were closest to the door shut their eyes. During the past seven hours, they had been in the dark, the only light provided by a few, dim lightbulbs.

While stretching and breathing in the fragrance of a damp jungle, José Ramón Pérez Peña saw several planes lined up on the runway. "What are they?" he asked Néstor Pino, beside him. "B-26 light bombers." "Why don't they have any markings?" Manuel Menéndez's question got no reply. An American instructor dressed in a green coverall took the group to have some breakfast. Bacon and eggs; ham, cheese and pickle sandwiches; juice; and coffee. A heavenly breakfast in the middle of the jungle. The men ate quickly — even Arturito, who set his heartache aside for the moment.

Some trucks were waiting for them, but, before climbing into them, the more curious looked at the back of them. They had Guatemalan license plates. Some wondered what the reason was for all the mystery; others thought it was more disinformation.

The trucks took around an hour and a half to get up to the Trax Base from the Rayo Base, in Retalhuleu, going through the town of the same name (population: around 4,000). The Cubans noted the poverty of its inhabitants. Half naked, barefooted children ran alongside the trucks, asking for cigarettes.

Before entering the town, the recruits were given a strange order: "Take your caps off." "Why?" somebody asked. Nobody ever learned the answer for sure. It seemed to be just one of the many crazy, impractical measures for fooling the Guatemalan Indians, who had extremely poor living conditions.

The Trax Base (which got its name from its purpose — training), on Helvetia Farm, belonged to Alberto Alejos, brother of the Guatemalan Ambassador in Washington. It rose on three terraces. The shooting range and parade ground were on the lowest level; the barracks, dining hall, kitchen, infirmary and some other buildings were on the middle level; and the CIA officers' barracks and offices were on the highest. They had their own dining hall and even a small projection room there.

It was August 1, 1960. The first 50 recruits had arrived at Helvetia Farm. Temporarily, they were lodged in the owner's country house. They left the house very early in the morning, heading for the mountains, and returned at dinner time. On August 15, the first barracks, called Section K, was ready, and the group was moved to Trax. Those founders of Trax, who had passed the course in Iusseppa, Florida, and at Fort Gulick, Panama, were appointed instructors of the exiles who were beginning to come in.

By early October, close to 500 men were being trained for guerrilla warfare at the base. Reveille sounded at 5:45 a.m., when the first streaks of dawn could be seen. The men had breakfast 15 minutes later and then began training. They did physical exercises and took daily 12-kilometer hikes at an altitude of 7,500 feet. They practiced arms handling, had shooting practice and were given classes in theory by U.S. Army Colonel Valeriano Vallejo, of Philippine origin, who had made a name for himself in the guerrilla struggle in the jungles of his country against the Japanese occupiers. Vallejo taught them intelligence, how to receive air drops, camouflage, propaganda and recruiting, among other things.

The Americans retained supreme command of the entire installation, the planning of the courses, control over the weapons and communication with Quarters Eye (where all the decisions were made). U.S. Colonel Frank J. Egan was the top-ranking officer at the base, and Oscar Carol, a former Lieutenant in the Cuban Army, was placed in charge of the Cuban instructors. José Andreu was Carol's executive adjutant; Manuel Blanco Navarro, head of military intelligence; Ramón Ferrer Mena, head of supplies; and José Pérez San Román, chief of operations. Their military service records reflected the importance which the CIA chiefs gave to the military aspect, leaving aside other considerations, such as the troops' possible rejection of those former military men because of their complicity in Batista's regime. The CIA had tried to recruit former military men whose service records were clean and who had been trained in its schools.

José Pérez San Román was a good example of this. He had enlisted in the Cuban Army in 1949 just after graduation from high school, when financial problems forced him to give up his dream of studying architecture at the University of Havana. A year later, he was accepted as a cadet at the Military Academy, and, three years later, graduated with honors and was promoted to Second Lieutenant in the infantry. Soon afterwards, he left for the United States, in a program of U.S. assistance to the Cuban Armed Forces.

In the United States, he took a combat engineering course for field officers. During the next four years, from 1954 to 1958, Pérez San Román was an instructor in the combat engineering corps. In 1956, he was promoted to First Lieutenant, second in command of a company. Once again invited as an allied officer, he went to the U.S. Army Infantry Center at Fort Benning, where he graduated from the infantry course for field officers. In 1957, the promising officer had an opportunity to apply his knowledge and the training he had acquired so painstakingly for the past eight years. In Cuba, an incipient guerrilla army was bravely challenging the regular troops. For several months, the young Pérez San Román commanded a company in the zone of operations. There, he witnessed abuses and excesses against the civilian population. Though he didn't himself take part in such acts, he felt an aversion toward those military officers who did.

In 1958, he felt relieved when he was moved out of the zone of operations in the eastern mountains and was appointed a professor at the Military Academy. That same year, he was promoted to Captain and named G-3 of the Infantry Division, a post equivalent to Lieutenant Colonel. He was arrested in December 1958, accused of conspiring against the powers of the state. He had been involved in an assassination attempt against Batista. Because of that and his clean service record, Pérez San Román retained his rank at the triumph of the Revolution.

He formed part of the commission that was created to cleanse the Armed Forces, but was arrested and accused in Case 39/59 in April 1959. Pérez San Román had helped former Commander Ricardo Montero Duque to leave the country. Montero Duque was wanted by the revolutionary courts, accused of having committed abuses against the civilian population during his service in Oriente.

In November 1959, Pérez San Román left for the United States and joined in the plans against Cuba. During the final briefing given to the Brigade before they set out, he insisted that they respect the civilian population in the territories they occupied. It is probable that he didn't know until the last minute that several of the dictatorship's notorious assassins had been included in the troops.

In the early days at the Trax Base, the future invaders were organized in infiltration teams.

The first pilots to be recruited reached the base in mid-August. They stayed at the farm until the air base was completed.

Training was officially begun on August 19. The men were divided into 12 teams — each of which, in turn, was split in two: a "grey team" and a "black team." Each of the grey teams had between eight and 10 men; each of the black, from 20 to 25. Each grey team had an intelligence officer, a psychological warfare officer, a weapons officer, a demolitions officer, a radio-telegraph operator and the head of the team. The intelligence officer's mission was to obtain all possible military information about military bases, weapons and military capability; data about those who wanted to join the counter-revolutionary forces; and information on the training received. The psychological warfare officer would be in charge of spreading destabilizing propaganda among the civilian population and in the Rebel Army and militia. The weapons officer would train civilians in weapons handling, and the explosives officer would be in charge of preparing sabotage actions and on the spot training. The radio-telegraph operator would keep in contact with the rearguard base, sending back all the information obtained and receiving instructions.

The grey teams would enter the country secretly and pave the way for the black teams, which would follow them after the grey teams had reported that the minimal security and support conditions had been achieved. The black teams' missions were to train those who had joined the struggle against the Revolutionary Government, so as to spread the anti-government guerrilla war.

After being captured, Eulogio Lavandeiro Torrijos described the action plans for guerrilla warfare that the teams were to develop:

In Oriente Province, they planned to land in three different places: near the Sierra Maestra Mountains, near the Sierra Cristal Mountains and at Guantánamo... In Camagüey Province, they were to land near the Sierra de Cubitas Mountains, and, in Las Villas Province, near the Escambray Mountains and then in the Zapata Swamp. In Matanzas Province, they planned to land a grey team and then another, a black team. In Havana, they would land two teams, which would operate in the city. In Pinar del Río Province, one team would land near the Sierra de los Organos

Mountains, and another, on the Isle of Pines. Its mission was to free the prisoners in the National Prison...

Lavandeiro was a member of this last team.

Each team was identified by a word from the international phonetic code: A-Alpha, B-Bravo, C-Charlie, D-Delta, E-Echo, F-Foxtrot, G-Golf, H-Hotel, I-India, J-Juliet, K-Kilo and L-Lima.

The recruits listened carefully to the stories which "Chino Vallejo", the European instructors (including Lithuanians and Ukrainians), and, of course, the Americans told them about their experiences.

The teams' specific missions would be determined by the characteristics of the zone in which they would operate in Cuba, but they had some general principles: unite the scattered groups and train them in guerrilla tactics, including ambushes, interrogations, attacks, reconnaissance, the use of weapons and explosives, underground tactics and communications. The main mission of those operating in the cities would be to establish contact with the various underground groups and train them.

The men were taken in groups to the base at San José de Buenavista Farm (which they called "Garrapatenango," or "Tick Heaven") to learn how to parachute out of planes. They had to make three jumps to graduate, and they made them at the Halcón Base, on La Suiza Farm.

The main base, Trax, was guarded by Guatemalan soldiers.

Every day, they took eight Guatemalan soldiers and posted them to guard the roads that connected Trax with the base at La Suiza and with the Aurora Base.[40]

In spite of that vigilance, the recruits escaped from the camp on Saturdays and Sundays by bribing or outwitting the Guatemalan guards. They headed for the town of Mazaltenango, where they sold their pistols to buy drinks and be with women. On one occasion, the chief of the rural police in the town reprimanded a group of Cubans because they were carrying rifles and disturbing the peace. The recruits retaliated by threatening him with their weapons and forcing him to do push-ups. Because such activities were said to endanger the secrecy of the operation — something already likely given the nature of the operation and the setting chosen for it — the men at the posts were ordered to fire over the heads of the those who tried to leave the camps. A small jail was built, surrounded by a wire fence, and those

---

40 Statement by Carlos Hernández Vega, invader.

who tried to escape were imprisoned there. The more dangerous were sent to Petén, a prison in the middle of the jungle.

The recruits watched movies, especially ones which had to do with war and the struggle against communism. On Sundays, priests held a Mass at 7:00 and 10:00 in the morning. Anti-Castro and anti-communist bulletins and propaganda were distributed in the camps, and the men listened to Radio Swan. They had been warned that their letters would be censored, and they were categorically prohibited from saying anything about where they were or the work they were doing. Pablo Organvidez Parada, a Cuban FBI agent, had been placed in charge of overseeing the Cuban recruits.

Letters from relatives were checked in Miami before being sent on to the Retalhuleu base. If they were problematical, they didn't leave Miami. Those sent by recruits were handed over to McQuady, the U.S. Military Attaché in Guatemala. McQuady told me and the other FBI agents which recruits were troublemakers, and we infiltrated their units to keep an eye on them.[41]

The training ended at the beginning of November 1960. The 12 teams, with close to 600 agents, were ready to be sent into Cuba. The men's morale was good. Every day, Radio Swan announced new outbreaks of insurgency and proclaimed triumphs against Fidel Castro's regime, which seemed to be disintegrating.

Arturito Menéndez, on the C-Charlie black team, didn't show much interest in infiltrating Cuba. He had written a lot of letters to his girlfriend and was yearning for a reply. The other men who had come to the base on the same flight were eagerly awaiting the order to depart.

During those first few days in November 1960, the alarm sounded at the base, and the recruits ran to form ranks. They were informed that the time had come — but, strangely, not for Cuba, but for Miguel Idígoras Fuentes, President of Guatemala, against whom several army units had rebelled, headed by a group of young officers. The rebellion was localized in Puerto Barrios. A hundred men were chosen to retake the military airfield there, which the rebels were holding. A hundred more remained at the Trax Base, ready to leave if necessary. The decision to use the Cubans had been made in Washington.

Roughly three months after I arrived, our unit saw combat for the first time. But not against Castro. We were called in to help put

---

[41] Statement by Pablo Organvidez Parada, FBI agent and invader.

down a coup attempt in Puerto Barrios, close to the Honduran border, against Guatemalan President Miguel Idígoras Fuentes... Two hundred of us were selected. We were issued weapons, then trucked to Retalhuleu air base where we were to board the planes that would take us to Puerto Barrios. We were somewhat nervous during the ride and we kept our submachine guns at the ready, pointed toward the jungle in case of an ambush. If somebody had fired a shot by mistake, we would probably have blown away a few hundred meters of roadside.

At the air base, we waited for our orders... The plan was for about a hundred of us to fly to Puerto Barrios — three C-46s of us, roughly 33 to a plane — take over the airfield after it had been softened up by our own Free Cuba air force of B-26 light bombers... Finally we arrived over Puerto Barrios, and the day's first screw-up occurred. The B-26s hadn't finished bombing and strafing the area, so we had to circle above the bay and wait for them to complete their mission... My friend Nestor Pino was in the doorway, one hand tight on the rope, the other holding a Thompson submachine gun. He would lead the way.

The rear wheels came down and as soon as we touched ground, the pilot applied the brakes. Quickly the plane taxied down the runway... Then, suddenly, a Guatemalan officer shouted above the noise: "We're taking fire! They're shooting at us!"

The plane reached the end of the runway and spun around, going farther away... Later, when we returned to Retalhuleu, I was one of the people who checked the fuselage of the aircraft thoroughly — and we discovered not a single bullet hole. Even though we hadn't actually seen any fighting, we were assembled the following day and the Guatemalan Minister of Defense showed up and congratulated us for our help.[42]

The men stayed at Retalhuleu for a week. They were on standby to assist the Guatemalan Government, but were not deployed. Idígoras sent messages of thanks to the Cubans at the base and promised that he would visit them soon. Years later, some researchers tried to create the myth that the Cubans' help, including the bombings by the Brigade's Tactical Air Force, had been of decisive importance in crushing the rebellion.

When everything seemed to indicate that the time for departure was near, the recruits began to observe unusual movement at the base. All of them were surprised when Colonel Vallejo, the expert in

---

[42] Félix Rodríguez, *Shadow Warrior*.

guerrilla warfare, was replaced by U.S. Marine Corps Colonel Jack Hawkins, who was introduced as "Frank" and who promptly became known for his severe discipline and poorly disguised scorn for the Cubans. Hawkins didn't know anything about guerrilla fighting. He had fought in World War II and had distinguished himself in the seizure of the beaches of Iwo Jima. Evidently, a decision had been made in Dulles's and Bissell's offices to change the strategy. On November 4, 1960, during the closest presidential election in the history of the United States, a coded message reached the Trax Base. It ordered a reduction in guerrilla training and the introduction of conventional training for an amphibious and airborne attack force.

The CIA had decided to wipe out the Revolution by means of a single, conclusive strike: an air and sea landing to obtain a beachhead.

At the base, the grey and black teams were dissolved, and the men were reorganized into squads, companies and battalions. Néstor Pino, Alberto Bolet and Manolito Menéndez Pou were assigned to Battalion 1, of paratroopers. Irán Gómez and José Ramón Pérez Peña were in Infantry Battalion 2, and Arturito Menéndez Rodil was put in the armored battalion. But Arturito had decided not to go to Cuba. His girlfriend had written, begging him to return. He thought only about seeing his girlfriend again and how he could escape from the camp.

A new language began to be spoken at the Trax Base: tanks, airborne troops, corps of engineers, heavy weapons.

The recruits didn't understand the reason for the change, and some of them still think that guerrilla warfare would have wiped out Fidel Castro. That was the result of Radio Swan's reports. At that time, no insurgent group in any part of the mountains in Cuba had managed to control even a tiny area from which the infiltration teams might have operated. The plane drops had been catastrophic, and most of the weapons and explosives had been seized by the militias.

Soon, however, everybody at Trax was enthusiastic about the idea of the invasion. It wouldn't be difficult to obtain a beachhead, hold it for a few days and then be supported by U.S. troops. Some of them tried to get cameras. It would be a great souvenir to have a photo of themselves on the beaches they had taken. "Colonel Frank" must have thought so, too, for he decided that a camera-toting war correspondent should accompany each battalion.

The CIA still planned to use the insurgent forces that were operating in the Escambray Mountains. The city selected for the landing was just south of the mountains. The insurgents would come down from the mountains to support the invaders. Thus, guerrilla warfare hadn't been entirely ruled out.

The cage

On October 14, 1960, before the conclusion of the military operations that had begun at La Campana Farm on September 8 to wipe out the groups of counterrevolutionaries in the Escambray Mountains, Prime Minister Fidel Castro signed a resolution creating the Escambray Plan (Las Villas-29 Agrarian Development Area), a state structure that would utterly transform that backward mountainous region. It was a region without electricity, but tens of thousands of thatched-roof huts; an astronomical infant mortality rate; malnutrition; epidemics of such diseases as gastroenteritis, tuberculosis and polio, which were direct causes of the short life expectancy in the area; no doctors or hospitals; illiteracy; cultural isolation; and no means of communication.

In a little over five years, several dozen towns were built under the Escambray Plan, in spite of the irregular war that was being waged there. The towns comprised comfortable, fully furnished homes with electricity and sewage systems; 17 rural schools and five other schools; five hospitals (with modern equipment and offering free service); 600 kilometers of roads; a public transportation service; dozens of sports installations; and several recreation centers.

Six movie projectors powered by electric plants mounted on double traction trucks began to circulate among the hamlets so the people could see movies — for the first time for the immense majority of the inhabitants of the Escambray. A theater group settled in the mountains, putting on plays wherever there were people to see them, no matter how far off the beaten track. Electricity began to be brought into the mountains, and, in a little over 20 years, the situation was vastly changed: electricity had been brought to over 80 percent of the territory. The first television sets appeared, and the number of radios multiplied. More than 7,000 young literacy teachers from the city were sent to the Escambray in early 1961 and, in 10 months, taught 28,000 people in the area how to read and write. These social improvements gradually and irreversibly reduced the bases for insurgency. But, back in late 1960, the Escambray Plan was just getting started.

In Quarters Eye, the CIA and Pentagon strategists had selected the area around an old city very near the mountains as the site of their invasion. Trinidad lay to the south, close to the sea, and only 15 kilometers from Topes de Collantes, the peak in the Escambray with the greatest insurgent activity. The existence of a port and beautiful beaches a little south of the city, and the fact that it had an airport, were key factors in its selection by the Agency.

The Guamuhaya Range was to play an important role in the new strategy. The aim was to create a group of insurgent forces that, at the time indicated, would complete the encirclement and isolation of the city in support of the invasion. Two insurgent chiefs, survivors of the pursuit activities that had begun on September 8 at La Campana, were the indisputable ringleaders: Evelio Duque Miyar and Osvaldo Ramírez.

In November 1960, Quarters Eye instructed the CIA station in Havana that José Ramón Ruisánchez was to quickly coordinate the new uprisings and be in charge of supplying the insurgents with weapons and explosives, both by air and by sea. In Miami, Howard Hunt would urge the leaders of the Democratic Revolutionary Front to get their respective organizations on the island — which had already created an underground network — to send some of their members to the mountains, though most of the members of the columns would be farmers from the area.

During November and December, several hundred counter-revolutionaries were sent from the cities to the spurs of the Escambray, where groups of collaborators took them through the area. Others who lived there were urged to join by friends and relatives already in the insurgent camps. On Swan Island, off the coast of Honduras, the radio station created by David Atlee Phillips stepped up its work of "psychological softening up," winning over some of the mountain people.

The Government was going to take our children away and send them to Russia. It was going to take away our money and replace it with vouchers. We would need a permit to go from one place to another. It had given us the land just so we could work it, and then it was going to take it away again. That's what the people were saying in those hills. Radio Swan came in more clearly than the Cuban radio stations.[43]

The CIA had ratified Ruisánchez's naming of Evelio Duque as Commander in Chief of the Escambray Front. During the dictatorship, Duque had been far from outstanding in combat. After the triumph of

---

[43] Testimony of José Reboso Febles, insurgent.

the Revolution, he'd had a short career as a revolutionary, but he didn't like the Agrarian Reform, which adversely affected old friends and relatives.

During the skirmishes in September and October 1960, he had managed to evade clashes with the militia and remained well to the rear, but, in the new stage, in which confrontation was inevitable, it wouldn't be easy for him to be chief. Clashes with Osvaldo Ramírez, who had a hot temper, weren't long in coming. On December 10, the two men met at a place known as Dos Arroyos.

Evelio reminded Osvaldo that he was the Commander in Chief, and Osvaldo asked how he could be, since he hadn't shot even once. "I have documents here that say so," Evelio replied. The argument heated up, and Osvaldo took out his pistol. Then we intervened and calmed him down. He wanted to shoot him. When we left, Evelio told him that his authority was recognized outside the country, and Osvaldo told him that, if he set foot in his territory, he'd blast him.[44]

"Commander Augusto" (José Ramón Ruisánchez) knew of the differences between Evelio and Osvaldo Ramírez, who commanded the strongest column the insurgents had at the time, and Ruisánchez had informed the officers in the U.S. Embassy about this situation. Things began to look very bad. Their plans required unity, so the actions that were to be carried out prior to and on D Day could be coordinated.

December 1960 was a crucial month for the CIA's plans in the Escambray. If it managed to structure the insurgent group and consolidate its positions, the invasion could be carried out in the first few weeks of the new year. Trinidad would be bound to fall. The insurgent forces would come down out of the mountains and attack from the north to surround the city and support its occupation by the invading forces; to the east, other insurgent groups would cut the Sancti Spíritus-Trinidad highway; and, to the west, a third insurgent force would prevent the arrival of reinforcements from the city of Cienfuegos.

It would take time for a substantial number of Rebel Army troops to arrive, because they would have to be sent from the city of Santa Clara, in the middle of the province, and the small groups that could be sent from Cienfuegos and Sancti Spíritus, to the west and east, respectively, would be stopped by the insurgents from the Escambray,

---

44 Testimony of Demetrio Clavelo Solís, insurgent.

in coordination with the battalion of paratroopers that would be dropped on the advance positions.

A short report that an anonymous Cuban State Security officer wrote at the end of the year described the prevailing tension and the real reason why many counterrevolutionaries took to the mountains.

CONFIDENTIAL
Re.: Information provided by infiltrated agent.
...He said weapons had a paper addressed to Commander Evelio Duque and signed by Commander Augusto, but the identity of the latter is unknown... Many of the elements in the organization will rebel in the next few days, to attack when the invasion occurs.

Waiting in the mountains for the Americans to come, rifle in hand, would guarantee a good position in the Armed Forces, police or — why not? — politics in the new republic. Then perhaps everything would go back to the way it had been before.

At Quarters Eye, the maps on the walls of the Operations Section showed that there were practically no revolutionary troops in the mountain territory around the city of Trinidad. Intelligence information stated that many members of the farmers' militia battalion that had been organized at La Campana had been appointed to civilian posts in the recently created Escambray Plan. Everything seemed to be going smoothly. By the time Fidel Castro became aware of the danger, it would be too late. At least, the CIA hoped so.

On one occasion, U.S. General Douglas MacArthur — one of the most outstanding U.S. military officers of World War II — said that the history of failures in war could be summed up in two words: too late. Too late in understanding the enemy's purpose, too late in becoming aware of mortal danger, too late in uniting all possible forces to resist...

In Cuba, after 1959, nothing was being done too late.

The conviction that the U.S. Government was preparing an invasion of Cuba; the persistence of insurgent movements in the Escambray Mountains; reports indicating an increase in those insurgent forces; the certainty that they hadn't been created spontaneously or as the result of a plan drawn up in Cuba and that, one way or another, they were to be involved in the planned invasion; and the death in combat of Major Manuel Fajardo, chief of the Rebel Army's operations in the region, unquestionably influenced Fidel Castro's decision to begin a powerful offensive — Operation Jaula (Cage) — in that mountain territory.

Fidel Castro at the Bay of Pigs

Fidel Castro at Bay of Pigs

Fidel Castro in Havana one day prior to Bay of Pigs invasion

José Ramón Fernández during Bay of Pigs invasion

Cuban militia heading to Bay of Pigs

Fidel Castro at Bay of Pigs

Cuban antiaircraft gun at Bay of Pigs

Road leading to Bay of Pigs

Fidel Castro during Bay of Pigs invasion

Cuban militia mobilized during Bay of Pigs invasion

Cuban soldiers inspecting weapons captured at Bay of Pigs invasion

On December 2, 1960, in the theater of operations itself, which he visited frequently, Fidel Castro gave precise instructions:

- Maintain a constant struggle, giving the enemy no time in which to recover.
- Don't move at night — only by day, to avoid confusion.
- If it is really necessary to move at night, move only along predetermined roads.
- Mobilize the farmers in the area again this month.
- Protect the people in the area. This measure will be accompanied by building towns on the recently created farms, to do away with isolation — always on a voluntary basis.
- Organize volunteer teachers to begin the enormous job of promoting education and culture.
- Concentrate the battalions' forces in strategic zones.

Angel Martínez was a Spanish Civil War veteran who, attracted by the Cuban Revolution, had arrived in Cuba some months before and was serving as an adviser to the chief of the Rebel Army in the central part of Cuba. In a 1977 interview he commented:

The plan was mainly political and military. There was even a principle, an element which determined the Commander in Chief's selection of the militia units from Havana: the proletarian nature of those Havana units.

The location of most of the insurgents' camps had been detected in September and October and kept up-to-date by reports from farmers living in the mountains; statements by prisoners; documents that were captured; and (to a lesser extent, because of its incipient organization and development) State Security, which infiltrated agents in those groups. These agents included Orlando Hernández Lema and Reineirio Perdomo, agents "Tito" and "Cabaigüan."

Orlando Hernández Lema had assisted the troops of the March 13 Directorate during the struggle against the Batista dictatorship. After the triumph of the Revolution, he decided to keep on farming as the city life didn't appeal to him, but peace didn't last long. The Escambray was on the CIA's agenda. In mid-1960, Víctor Manso, whose grandfather was a large landowner in the area who resented the fact that the Agrarian Reform had reduced the size of his holdings, told Orlando that four captains were preparing an uprising. Orlando didn't think twice about it. He went down to Trinidad and took a bus for the capital. Wasting no time, he sought out Major Faure Chaumont, the leader of the March 13 Directorate, whom he had guarded in the mountains, and told him about the plot. A few hours later, he was having lunch at the Maracas Restaurant in Havana with Major Ramiro Valdés, the head of Cuban State Security, who gave him a mission.

In early November, Orlando left his house and headed for Manacal de Piedras, another mountain area, where Evelio Duque, Commander in Chief of the insurgent forces, had his camp. Orlando, agent "Tito," was perhaps the first agent Cuban State Security had in the Escambray. Duque remembered him from the previous war, the anti-Batista struggle. He knew that Orlando was a courageous, honest, exaggeratedly modest man; he wasn't ambitious, and he had a fairly high cultural level. Therefore, Duque didn't trust him. There was something about him that didn't fit in with that war. And his mistrust grew when Orlando offered him a load of weapons. "Don't worry about weapons. I have enough, and more will be coming soon." Orlando stayed at the camp, but he wasn't given a weapon. He worked with a Spanish priest who made a big thing out of having supported Franco and who held Mass for the insurgents. Orlando read for him during the services. He still remembers how, at night, while lying in his hammock, he used to go over the events of the day, repeating every detail: which messengers had come and gone, the weapons, the plans, the discussions on internal differences, the references to the Americans, even the slightest bits of conversations.

One day, some photos were taken. One of them reached the U.S. Embassy, which sent it on to Quarters Eye. David Atlee Phillips, the CIA officer in charge of propaganda, had it sent around the world, with a caption stating that it was of the staff of the insurgent forces in the Escambray. Agent "Tito" appeared clearly in the photo.

Near the end of December, a few days before Christmas, Orlando and another insurgent went on a mission. A few hours later, they came to a farmer's thatched-roof hut. "The area is full of militia," the man said, not looking at their faces. From their clothes, he realized that they had to be insurgents, and he was confirmed in that belief when they ran out of his hut. Deliberately, "Tito" fell behind and, when his companion was out of sight, turned around and went back to the hut. "Where are the militia?" he asked the farmer, who looked at him blankly. After a few seconds' silence, "Tito" added, "I want to surrender." The farmer looked down again, lit a cigar butt and stated firmly, "There isn't any operation near here. The militia are a long way off, so you can surrender to me. I'm the only militia there is anywhere around." Two days later, Orlando was talking with Lieutenant Luis

Felipe Denis, who had been named as head of State Security in the Escambray not long before. His information was added to that from other sources which reached Fidel Castro.

Some of the most important information was provided by Reineirio Perdomo, who had no hesitation about what to call himself in his work as a secret agent. He adopted the name of the town where he had been born: "Cabaigüan."

"We don't have any liaisons, so don't identify yourself to anybody; remember everything you see and everything you hear; if you get hold of an important document, hide it on your body. When you get enough data, come out. To make sure nobody shoots you, take off your shirt and turn yourself in with your hands up, completely unarmed." "And the Bible?" I asked him. "If it doesn't fit in a pocket, throw it away, but turn yourself in with your hands up and without wearing a shirt. And remember, you mustn't fight, even if they tell you you have to." I couldn't fight, in any case, because I'm cross-eyed and wear glasses as thick as the bottom of a bottle. Those were the instructions Aníbal Velaz gave me.[45]

On December 24, while pork was being roasted over fires in back yards in the small town of Caracusey, near the Escambray, and beer and rum were wreaking havoc, "Cabaigüan" greeted Julio Emilio Carretero's nephew, a former policeman of Batista's who was now Commander Osvaldo Ramírez's deputy. Reineirio Perdomo didn't accept a glass of rum. He was a Pentecostal missionary, and his sect didn't drink alcohol. As soon as it was dark, the two set out for San Ambrosio, an isolated mountain region where the insurgent column was.

They walked all night, stopping to rest twice, at the homes of relatives who collaborated with Ramírez. At dawn, they reached the camp. Almost immediately, Perdomo was taken to the chief of the column. "Cabaigüan" quickly realized that the man didn't like him. He knew that his appearance — a little awkward and weak — didn't help. Reineirio wasn't a man of action.

After checking that he had been sent by people he could trust, Osvaldo Ramírez was about to assign him to a group of men, but Reineirio said, "I can't fight, Commander. I'm a missionary, you know." Osvaldo looked him up and down and put his hand on his shoulder. Then he looked at Carretero, who was standing next to him. "Give him a Winchester and have him do guard duty."

---

[45] Testimony of Reineirio Perdomo.

In his free moments, "Cabaigüan" went through the camp with his Bible open, carefully recording in his head everything he saw.

The final details of the Government's Operation Cage were worked out during the first week of December. The area that would be encircled initially was around 2,400 square kilometers in size, and it was divided into thirds. The tactic to be followed in those traps was to divide them up into areas or sectors and check each one, little by little, to control the sources of water and supplies and the roads, to besiege the insurgents and to set ambushes to catch them on the move — which was usually at night.

During the latter half of December, the battalions of militia began to arrive. After some on-the-spot adjustments to enlarge the original ring, the Escambray was surrounded by militia from the sea, to the south, up to close to the city of Fomento, 40 kilometers to the north, and from east to west through 80 kilometers of wilderness. The support that some of the people — who remained true to the Revolution in spite of the intensive radio propaganda and the protests of old friends and relatives, ties that were very strong in that part of the world — gave to the operation was decisive for its success.

Therefore, the instructions governing the relations between the troops and the farmers were extremely important. Those instructions were: protect the families and their possessions, teach them how to read and write, tell them what the Revolution has done, teach them first aid, help them in their agricultural work and promote sanitation. All farmers would be treated with absolute respect, even when it was known that they had relatives who were insurgents or that they themselves were sympathizers. The farmers who supported the Revolution should be protected against all attempts at intimidation. A squad of militia was stationed in each thatched-roof hut. At night, ambushes were set around them.

Batista's troops didn't go into the woods, but the militia did. When the Government launched its offensive, we hid wherever we could. I hid on a rocky islet a long way from a friend's house and went to get food behind his house every other day. I had to watch the militia until they weren't paying attention and then signal my friend, and he would bring me something to eat. We slept on the ground, covered with plastic bags. We had a bath perhaps once every 15 or 20 days. There's fruit and other food all over in the Escambray. There are a lot of plants that have fruit you can eat. Some of them are bad for you, but others aren't. If you're an insurgent, you have to eat whatever you can get. We couldn't go to the houses, because there were militia in all of them. One night, we went out to walk after midnight, and the militia caught us in an ambush. The first warning we had was the shooting. I was between Gavilán and Berto. Berto dropped in front of me, and Gavilán, behind me. When somebody drops and doesn't say anything, it's because he's dead. You die when your time has come. Every so often, people would tell us that a certain man was an informer, but sometimes they said that because the man owed them 2,000 or 3,000 pesos, and they wanted us to kill him. Men were killed without any major investigation of the facts.[46]

At Quarters Eye, the maps of the Escambray began to be filled with colors showing concentrations of enemy forces, and some officers began wondering what would happen if, on the day of the invasion, that enormous concentration of troops was still there, just a few kilometers from the city of Trinidad. Others wondered if Fidel Castro had any proof of the Agency's aims. But that was utterly impossible. Knowledge of the area chosen for the landing was limited to a very select group of high-ranking officers and, in the White House, was known by only a few members of the President's team. No, no leaks were possible. In fact, what was happening and was beginning to worry some of the members of the Agency's staff was that the Cuban leader was proving to be an excellent military strategist.

Perhaps the danger threatening the Escambray was what led Bissell to decide to push through an operation to make a large arms drop on the camp of Osvaldo Ramírez, who had just been named Commander in Chief of the Escambray Front. The insurgent chief had requested the weapons in repeated messages addressed to "Commander Augusto," and he, in turn, had sent the request on to the U.S. Embassy.

Ramírez's camp was in the San Ambrosio area, a practically inaccessible region with abundant vegetation and steep elevations. When he received Ruisánchez's message, he gave instructions for a landing strip to be improvised at Paso Hondo. It was December 31, 1960. It had been a great year for the Cuban Revolution, but the decisive one would be the year that was about to begin.

While one group cut down underbrush to make the landing strip, the news spread. A communist teacher lived in the area. Even though the young man was certainly unaware that Osvaldo Ramírez's column, consisting of more than 300 men, was nearby, Ramírez ordered Julio Emilio Carretero, one of his deputies, to bring him in.

---

[46] Testimony of José Reboso Febles.

Carretero hadn't been chosen by chance. He had captured a lot of people. Carretero had been a policeman for Batista's government and had a natural bent for this kind of thing. Even though "Commander Augusto" had instructed the insurgent chiefs not to accept anyone who had worked for Batista, Osvaldo had taken Carretero with him when he had gone to the mountains five months earlier.

That night, the last in the year, Carretero and three of his men — Macario Quintana ("Flatfoot"), "The Sailor" and Tomás San Gil — broke into the hut of Ireneo Rodríguez, the farmer who was putting up the volunteer teacher, one of the many young people who had gone to live in the most isolated parts of the island to open schools and begin teaching children and adults.

"Not only a Communist, but a nigger, too," Carretero snorted as soon as he saw him. The teacher had leaped out of his hammock and was trying to put his boots on. "Let's go," Macario snapped and shoved him. The teacher fell down. "Where are you going to take him?" the farmer asked timidly. "You bastard!" Carretero replied, and took him along, too, in spite of his wife's pleading and his children's tears. The teacher and farmer were quickly taken to the camp. Carretero's men were in charge of guarding the prisoners. Ramírez had decided to take care of them the next day. He couldn't allow revolutionary teachers to take over the Escambray or farmers to give them shelter. He decided to set a precedent for those who dared to defy his authority.

But the problem couldn't be solved the next morning. The first clash with the militia who were coming to drive the insurgents from San Ambrosio took place in the early hours of January 1.

The messages which Ruisánchez sent to Ramírez testify eloquently to the drama that was unfolding in the mountains:

"Important not let yourself be seen or clash with enemy. Could hamper Operation Silence."
Commander Augusto

"Friends designated Kings' Day and three more days: 7, 8 and 9."
Commander Augusto

"Arms drop will be made around 500 feet in 800-pound bundles."
Commander Augusto

The fighting grew more intensive on January 3. The insurgents' situation deteriorated. Ramírez had to stay there. If he left the area, he would lose the load of weapons and explosives, a large part of which were to be used to strengthen other columns and enable them to support the invasion when it came. He had to hold out for only three days more, but the situation became desperate on January 5. The militia and Rebel Army soldiers were preparing for the final attack. The topographical conditions, which seemed exceptionally good for irregular warfare, weren't insurmountable for the revolutionary forces. On January 6, when the weapons sent by the CIA were parachuted in, it was the militia who retrieved them. The messages exchanged on the next day showed how the situation ended.

"Today's newspapers show photos captured weapons dropped by plane Escambray. Suppose are of Operation Silence. If Operation Silence fell into enemy hands, we are lost. Am confused. Investigate and report."
Commander Augusto

"Situation has changed. Trying encircle us. All Operation Silence packages fell to enemy. Enemy preparing offensive with thousands militia. All seems lost. Even life."
Commander Osvaldo Ramírez

Meanwhile, as Reineirio Perdomo testified later:

Before going to sleep, Ramírez gave instructions for the teacher and farmer to be tried. He was irritated.

He needed to raise the morale of his troops, and the teacher gave him a perfect opportunity. Before the trial, an emissary went over to the cage and told him that if he retracted his communist ideas and denounced Fidel, he could save his life.

At dawn on January 4, the two men were put on an improvised platform. Close by, an insurgent kept a record of the proceedings on an old typewriter.

The "secretary of the court" set about taking statements from the two men. A hundred armed men exhausted by the dawn fighting were there.

The teacher's hands were tied. He was nervous. No doubt about it. The 18-year-old was afraid. He said he came from the city of Matanzas and that he had decided to leave his studies and take the course for volunteer teachers because teaching reading and writing to children who had never had any teachers was a good thing. The "prosecutor," waving a teaching booklet that had been seized in

Ireneo's hut, interrupted him, shouting that he must have known it was communist indoctrination. The teacher raised his voice a little so he could be heard over the ever louder insults hurled at him by his audience, saying that he was teaching the children the vowels and making words with them. Once again, the "prosecutor" made him stop talking when he read a sentence from the booklet: "The Agrarian Reform is progressing." Once again, the shouting became deafening. The teacher looked at the men who had come toward him threateningly. "Are you a Communist?" the "prosecutor" asked him loudly, and the crowd grew quiet. Suddenly, there was silence. The teacher bowed his head and then looked at the farmer next to him. Somebody threw a stone that hit him in the face, and he staggered for a moment but didn't fall. Then Macario went up to him and hit him on the ear, and he fell down. Others climbed up on the platform and kicked him, calling him a red, a nigger, a supporter of Fidel. The trial had ended.

That night, while a heavy silence presaged the militia's final offensive, the teacher lay in the cage. He was breathing with difficulty, and blood dribbled out of his ear. His nose was broken, and his face was terribly inflamed. Several of his ribs were broken, and he couldn't stand. But the worst pain was in his testicles, which Macario Quintana had squeezed several times in his powerful hands. Kneeling next to him, the farmer cleaned his face with a handkerchief. The guards had gone a little way off, so as not to be bothered by the boy's moans. Every so often, one of the insurgents walked up close to the cage, insulted the teacher and went on his way.

When dawn was breaking, a silent man came by. He opened a Bible and began reading from it. From a distance, one of the guards, sitting under a tree, shouted something to him. "I'm going to give him a service," the new arrival answered, and the guard shut his eyes again. After making sure that he couldn't be heard, the man with the Bible put his face up against the mesh that separated him from the prisoners. "I'm not an insurgent," Reineirio Perdomo, Agent "Cabaigüan," who had witnessed the "trial," recalled that he said, "but I can't do anything for you." The teacher opened his eyes and looked at him with a crazed expression for a few seconds, which seemed like forever to Reineirio. Then he moaned again and closed his eyes. "Cabaigüan" saw a tear run down his cheek. The farmer asked for some water, and Reineirio threw his canteen over the stockade. "Finished?" asked the guard, who had walked closer and now stood by the agent.

Reineirio recalled:

At dawn, when the shooting began and it was obvious that the militia were advancing, the order to withdraw was given. Then Carretero, Macario, "The Sailor" and Tomás San Gil dragged the teacher and the farmer out of the cage and hit them with their fists and rifle butts. They vented their spite on the teacher again. They even bayoneted him and cut off his genitals. I think the teacher was already dead when they hanged him. Then they hanged the farmer.[47]

A few hours later, the column of insurgents left San Ambrosio.

A week later, Agent "Cabaigüan" managed to leave the insurgents and turn himself in to a troop of militia. At his insistence, he was taken to the head of State Security in Las Villas, who was at Topes de Collantes, general headquarters for the Escambray campaign. "You crazy man, are you still alive?" Captain Aníbal Velaz, the man who had trained him as an agent, asked.

He stayed at Topes for three days, dictating what he had seen and heard. While he was doing that, somebody came and said that Fidel had arrived. Shortly afterwards, Aníbal took him to Fidel Castro. "Tell me about the murder of the teacher. I want you to write down the names of the men who hit, tortured and abused him — even those who threw stones," he said.[48]

The murder of the young teacher caused a great stir and had a catalyzing effect on the contending forces. The CIA's Richard Bissell hadn't foreseen or encouraged the crimes. He was convinced that such things would increase the Cuban people's — especially the Escambray farmers' — support for the Revolution and aggravate the insurgents' isolation.

Fidel Castro knew how to make the most of the low morale which began to afflict many of the Cuban insurgents.

During the first few days of the battle, a group of Rebel Army officers met with Commander Fidel Castro. Raúl Menéndez Tomassevich, now a Major General, made a report on the situation of the insurgents. He recalls that he used both the words *insurgents* and *guerrillas* but didn't come up with a really good name for them. Then Fidel interrupted him and said, "Don't call them *guerrillas* any more; we're the guerrillas. They're counterrevolutionaries."

---

47 Testimony of Reineirio Perdomo.
48 Ibid.

The camp of Column 7, which Ramírez headed, was seized on January 6. Over 300 insurgents had been there. The militia and farmers immediately set off in pursuit of them. The enemy chief divided his troops in two groups. The group with him — around 100 men — was defeated a week later at a place known as Limones Cantero, and his troops were decimated. The second group, of about the same size, began to withdraw slowly, at night, toward the central region of the Escambray, where, as a result of successive clashes with the militia, it began to disintegrate. Thus, the strongest column was defeated. Other columns met the same fate. Columns 1 and 2 were decimated, but their chiefs — Evelio Duque, Edel Montiel and Joaquín Membrive — managed to escape and fled the country. Captains Zacarías García, Juan Cajigas and Nando Lima, the chiefs of Columns 3 and 6, were taken prisoner in February 1961. That same month, Ismael Rojas and Carlos Duque, the chiefs of Columns 5 and 8, were surrounded during some skirmishes and captured. Captain Ismael Heredia, the chief of Column 4, had been killed in an ambush. By the end of March, 25 groups of insurgents had been defeated.

Even though the Escambray had been occupied by revolutionary forces, in January 1961 the CIA resumed the air operations it had programmed for strengthening its forces in those mountains. It made a drop over the Santa Lucía area, near the city of Cabaigüen, in early February; on February 13, several parachutes opened over the Naranjo area; four days later, another large load descended on La Sierrita, in the southwestern part of the Escambray; and, on March 4, a drop was made on Charco Azul. The militia retrieved all of the matériel from those drops.

In his book *Operation Puma*,[49] CIA pilot Eduardo Ferrer reported that 68 missions were carried out dropping weapons and explosives in the Cuban mountains between September 1960 and March 1961 — and that 61 of them were resounding failures.

Even though he stayed far to the rear, in Havana, José Ramón Ruisánchez, "Commander Augusto," realized that the cleaning-up operation in the Escambray might reach him. Some of the insurgent leaders and liaisons who were on the run knew him, and, if they fell prisoner, they might identify him. He decided to leave clandestinely for the United States.

The offensive in the Escambray was too much for the insurgents, who had been preparing to play an important role in the city of Trinidad during the invasion. Incessant pursuit, a well-planned system of ambushes, rigorous control over sources of food and water, the

---

[49] Eduardo Ferrer, *Operation Puma*.

revolutionaries' constructive relations with the farmers who weren't committed and the neutralization of those who supported the insurgents put a lot of pressure on the insurgents. The diary of one of those chiefs testifies eloquently to the brevity and intensity of that military operation:

> February 20. Matasiete deserted, and we had to move camp. February 25. Pedro and I went out today to see if we could escape; there are militia all over. We're surrounded and short of ammunition, and we haven't eaten for many days... There are only eight of us left of what was a column of over 40 men, and the others are discouraged... It's March 1, and it seems that nobody is going to come and help us. The exiles live too well to come here, where things are more difficult... Tonight, the two of us who are left will go out to see if we can find an area that's better than this one. If everything is the same, we will have to either shoot ourselves or surrender.[50]

By the end of March 1961, it became evident that the strength of the insurgent forces in the Escambray had been considerably reduced. Meanwhile, information was being gathered about an imminent invasion. In early April 1961, all of the forces that had taken part in the Revolutionary Government's Operation Cage were ordered to return to their own provinces.

The war in the Escambray would continue for four years and would cost the nation around a billion pesos. At its height, 100,000 militia and soldiers were involved. The last group of insurgents, consisting of around a dozen men, was captured in early March 1965, hiding in a cave. When their chief was brought before Major Lizardo Proenza, chief of operations, he wore a wide-brimmed hat with a star on it, a symbol of his military rank. Proenza teasingly came to attention and asked, "How are you, Commander?" To which the man replied, "The only commander here is Fidel."

---

[50] Campaign diary of Julián Oliva, insurgent.

Intelligence and disinformation

Pedro Rodríguez Díaz, 19, was an officer at the main office of the Investigation and Information Department of the Revolutionary Armed Forces (DIIFAR) when, one morning in October 1960, he was ordered to go to headquarters immediately. Pedro was annoyed with his bureaucratic job and had told his superiors he wanted to do operational work. He wanted action.

Therefore, he felt a mixture of anxiety and curiosity when he received the order and forgot to put away the documents stamped "Confidential" that were strewn all over his desk; he simply hurried from the office.

At that time, a secret section of DIIFAR was housed in an office separate from headquarters. The simplicity and banality of its cryptonym, M, would confuse even the most experienced agents in Washington. It was the embryo of the Cuban Revolution's intelligence services.

"You're going to Costa Rica today," Tomás, one of the chiefs of M, whom Pedro had known since their days in the underground struggle against Batista, said quietly. "There, you will make contact with an officer in the Costa Rican National Guard who says he has some information that should interest us. Be careful."

Filled with the strange sensation of apprehension which rookie agents feel, Pedro settled himself in his seat in the four-engine Super G Constellation. Only then did he admit that all he knew about espionage was what he had seen in the movies. All the training he had been given was limited to what Tomás had told him when saying good-bye at the door of his office: "If you have to go to the Embassy, don't take a taxi, because they're controlled by the police."

Pedro's problems began almost as soon as he sat down in the plane. By chance, the passenger sitting next to him was a minister in the Costa Rican Government, who was returning home from a trip. The man was quite a talker and bombarded the Cuban with questions. Pedro did everything he could to impress the man while glancing at his watch every so often. When he walked down the plane's ramp four hours later at Los Cocos Airport, he was sure his cover was blown.

Therefore, he thought the worst when the immigration officer "invited" him to follow him. Shortly before, the gendarme had exchanged a few words with the Costa Rican minister, Pedro's traveling companion.

The immigration officer checked Pedro's passport meticulously, page by page, stamp by stamp, and finally gave him a wry smile. Pedro thought the end of his adventure had come. "You don't have a vaccination certificate." Ten minutes later, the young Cuban agent left the airport after having been given three injections.

"Just under 350 meters east of the old Masonic Lodge." Pedro didn't think that anybody could get where he wanted to go with instructions like that, but the taxi driver took it in his stride and soon left him in front of the house where a Cuban couple lived. After they introduced themselves, Pedro took the husband aside, told him some details of his mission and asked for a Thompson submachine gun and a pistol. The man's eyes nearly popped out, and he shook his head. It was too much to ask, right at the beginning.

Finally, Pedro managed to convince him of the importance of the mission and, after planning the details for carrying it out, went to bed. The room he had been given was next to the garden. The woman of the house warned him not to go into the garden, because of the snakes. The agent made a face but quickly recovered and, with a wry smile, told her he wasn't afraid. As soon as he was alone, he hurried to close the door to the garden and was amazed to find that it wouldn't shut. It was broken. Then he decided to put several glasses and cups on the floor, placed in such a way that they would fall over if one of the reptiles brushed against them. He lay down and put his pistol on his stomach, loaded and with the safety off.

Two days later, after contacts had been made, the meeting with the Costa Rican officer was held. One thing worried Pedro and his Cuban host: the man had insisted that Pedro go alone.

Pedro arrived on time at the place agreed on for the meeting. It was an old abandoned warehouse on the outskirts of San José. He walked confidently through the doorway and into the dark building, which seemed better suited for a trap than for a talk.

The captain was waiting for him behind the counter. He, too, had promised to be alone, but he was flanked by two soldiers armed with rifles. "Did you bring the money?" he asked. Pedro wasn't flustered; he simply said, "No."

This reply infuriated the officer, but Pedro demanded that he first see the information and assess its worth. After an angry exchange, the captain, a short, stocky man around 40 years old, cut off the discussion, pointing out that he had more men and firepower. Pedro replied by simply opening his jacket and showing him his .45. For some seconds, a heavy silence reigned in the warehouse. The Costa Rican officer was the first to break it. "Everything's here," he said. "Bring me the money tomorrow."

On leaving the warehouse, Pedro felt prickles along the back of his neck, as if the captain and soldiers had it in their sights. He quickened his pace and sighed with relief when back in the car. His Cuban host stepped on the accelerator.

As soon as they got back to the house, he started reading the papers. They mentioned the camps in Retalhuleu, Guatemala, and Puerto Cabezas, Nicaragua, and spoke of the movements of thousands of mercenaries and of support by the governments of Somoza and Idígoras Fuentes. Except for some minor details, the information was nothing new for the Cubans. Only two weeks earlier, on October 7, Foreign Minister Raúl Roa had declared in the United Nations that preparations were being made for an invasion and had named those same places:

> In late August and early September [1960], troops and barges of the Guatemalan Army were concentrated along the country's Atlantic coast. On Helvetia Farm — in the municipality of El Palmar, bordering on the departments of Retalhuleu and Quetzaltenango, in the western part of the country — recently bought by Roberto Alejos, brother of Carlos Alejos, Guatemala's Ambassador to the United States... U.S. military men are giving special training to a large number of exiles and adventurers. There are 185 foreigners, 45 of whom are U.S. citizens. A concrete runway with underground hangars has been built on the farm, and a highway to the Pacific coast is under construction. Detection apparatus has also been installed. The roads leading to Helvetia Farm are controlled by Guatemalan Army soldiers. The foreigners aren't allowed to mix with the local population... Bombers with Cuban insignia have been seen at the La Aurora Airport. The people say that they will be used either to attack Cuba or to simulate a Cuban attack on Guatemala.[51]

The importance of the information Pedro had obtained lay in the fact that it backed up other information, reaffirming that the plans for aggression were real. Moreover, it was the first indicating that Puerto Cabezas was involved in the affair.

---

[51] Archives of the Cuban Ministry of Foreign Affairs.

Pedro went back to his contact point the next day. The captain was alone — perhaps because he didn't want to give the others a share of the money, or maybe because he felt more confident. Even so, their short conversation was far from friendly. Pedro told him that what he had given him wasn't worth the amount of money he wanted for it; they bargained and finally came to an agreement.

That night, the last one Pedro had planned to spend in San José, the Cuban couple invited him to visit someone who was a friend of Cuba. Convinced that he might be able to obtain new data on the enemy's plan, he agreed to go, after taking the precautions required by his secret mission. When he arrived, he was amazed to find an enthusiastic crowd, that greeted him with applause and shouts of "Long live the Revolution!" Pedro was overwhelmed and had to speak extemporaneously about the latest happenings on the island. From an agent, he had become a revolutionary agitator.

That night, he found it hard to sleep, because of a nagging fever that wouldn't abate, in spite of all the remedies his hostess concocted. He had to stay in San José three days more, gathering data on the invasion plan, which sympathizers with the Cuban cause offered spontaneously.

A week after beginning his mission, Pedro returned to Cuba. Tomás was waiting for him at the airport, and he quickly reported to him about what he had done. Tomás was pleased, but Pedro had to be hospitalized immediately. The injections he'd been given at the San José airport had given him an infection.

By the time of Pedro's trip to Costa Rica, the CIA no longer considered it a priority to keep the Cubans' training camps in Guatemala a secret. In any case, it was impossible to do so for long. The Agency's main interest at that point was to camouflage the U.S. Government's participation in the project and to maintain the secrecy of the magnitude, date, time and place of the operation. Even though it was very difficult to believe, the Democratic Revolutionary Front made enormous efforts to make world public opinion think it was responsible for the invasion. And, though many doubted its claims, no one was able to prove that they were false.

In fact, the CIA couldn't hide its participation in the project for long. It became impossible to hide the training camps with U.S. instructors and other personnel, guarded by hundreds of soldiers belonging to the Guatemalan National Army, with men and military equipment constantly coming and going and planes landing and taking off from the jungle, surrounded by thousands of farmers' houses. As an intelligence maxim has it, "You can't hide a hippopotamus under a handkerchief." Nor is it easy to hide a hippopotamus when it has to be moved from one place to another in the city of Miami; have medical checkups; leave its family; disappear mysteriously one night; and then begin to send letters which, though censored, gave hints about why it was away.

But what damage could be done by the talk of the Cubans in Miami or New York — if they did talk — compared to that of the thousands of coffee workers who surrounded our camp in the Guatemalan mountains and who earned a mere 40 cents a day for their labor? The base which the U.S. Government officials chose was just a mountain ridge west of the Pan American Highway. Where was the Cuban air base? Its site, like everything else not chosen by the Cubans, was in the middle of the town of Retalhuleu, which had a population of around 4,000, with questionable political leanings: a secret base for a secret operation... Moreover, when, in history, has it ever been possible to hide the massive preparations for a frontal, conventional attack from the enemy? Could General Eisenhower keep the preparations for the invasion of Europe during World War II hidden from Hitler?[52]

Some of the Cuban-American writers and participants in the Bay of Pigs invasion who have touched on this topic state that Cuban State Security had infiltrated agents in the Trax Base. The most quoted version points to Benigno Pérez Vivanco, a recruit who was later selected to head one of the infiltration teams, as a Cuban State Security agent. In his book *Shadow Warrior*, Félix Rodríguez stated:

Even though every precaution had been taken when the first selections were made, at least one of Castro's agents penetrated the grey teams. His name was Benigno Pérez. We knew that he had been a lieutenant in Castro's armed forces and that, like many of his officers, he had deserted and gone to the United States.
Pérez was a hardworking individual. I remember him as a small man who drove trucks and bulldozers, a cigar always seemingly clenched permanently between his teeth. But one thing about him made me wary: the guy would never look you in the face. When you spoke to him he would avert his eyes, as if he was ashamed of something. He was older than most of us, and I wondered why he was selected for the grey teams. At the time I

---

[52] José Pérez San Román, *Respuesta*.

guessed it was because they believed he would still have good contacts in Cuba as a former Castro officer.

I was happy when he was finally assigned to someone else's unit — I would have refused to have him in mine simply because I had a queasy feeling in my gut whenever Pérez's name was mentioned. But it wasn't so good for the guys he worked with, because Pérez didn't have good contacts in Cuba, but great contacts — many of them members of Castro's secret police — and every one of his fellow team members was captured. Today, Benigno Pérez lives the good life in Cuba as a high-ranking officer of the DGI [State Security].[53]

Benigno Pérez Vivanco had fought against Batista's forces in the Rebel Army's Second National Front of the Escambray, which was headed by Eloy Gutiérrez Menoyo. After taking part in eight battles, he was made a captain. After the 1959 revolution, Menoyo reduced his rank to first lieutenant, saying he needed to give his rank of captain to another comrade. Pérez complained to Major Camilo Cienfuegos, who, on learning that he had been a heavy equipment operator, sent him to the development area of the Isle of Pines. Months later, in July 1960, after some arguments with his chief, he and some of his friends went to the United States. A week later, he began working for the United Fruit Company as a crane operator. In August, the FRD recruited him, and he left for Guatemala, where he worked on building the Rayo Air Base's runway, in Retalhuleu. He soon became one of the favorites of Filipino Colonel Valeriano Vallejo and the U.S. head instructor, "Carl."

I went all over with Vallejo and Carl. They trusted me a lot. I got along well with everybody except those who had been military men in the other army and Batista's supporters. I didn't have problems with any of them, but they weren't my friends. I had fought against the Batista dictatorship, and it wasn't easy for me — as it was for some of those guys — to consider them my comrades now. And there were a lot of Batista supporters in the camp.[54]

In late November, when the original teams were dissolved and Attack Brigade 2506 was being created, Pérez was among those selected for training and coordinating actions with the underground groups supporting the invasion. Pérez once again underwent rigorous training in the Panamanian jungles.

---

[53] Félix Rodríguez, *Shadow Warrior*.
[54] Testimony of Benigno Pérez Vivanco.

He entered Cuba illegally along Havana's northeastern coast on March 22, heading the Inca team. They brought 17 tons of weapons and explosives for the underground groups. After some vicissitudes, Benigno Pérez and Rafael García Rubio, his radio operator, were hidden in Apartment 6-B in the Almar building, in Miramar.

During April, he trained three underground groups in how to handle explosives and advised in several acts of sabotage in the capital, which were carried out successfully. At around 6:00 a.m. on April 21, after a week of intensive roundups of conspirators and two days after the Brigade's defeat at the Bay of Pigs, Pérez and García Rubio were returning to the apartment where they had been hiding. They had spent the night at a motel with two women, trying to avoid being caught in the apartment in the early morning hours, which were the most dangerous. They didn't know that neighbors in another apartment in the building who belonged to the Committee for the Defense of the Revolution had noted the extra movement to and from that apartment and had been asked by State Security agents to keep close tabs on the people staying there.

Shortly after 6:00, having been told that the suspicious individuals had returned, four State Security agents appeared at the building. Two of them remained by the street door, and the other two went up to the apartment. Those men had been taking part in operations for a week and were exhausted. Marcial Arufe, who was inside, looked through the peephole before opening the door. On seeing the unshaven face of a stranger wearing an olive-green cap, he asked Pérez and García Rubio to leave by the freight elevator. The two men heard the shooting as they descended to the first floor. They didn't reach the street, however, but were arrested at the door. In the office of Cuban State Security, Pérez's old comrades from the guerrilla struggle against Batista were amazed to see him there, accused of being a terrorist and counterrevolutionary.

Pérez was condemned to death by firing squad, but his sentence was commuted to 30 years' imprisonment. Fourteen years later, he was released on parole. Soon afterwards, he got married. Benigno Pérez now lives in Matanzas Province and works as a sugarcane harvester operator on an agricultural production cooperative.

In fact, there had been no Cuban agents at the Trax Base.

The first reports about the existence of the camps in Guatemala came from the Guatemalan press and from public protests. As early as June 1960, the Guatemalan Workers' Party made several denunciations and statements. Law students and members of the Salvador Orozco Club, in Quetzaltenango, made public statements which had repercussions in the Central University of Guatemala City. The matter was taken to Parliament, and several deputies asked the government for an explanation and issued public letters of denunciation. The camps thus became a topic for discussion in the streets. A student demonstration protesting the presence of anti-Castro Cubans being trained in the country wound up with a protest in front of the U.S. Embassy in the latter half of October 1960. Colonel Carlos Paz Tejeda's denunciation of the camps and military bases in Guatemalan territory — which was given a whole page in *Prensa Libre*, a Guatemalan daily with a circulation of 30,000 copies — took the issue to the garrisons.

Meanwhile, reports from the Guatemalan press were accumulating in the office of Section M, in Cuba. They were sent in by sympathizers with the Revolution and even by Cubans living in Miami and New York. Moreover, there were some reports from agents of Cuban State Security. All had one thing in common: they denounced the invasion plan and stated where the camps were. Nothing more. It was clear that some of them included information that the CIA officers in charge of disinformation activities had prepared in Quarters Eye to confuse Fidel Castro and keep him off the scent.

As early as September 30, a State Security agent who had infiltrated a branch of the Movement of Revolutionary Recovery (MRR) in Havana reported:

> This report is the most important of all, so far, because the abortion of the U.S. Embassy's plan will depend on the magnitude of the things set forth in it. All of the teams will come on October 15, at the following points: Sagua de Tánamo, northern Las Villas Province and the Sierra de los Organos Mountains. The teams will be brought in by U.S. Air Force planes with 70 Cuban pilots. They will try to reinforce old and create new fronts. Seventy planes and attack commandos will take part in the general attack — that is, the landing and bombardment — which will take place on the morning of October 25. Assassination attempts and acts of sabotage will begin on the first of that month.[55]

Nothing happened. Brigade 2506's planes carried out just one mission in the month of October, which consisted of dropping a load of supplies in southern Las Villas Province, in the Escambray Mountains.

---

[55] Archives of the Cuban Ministry of the Interior.

It is clear that Richard Bissell and his principal collaborators analyzed in great detail Raúl Roa's statement in the United Nations on October 7, 1960, and used it to initiate new disinformation campaigns.

Thus, on October 30, just three weeks after the Cuban Foreign Minister's denunciation of the plans in the United Nations, Cuban intelligence received a cable from Mexico which stated, "Our Guatemalan friends report 6,000 men transferred from Helvetia Farm to Nicaragua..."[56] A report to the headquarters of Cuban State Security dated December 29, 1960, stated:

> In response to your question as to whether we have a concrete report about the mercenaries who left aboard 13 ships on October 27, 1960, we in this section received a report dated November 26, 1960, which stated the following: "It has been verified that the 6,000 or so men were moved as follows:
>
> "a) Only the foreign mercenaries (especially Cubans, Salvadorans, Hondurans, etc.) were sent to Nicaragua on October 27.
>
> "b) Others were taken to a camp at the Chinajá airstrip, where they were seen on subsequent days.
>
> "c) The Guatemalan Army troops, who were included in the total, remain at Helvetia Farm, and another contingent of regular troops — around 500 men — was later sent to the farm. Many U.S. citizens also remain at the farm.
>
> "d) The agricultural workers and farmers enlisted in the army were demobilized and went back to agricultural work, but close watch is kept over them. It is supposed that they have remained in that situation temporarily.
>
> "Otherwise, everything continues much the same at the Helvetia base and on the farms surrounding it. There are always 150 planes [without specifying what kind], a figure which coincides with what Idígoras told the Guatemalan Air Force pilots on October 13, 1960.
>
> "Those who are still there are simply training in parachute jumps, using a very large transport plane; therefore, the other aspects of their training seem to have been completed."
>
> In addition, we received a cable from Mexico on October 30, 1960, in which our Guatemalan friends reported that 6,000 men had been moved from Helvetia Farm to Nicaragua. It was certain that the transfer was made from Puerto Barrios. From earlier

---

[56] By the end of October, there were fewer than 600 recruits of the future brigade at the Trax Base. It is clear that the CIA multiplied by ten. (Author's note.)

reports, we had known that 13 unregistered ships which flew no flags were in Puerto Barrios.[57]

The disinformation is obvious. No movements had been made, and the Brigade had considerably fewer men than reported. In Cuba, Cuban Security analyzed all of the information and reached its own conclusions. The troop movements and the figures on the number of mercenaries, planes and ships were taken with a grain of salt, but the existence of the camps and the invasion plan were again confirmed.

In January 1961, in response to the public denunciations of the existence of the camps and the conflict this had caused in the Guatemalan Congress, the Guatemalan Government engaged in a misleading ruse. It invited members of the press and several opposition deputies to visit the supposed training centers to see for themselves that no Cubans were there. Eduardo Ferrer, a pilot in the Brigade, recalled the day they visited:

> In early January, we were told that the next day a group of 50 reporters from all over the Americas and Europe was coming to Rayo. Their purpose was to report the truth about the base to the outside world... The flight bringing the newsmen to Rayo was due to arrive at precisely 11 a.m. By 9 a.m. there was no one at the base. Very early that morning, we had received orders to pack our knapsacks and canteens and proceed three kilometers into the jungle. We spent the morning in hiding. To justify the existence of the base, a detachment of Guatemalan soldiers was brought in. Four hours later, a scout found us and reported that the *Constellation*, with all the newsmen aboard, had departed on its return trip with a "no-news cargo." We stumbled back to Rayo, having covered six kilometers of steaming Central American jungle.[58]

On March 2, 1961, when the CIA still had the city of Trinidad as Brigade 2506's goal, the regular edition of the *Diario de Costa Rica* published a denunciation of Costa Rican Deputies Marcial Aguiluz and Enrique Obregón. The Deputies presented copies of a letter dated February 24 in which Cuban counterrevolutionaries Orlando Núñez Pérez and José Miguel Tarafa, delegates of the Democratic Revolutionary Front, reported on what they had done to organize training bases in Costa Rican territory. Aguiluz and Obregón Valverde added that the Cubans had three farms at their disposal: Playa

---

[57] Archives of the Cuban Ministry of the Interior.
[58] Eduardo Ferrer, *Operation Puma*, Chapter 10.

Hermosa, in Limón Province; La Cañera, between Guaipites and Rosanna; and another at Sixacla River, near Panama. The newspaper article pointed out:

> Around then, a group of Cubans and Costa Ricans who had been trained in a place 10 minutes from the Matina railway halt on the Limón-San José line had prepared a landing stage from which to go to the Bay of Pigs (Cuba). For their invasion purposes, they can use the river, going aboard the *Don Fabio*. To help judge the authenticity of this report, we are publishing excerpts from the reports we have on a message which one of the San José chiefs sent to the man in Puerto Limón who is the chief or commander of the group.

Shortly afterwards, a Cuban official sent a cable stating:

> Carlos Luis Falla, the author of *Mamita Yunai*, went hunting at Tortuguero Lake and took a look for himself. Then he came to the Embassy and told me that there was nothing of the sort there.[59]

Section M didn't give much importance to the Costa Rican deputies' statement about the Bay of Pigs. Other quite recent information pointed with a watchmaker's precision to another spot along the Cuban coast for the D Day landing.

In fact, it wasn't until March 14 that the CIA and Pentagon experts chose the Bay of Pigs for the landing. The Bay of Pigs then changed from a point on the map which, everything indicates, the Agency used for disinformation purposes, to the final destination of Brigade 2506.

In late March and the first few weeks in April, the Cuban leadership decided to send the more than 50,000 militia who were in the Escambray back to their homes. Just one of the over 70 battalions, with inferior armaments and scanty military training, was sent to defend the coast at the Bay of Pigs, and only one platoon and five men from a squad were situated at two points along that coast. The bulk of the battalion was sent to the Australia Sugar Mill, 29 kilometers from Larga Beach and 68 kilometers from Girón Beach. The port of Casilda and the area around it, near the city of Trinidad, were given top priority for the defense of their coasts.

A long confidential report prepared by Cuban State Security on the "mercenaries' bases and camps in Guatemala, Nicaragua and Florida," was sent to Fidel Castro and subsequently returned to the offices of State Security on April 7, 1961. It had been drawn up on January 12,

---

[59] Testimony of Major (R.) Héctor Gallo.

and it confirmed that there were camps in Guatemala. The figure it gave on the number of mercenaries was 10 times the real number. The report stated that the enemy had jet planes and B-29 superfortress bombers. In fact, Brigade 2506 had B-26 bombers, not B-29s, but unquestionably it had planes for bombing military targets. For its part, the Cuban Government rushed to prepare courses for antiaircraft artillery.

The report also contained a synthesis of the information that had appeared in the international and U.S. press on the camps and invasion preparations. In assessing this media coverage of the invasion plans, one of the last pages of the long report of Cuban Security stated:

> As you may have noted, the reports by U.S. correspondents which caused an international uproar contained only a very few details on the mercenaries' bases in Guatemala. This Department already had complete information about them, as noted in the first part of this report. The Cuban Government and Dr. Raúl Roa, its representative in the UN, had already denounced those activities.[60]

One of the last pages of the confidential report to Fidel Castro summed up one of the plans the CIA had drawn up in its disinformation campaign, aimed at making Cuba believe that the invasion would occur at several points simultaneously rather than at only one place:

> The plan is to drop small commando-type groups at several points in the island, synchronizing them with assassination attempts and acts of sabotage in the cities. Those groups will leave from Florida, some adjacent keys and possibly Swan Island. While the landings are being made, the mercenaries camped at the Guantánamo Naval Base will head for the Sierra Maestra, which they will use as their center of operations for attacking several cities in Oriente Province, supported by aviation based on Swan Island and in Guatemala.

On receiving confirmation that the invasion was taking place at the Bay of Pigs, combined with a landing at Baracoa, Fidel Castro didn't hesitate. Witnesses at Point One say that, after receiving the two reports in the early morning hours of April 17, Fidel told the officers who had met there that it was absolutely necessary to defeat the invaders at Girón and Larga Beaches without loss of time, and he immediately ordered forces mobilized to confront the attack. He was convinced that it was the main landing.

---

[60] Report from Cuba's intelligence services to Fidel Castro dated January 12, 1961.

"We have a road in here"

"Many women die in childbirth," Victorino Sierra thought, sitting at the foot of the tree. "Basilia Blanco went into labor and took a long time. She lost a lot of blood. People went to Covadonga to get the doctor, but he didn't want to come. Then her husband went to the Rural Guard, and they brought the doctor, but she was already dead. Little babies die, too." Victorino thought of his two children who had died, one of gastroenteritis and the other, a girl, when she was two years old. "The doctor from Covadonga said it was meningitis," he murmured. "Four days after Encarnación went into labor, they got her out through Buena Bay and took her to Cienfuegos. She died there. The same thing happened to América. When they took her out through Aguada, she was nearly dead. Yes, many women die in childbirth."

Victorino suddenly stopped thinking and looked toward the pile of charring wood a few meters away. He thought he had heard a tiny explosion. His face looked drawn. Another explosion, this one louder, told him that somewhere the dirt which covered the wood and kept oxygen from getting to the coals had shifted. Victorino stood up and grabbed the rustic ladder. A few minutes later, he covered the hole in the dirt. Carefully, he went down the rungs of the ladder leaning against the pile of charring wood. One false step, and his foot, covered only by a cloth slipper, would plunge through the thin layer of earth which kept the temperature inside the pile at over 100 degrees. Seconds later, he settled himself once again under the tree.

Victorino had begun to make the charring pile a month earlier. The first thing he had done was look for a good place in the forest in which to build it. Then he and his 11-year-old son had cleared the area. They took away most of the stones and buried the half-buried ones. Then they covered the ground with branches and dry firewood and set it on fire. Lastly, they spread cinders from other charring piles and cut paths in various directions, all leading to the spot. That made the base for their pile. Then they put down their machetes and took up short-handled axes and began to cut firewood in the surrounding woods, lengths from five to six feet long, and drag them to their pile. The wood in that area wasn't the best quality, but neither was it the worthless, thin stuff.

When Victorino was still a small boy, his father had made a *burro* for him. It was a piece of wood on which around 30 kilograms of firewood could be placed. It was tied to a rope which he put under his armpits and then across his forehead. That's how firewood was dragged from where it was cut to the charring pile — a longer and longer distance each trip. The person who dragged the wood was the *burro*. And that had been the only "toy" Victorino had had as a child.

They raised the charring pile by placing the wood in a circle, each piece close against the next, slightly inclined, one floor of wood on top of another. At the top, the "mouth" remained open. That's where they put in red-hot firebrands until they were sure that the green wood had caught. Then they covered it and made some openings around the edges so the charring pile could "breathe." The color of the smoke that came out of those openings showed how the wood was burning. If the fire was hotter toward the south, the openings on that side were closed, leaving the ones on the north open. The fire had to be watched 24 hours a day to keep the pile from exploding. If you were careless and the "mouth" opened and you didn't shut it in time, the charring pile would erupt like a volcano. That's why Victorino had spent 12 days in the woods, by the charring pile, relieved every so often by his son, whom he didn't trust enough yet to leave in charge all night long.

In the rainy season, when the water in the swamp was higher, Victorino and his son would get up at 4:00 in the morning and, after a cup of coffee, put a bar of guava paste, some sowbelly and some ship's biscuits in a can. They would take a flat-bottomed boat or barge and, poling it like Venetian gondoliers, would go far, very far into the swamp, toward the cays where they could still find hardwood trees. When they reached the shallows, they would leap out of the boat and push it with their backsides. The water came up to Victorino's waist and his son's chest. Often, they stepped into potholes and plunged deeper.

Several hours later, they reached the cay they had chosen. Then began the real work of lumbering. When a tree fell, Victorino and his son would climb up on it and use their axes to smooth the edges. If the tree was to be used as a railway sleeper, they had to work it along the four sides as a carpenter would with the help of a saw. Then they would drag it to the barge and go back and cut another. They would keep that up until they had 10 or 15 of them. They also cut *bolos*, to be used as props for curing tobacco; Santa María trees, for crossbeams; and other precious wood trees, for making funiture. But these last were getting harder and harder to find. After several hours of hard work, they would take a break to eat bits of sowbelly on crackers, followed by the guava paste to get rid of the nauseous taste of the sowbelly and keep it from repeating on them.

When the barge was heavily laden, Victorino and his son would begin pushing it through the shallows back to the channel. When they reached it, Victorino would stand on the bank and put a rope across his chest, the other end tied to the barge's painter. Then he would haul on the line until the barge began to move slowly. His son, standing a few meters behind him, would use the pole to keep the barge away from the bank. By the time the sun was going down, father and son, utterly spent, would reach home, where Victorino's wife would have supper ready.

While gulping down his small portion of cornmeal with sugar water, Victorino would figure out how much he could charge for the load. Victorino knew that he wouldn't be able to sleep that night, because of his aches and pains. In a corner of the room, his son removed the chiggers which had burrowed into the soles of his feet. If he didn't do that right away, they would lay their eggs there, and the itching would be unbearable.

The man who bought the charcoal and wood would pay 50 centavos for each tree. Victorino had never seen any real money, however. The man would give him a voucher, which Victorino would use at the store belonging to the man who also owned the land, the woods and the railway line. He would exchange it for enough salt, sugar, coffee, lard, sowbelly, crackers, guava paste, rice and dry beans to keep going.

Victorino Sierra was a charcoal maker, and charcoal makers don't talk a lot. The loneliness and silence imposed by their hard work and the muddy water and lush vegetation made the swamp a realm of silence. Victorino liked to be alone, sitting under a tree and keeping watch on his charring pile. Then he would remember all the thoughts which stored up the memories of his life.

Victorino's father had been a Galician emigrant who arrived in Cuba without any papers. Because of that, he went to live in the Zapata Swamp, the most desolate place on the island, whose vegetation seemed to have died on the threshold of civilization. There, nobody would go looking for him.

The Zapata Swamp seems to have been formed by the branches of rivers which, like the Hanábana, ran toward the south, and others that, like the Hatiguanico, ran westward. Those rivers flowed over a thin, almost horizontal stratum of rock where shallows, kamenitzas and caves acted as drainage points for rainwater and the water from other rivers. When the shallows were clogged by excess sediment, drainage began to be hindered, the water became dammed and enormous lagoons — such as Treasure Lake — were created. Instead of emptying into the Bay of Pigs, the Hanábana River spread its water over the Zapata Swamp, and the upper course of the Hatiguanico River was covered with mud.[61]

The swamp is in the southern part of Matanzas Province, near the central region of Cuba. It contains the Bay of Pigs. To the east is the Bay of Cienfuegos; to the north, the Havana-Matanzas plains; and, to the west, Broa Bay and the Gulf of Batabanó. The swamp is traversed by long, narrow channels which charcoal makers dug so they could take the wood and charcoal out. The region consists of three zones: the Zapata Swamp; the Western Zapata Swamp, which consists of southern Matanzas Province and part of Havana Province; and the Eastern Zapata Swamp, the area east of the Bay of Pigs.

At the Bay of Pigs cove, a coralline strip of solid ground containing some beautiful beaches and sparse vegetation lies between the swampy area, which is covered with mangrove and other trees, and the shore. The CIA and Pentagon strategists chose that strip of land for the invasion — which is separated from the rest of the island by the swampy area, that extends northward for 12 kilometers and eastward for six kilometers — thinking it would be a magnificent beachhead. But the CIA experts weren't the first to exploit the exceptional natural attributes of that strip of land. That coast had already been a refuge for pirates. Gilberto Girón, the most famous of them, had established his camp on the beach which now bears his name.

There are more than 900 species of indigenous plants in the Zapata Swamp, and 100 of them are unique to Cuba. The fauna, which is impressive for its diversity and indigenous nature, includes such mammals as the *conga, carabalí* and dwarf hutia. The Zapata Wren, Zapata Rail and Zapata Sparrow also enrich that superb area 4,520 square kilometers in size.

Unquestionably, the crocodile is the ultimate expression of the mysterious enchantment of that area. It is the king of the swamp, fearsome and silent as its most powerful rival: the charcoal maker. The Cuban crocodile (*Crocodylus rhombifer*), a freshwater animal, is endemic to the island, but the American crocodile, which prefers the

---

[61] Núñez Jiménez, 123.

salt water of the coastal areas, may also be found in the Zapata Swamp.

Crocodiles are very patient; so are the charcoal makers. A crocodile will lie immobile for hours, waiting for its prey. When the hutia finally climbs down from the tree to get a drink of water and moves close to the edge of the inlet, the crocodile moves with amazing speed to crunch it in its jaws. Crocodiles have always considered charcoal makers to be prime targets, and many of the latter have lost their lives to those beasts.

On May 25, 1959, sitting by his charring pile, Victorino Sierra had another worry. The owners of the land, the railway companies and the stores had said no more wood should be cut. Victorino didn't know why and was worried because it was the first time that the owners had suspended the activity that was the mainstay of his existence. He didn't know the owners, because they lived in the capital or in Cienfuegos, but nobody questioned the decision, because the foremen who represented the owners had said that was what they wanted.

Several months earlier, Victorino Sierra had heard — first as a rumor and then as news on a small battery-powered radio in the settlement — that Batista had fled and that Fidel Castro was in charge of the government. Later, Alejo, "The Moor," who had gone to Aguada de Pasajeros, brought a newspaper, in which Victorino and the others could see a photo of the bearded man from the Sierra. But Fidel didn't mean anything to Victorino, even though Alejo, who was normally a man of very few words, now spoke about him nonstop whenever he was mentioned. Victorino simply listened. Nothing in the swamp had changed, though some people said they had seen the bearded man going around Treasure Lake in a helicopter. But, if the owners put a stop to the cutting, Fidel Castro couldn't do anything, because it had always been the owners who ruled in Cuba.

Victorino was thinking about this, and about how hungry he was, when he heard a new sound. First he looked at the charring pile and then at the sky. Yes, that thing was the helicopter he had seen two or three times crossing the Zapata Swamp. "It's going to land at Cayo Ramona," Victorino said and, in a spurt of energy, ran to the settlement.

In May, the owners halted all work. They did that to turn the charcoal makers against the Revolution, hoping they would blame the Revolution. The charcoal makers were hungry, but, since nobody was buying their wood or their charcoal, they didn't have any vouchers. I went to Aguada and spoke with the revolutionary authorities there. They took me to Santa Clara in a small plane, and I told them what was going on and then returned to the swamp. A week later, on May 25, I saw a helicopter circling over the settlement. I ran out of my house barefoot and without putting my shirt on. Then I saw him. It was Fidel. I gave him a big hug even before he got out of the 'copter. Fidel asked me, "Do you know Alejo, 'The Moor'?" "That's me." "What's going on here?" I realized that they had told him what I had said in Santa Clara. Well, I told him what things were like. I remember that, when I finished, I told him I didn't have anything to eat. "We're going to solve this," he replied. I stayed next to him, but everybody in the settlement — men, women and children — crowded around. It was really something! He told us that they were going to give each family 100 pesos so the immediate problem would be solved, and he asked me to make a census and go to Havana to get the money. Right there, the first cooperative was organized. Every sack of charcoal weighed 325 pounds, and the owners used to pay us 95 centavos a sack. We got 10 centavos for every thousand pounds of firewood, or 12 centavos if it was from myrobalan or button trees, and you had to haul a full load of firewood to get enough vouchers to buy in the store. I told Fidel about all those things that day. I remember I told him no priests ever came to the swamp, except for one who came once a year to baptize everybody all together.

Fidel told me he wanted to go to Girón Beach, and he asked my help. I found an old '46 Chevy pickup truck, and we set off. Pedrito Miret — that's what Fidel called him — and Núñez Jiménez were with him. The pilot, Díaz Lanz, who became a traitor later on, flew the helicopter back to the Australia Sugar Mill to get gasoline. Fidel had told him to pick him up at Girón Beach at 5:00 p.m. We got there, and the few charcoal makers who were in the area all put a little something in the pot, and we got enough food together for a small meal.[62]

Manuel Alvariño, who lived in that part of the swamp, accompanied Fidel on that trip. His account, repeated and polished many times later, is worthy of a good storyteller, such as abounded in the rural parts of Cuba.

He had lunch at Aniceto's place. Aniceto made Navy beans with the only hog's foot he could find. When he put the plate of beans on the table, the foot was aimed at Fidel. Then Pedrito Miret said,

---

[62] Testimony of Alejo ("The Moor"), a charcoal maker.

"Look, Fidel, we're going to have to try to straighten out the world," and he turned the plate around so the foot pointed at him. Then Fidel turned the plate so the foot pointed at him again and said, "Pedrito, you'd better leave the world the way it is."

Xiomara, one of Alvariño's daughters, was watching from a window. Even though she didn't really understand who the man was, she felt an unusual admiration for him. She saw him once more, a year later, in Havana. That was at her graduation from a dressmaking course. Hundreds of daughters of charcoal makers took courses in the capital during those years.

Alejo, "The Moor," continued:

At around 5:00 p.m., he began looking at the sky and, after a while, he asked me, "'Moor,' if something's wrong with the helicopter, how can you get me out of here?" "In the pickup truck," I replied. "No, I don't mean to Cayo Ramona. I have to get to Covadonga." "Commander, I'm going to Covadonga to get the hand car." He stayed overnight, because something was wrong with the helicopter. I arranged a guard to watch over Fidel. I told the charcoal makers who were there, "Those of you who have machetes, cut clubs for those who don't, and everybody guard the Commander. If you all stand guard around the house, not even a mouse can get through." Everybody stayed awake, with machetes and clubs, guarding Fidel.

At Cayo Ramona, that night, Victorino Sierra worked on sums, talking his way through them: "Not 350 but 250 pounds per sack. Fidel said the work would be humanized. Not 95 centavos but three pesos a sack." Victorino kept on doing sums until the sun came up. The charcoal makers in the settlement had elected him administrator of the first cooperative in the swamp. Meanwhile, his son was watching the charring pile. Victorino smiled.

At Girón Beach, Fidel had said something that seemed crazy to many of the charcoal makers who were listening to him attentively. A road would be built from the Covadonga Sugar Mill, on the other side of the swamp, to Girón Beach, to make it easier to take the charcoal and wood out and to improve the charcoal makers' living conditions. Highways would replace the only means of transportation there was in the region at the time: a narrow-gauge railroad which had been built to take the sugarcane grown on the farms on the solid ground to the Covadonga and Australia Sugar Mills. The train came in once a day. When the swamp was high, in the rainy season, it was the only means of communication, even though it was often derailed, which put the line out of service for several days at a time. Then, if you were sick, the only way to get out was to have friends and relatives carry you by stretcher to the sugar mill, over 30 kilometers away.

The new roads, the first proof of progress, would end nearly a century of isolation, loneliness, pain and death. In addition, that decision of Fidel's would mean that the invasion — which the United States hadn't yet thought of — wouldn't be a mortal blow against the Revolution. The battalions of militia, tanks and antiaircraft and other artillery would advance along the three roads that would cross the swamp from the northwest and northeast to the southern coast and along a fourth road which would run along the coast. If the roads hadn't been there, it would have been extremely difficult to reach the beachhead through the swamp. Years later, Fidel commented:

> They landed at a place where they could hold out for a while, because it was very difficult to regain. The access roads had to cross several kilometers of swamps, which made it impossible to carry out any military maneuvers. It was a Pass of Thermopylae.

The Revolution didn't limit itself to building those highways. They were just the beginning for a project that seemed like the awakening from a nightmare. Fourteen cooperatives were created, and the prices paid for charcoal, wood and crocodiles quickly rose. The charcoal makers' average daily wage rose from one peso to 10. The members of the cooperatives were entitled to receive the benefits of the Association of People's Stores, which sold food and clothing at cost and on credit. The National Institute of the Agrarian Reform supplied the stores. For the first time, the charcoal makers could afford to wear shoes and dressed and ate like human beings. Weekly and annual vacations were established, and other labor and social rights were extended, as well. Hunger and misery, the charcoal makers' inseparable companions in the past, disappeared at a stroke.

Work on the only hospital in the region, which was located in the Cayo Romana settlement, had begun in 1952. It had been given a lot of fanfare in the press, because it was built at the initiative of the First Lady of the Republic; in 1959, the unfinished structure was being used as a pigsty, but it was completed soon after the triumph of the Revolution. The 1961 invaders seized it and used it as a field hospital. Thirty years later, that hospital in the Zapata Swamp offered general medical care, minor surgery and acupuncture and had a maternity home for expectant mothers. The area also has 12 family doctors. Infant mortality in the Zapata Swamp has been reduced to zero.

Three months before the invasion, a contingent of volunteer teachers was assigned to work throughout the swamp. Dirt-floored, thatched-roofed and -sided schools with benches made out of palm trees were opened in nearly all the settlements. For the first time, the thousands of children who lived on the Zapata Peninsula began to go to elementary school. Water filters, sanitary instructions for preventing disease, scholarships, the construction of rubblework houses, rural transportation and health services were introduced. The old swamp, which had produced some of the most tragic accounts in Cuban literature and had inspired Cuba's first feature film (*Mégano*), was buried once and for all.

When the 1961 invasion took place, 300 sons and daughters of farmers from the Zapata Swamp were studying in Havana, and many young people from the city had gone to the swamp to teach its adults how to read and write. Several dozen farmers' children had received scholarships for studying arts and crafts.

In Soplillar, one of the settlements nearest Girón Beach, Nemecia Rodríguez was going to the new people's store with her mother. She had her heart set on a pair of white shoes. Her mother told her it wouldn't be a good idea to get them, because of the mud. Nemecia kept pleading and her mother — who had never before had enough money to buy her any shoes — finally bought those she wanted.

Nemecia liked to listen to the stories told by "Baldy," a neighbor in the settlement. "Baldy" was one of the poorest charcoal makers in the area, and he spent a lot of time birdwatching. He liked talking about birds with the other people in the settlement:

> The Florida duck emigrates to get away from cold fronts. That's why it leaves before December. More flamingos come than any other bird; there are thousands of them. It's large, with long legs; some of them are always here. The Brown Woodpecker's always walking around in the mud; that's how it got its name. There are four species of woodpeckers in the swamp: the Green, the Brown, the Scapulary and the West Indian. Anybody who tells you different doesn't know anything about the birds in the swamp. Ah! The Zapata Wren isn't the smallest bird; that's a lie. The smallest one is the Bee Hummingbird. But the Long-Tailed Hawk is also very small and is the most beautiful.

Much to "Baldy's" surprise, the Prime Minister of his country had dinner with him on December 24, 1959 — not at the Presidential Palace or in any mansion in the capital, but with him and his family in his untidy hut. "Baldy" recalled:

> I was shaving under a tree, when I saw a helicopter flying low and then landing. There I was, with my razor in my hand. Núñez Jiménez got out. I didn't know who he was. He asked me if a group of them — there were 14 in all — could eat at my house. I said OK. He didn't tell me Fidel would be in the group. When the helicopter came back, bringing Fidel, I was getting a sack of charcoal. He asked me a thousand questions — if I earned a lot or a little, that kind of thing. The first cooperative had already been created, and the swamp had begun to change. He asked me if I had worked a lot under the other government. I told him I had. He told me he wanted to spend Christmas Eve with me. He brought a pig and a half, but we didn't touch it except for the tail, which Fidel ate, because he liked that part. He brought beer, malt drinks and soft drinks for the kids. He was very happy. I remember he told me, "You're going to see buses from Havana coming here." I thought he was crazy, but, sure enough, buses from Havana came to the swamp on Christmas Eve of 1960, after the road had been built.

"Baldy's" youngest daughter will never forget that Christmas Eve with Fidel: "I was a little girl, but I remember it perfectly. I sat next to Fidel and had malt and soft drinks. I was given a pair of white socks. After dinner, a farmer from the neighborhood came in to play the guitar. I still remember the ballad he sang for Fidel that night."

> "Thanks be to God and to Fidel,
> We have a road in here,
> So childbirth is no cause for fear;
> Our women now get well.

> "Commander, 'cause of what you braved,
> You freed us from that threat.
> It's something that we won't forget —
> The many lives you've saved."

Attack Brigade 2506 landed just a few kilometers from that hut in the settlement of Soplillar.

Mission: Paralyze Havana

A bell rang in the five-story building, one long peal, announcing that the store was closing. Automatically, the central air-conditioning system switched off, and the temperature began to rise. Half of the inside lights were turned off, and the elevators stopped after reaching the ground floor. The doormen kept new clients from entering the store, but the nearly 300 who were already inside weren't bothered. The clerks who weren't waiting on anyone at that moment got ready to leave. The remainder in the store's 19 departments would follow them as soon as they finished waiting on their present customers. In five minutes, the store was practically empty. It was 6:00 p.m. on April 13, 1961.

Carlos González Vidal took care of his last customer, left the record department and hurried to the fabric department. His face was red, and he seemed very intense. He touched the gold medallion of Our Lady of Cobre, which he wore on a chain around his neck. Three employees still remained in the fabric department, which was one of the largest in the store. They thought nothing of the fact that González was there. He was friendly and jovial. The only drawback to his character was his growing hostility to the Revolution. In recent days, however, he had been attentive, chatty and friendly with them. He helped them close several sliding doors in front of the shelves of fabrics, protecting them from dust, while he talked about record sales. "Fewer and fewer people are coming in from the United States."

After shutting one of the sliding doors, González was alone. Then, from his briefcase, he took a pack of Edén cigarettes and bit one end of it until he felt the calamine crush between his teeth. In fact, it was an incendiary bomb containing a high explosive.

One week earlier, Mario Pombo Matamoros, chief of the People's Revolutionary Movement (MPR), a counterrevolutionary organization with a base in the commercial sector, had gone to 156 Paseo Street and worked out the details of the most important act of sabotage the organization would carry out: the destruction of the El Encanto Department Store. Shortly afterwards, he talked the matter over with

González, who agreed to do the job — if he were sent to the United States immediately afterwards.

His phone rang on the morning of April 13, getting him out of bed. Soon afterwards, Arturo Martínez Pagalday, his contact with the organization, met him in the street and gave him two incendiary bombs, telling him to put them in vulnerable spots in the store. That was why Carlos was in the fabric department, an ideal place for starting a large fire.

González put one of the bombs between two bolts of cloth and went back to the aisle. A few steps farther along, he did the same with the other. He felt confident. He had asked his contact if the bombs were U.S.-made, and Martínez had nodded: "Somebody who came from there gave them to me. They have the explosive power of 100 Molotov cocktails." Martínez wasn't exaggerating. Jorge Comellas ("Cawy"), a member of the infiltration teams, had given him the bombs and taught him how to use them. "Cawy" was a special agent who had entered the country with a load of arms and explosives, including nearly 100 incendiary bombs.

Minutes later, González left the store. Two hundred meters away, he got into a car. "Well?" the driver asked. "I did it," González replied, but he couldn't control the anxiety that began to overcome him. He thought he would feel better the following night, when he would be far from Cuba. The car headed for the Malecón waterfront drive, turned left and then drove toward one of the beaches on the northern coast west of the city.

Inside El Encanto, first one explosion and then another started a fire in the fabric department. An hour later, smoke began coming out of the doors and windows. Firemen, helped by hundreds of volunteers, worked until dawn and until they were too exhausted to move, pouring tons of water over the burning building, holding the long hoses over their heads and carrying out those who were asphyxiated by the smoke. Meanwhile, hundreds of people saved the merchandise that was in the basement and threw buckets of water on the windows of neighboring stores so they wouldn't explode. But, when dawn broke, the largest store in Cuba was no more. The place where it had stood had become a tangle of iron, bricks and burned wood. Several days later, the charred body of a clerk was found in the rubble.

Nobody there asked how the fire had begun. Everybody knew. The arson bore out a maxim which the CIA officer in Florida who was in charge of sending explosives to Cuba had told the anti-Castro Cuban agents: "One man alone with one of these explosives can cause quite a commotion in a big city."

El Encanto was very beautiful, very elegant, but old. It had been built at the end of the last century and remodelled and enlarged several times. That's why it completely collapsed. Cloth makes a lot of smoke, and, since the doors and windows were closed, it covered everything. Total losses were estimated at 20 million pesos. It was the largest store in the country, with 930 employees.

The next day, we found that Fé del Valle was missing. After my investigation, I came to the conclusion that she had gone up to the fourth floor, to the Federation of Cuban Women's office — where the local organization's funds were kept. She must have gone up by the escalator, using it as stairs. When she tried to get down, the smoke which was filling that floor must have made it hard for her to find the escalator again. She couldn't get down any other way, because the emergency stairs were behind the escalators, and the whole area must have been shrouded in dense smoke. That's how Fé del Valle was trapped.

We began our investigations immediately, and we were in the midst of them when the airports were bombed. That's when counterrevolutionaries began to be arrested. I was in Security Operations. Then I found that Carlos González Vidal was there, under arrest. I had begun to work in State Security only a short time before. Before that, I had worked in El Encanto and knew a lot of people there, including Carlos. I'd had several political discussions with him. Well, I asked for his card, which said that he had been picked up at Baracoa Beach at around midnight while signaling out to sea with a flashlight. He was unlucky that Peña, the head of the militia group that was guarding that part of the coast, had also worked at El Encanto and recognized him immediately. Well, they sent him to 5th Avenue and 14th Street, where he was detained subject to investigation.

He was surprised when he saw me. He didn't know I was in State Security. When he had been picked up, he had his two weeks' salary on him, and it wasn't payday yet. When I asked him how that was possible, he told me he had asked for an advance. That wasn't normal or very logical. I began to be suspicious. I had been told that 50 machine guns had been seized at the Tikoa Club, and, even though that turned out not to be true, I knew that a relative of Carlos's owned the Tikoa. I accused him, point blank, "You're mixed up with the machine guns they seized at the Tikoa." "No, not that," he said quickly, not thinking. I asked the other comrade who was taking notes to go out of the room. When we were alone, I looked him straight in the eye and said, "But you were involved with the fire." He burst out crying. Soon after that, he pulled himself together and confessed. He told me he had been given the incendiary bombs at 2:00 in the afternoon, and he told me everything he had done.[63]

At the beach, Carlos González had been arrested by a militia who had worked at El Encanto. In State Security, he had been interrogated by another former El Encanto employee. It seemed that everybody knew everybody in Cuba, and the people's and State Security's knowledge about counterrevolutionaries would be a key factor in halting underground activities on the island.

The destruction of the store was the high point in subversive activities, but the counterrevolutionary organizations were weakened by the time the invasion took place and couldn't give it as much support as had been expected. Unquestionably, the worst calamity had been the arrest of the Staff of the Revolutionary Unity Front (FUR) and of Rogelio González Corzo ("Francisco"), the CIA's main agent on the island, while he was trying to unify the actions of around 30 subversive groups.

During the last three months, the underground had engaged in intensive activities to make itself felt, but the massive defense put up by the people was overwhelming. They responded to the acts of sabotage and terrorism with spontaneous demonstrations and calls on the Committees for the Defense of the Revolution (CDR) to redouble their vigilance. The CDR, which had a branch in every city block and on every farm, had 104,000 branches throughout the country by the end of March.

On March 31, 1961, when the invasion was imminent, President Kennedy invited Senator James William Fulbright, Chairman of the Senate Foreign Relations Committee, to spend Easter with him at Palm Beach. Fulbright drafted a memo which he gave to the President when he got on the plane that was to take them south. After analyzing the pros and cons — for the United States — of each possible course of action regarding Cuba, Fulbright stated that an invasion of Cuba by exiles might come up against such strong resistance that the exiles wouldn't be able to overcome it by themselves.[64]

---

[63] Testimony of Colonel Oscar Gámez. Carlos González Vidal was tried, found guilty and sentenced to death.
[64] Karl E. Meyer, *Senator Fulbright*, 198.

On April 15, after the airports had been bombed, files containing data on many of the conspirators on the island were turned over to the State Security agents assigned to arresting them. In his book *Cuba: the Pursuit of Freedom*, Hugh Thomas states that around 2,500 CIA agents or collaborators were picked up. In fact, the neutralization of the internal counterrevolution was more extensive. The most active counterrevolutionaries were known.

Acting on their own, people began stopping counterrevolutionaries on the street and taking them to the Rosita de Hornedo Theater. We had to make it clear that if those who were brought in weren't accompanied by a document signed by "Chicho" or "Chicha," they couldn't be arrested. "Chicha" was Ana, the other chief, and I was "Chicho." Thus, we held back the people's reaction a little.[65]

Later statements by some of the main agents of the counterrevolution corroborated the effectiveness of the neutralization and of the attacks made on the eve of the invasion:

By the time of the Bay of Pigs invasion, the Unity Front (FUR) was disorganized, and the massive flight of its office holders and of the organizational leaders ended everything. The few of us leaders who remained were being arrested, and I think I'm the last one left.[66]

The capital, where the CIA had wanted to create strong opposition to the Cuban Government so as to destabilize it by means of a wave of sabotage and terror, remained calm, alert and staunchly behind the Revolution. The situation was just as favorable in the rest of the country on the morning of April 15.

---

[65] Testimony of Lieutenant Colonel (R.) Israel Behar.
[66] Statement by Octavio Barroso Gómez to Cuban State Security.

"Gentlemen, this is it!"

The news of a pre-mission briefing spread quickly throughout Happy Valley. Emotions were at a peak. Everyone was tense. It was 1000 hours the morning of April 13 when "Gar," the new chief adviser of the base, together with Reid Doster[67] and other advisers, called the pilots of the B-26 squadron to Flight Operations. The pilots sat expectantly, silent and waiting. Finally, in a voice that filled the wooden building, "Gar" announced, "Gentlemen, this is it!"[68]

Two hours later, after a detailed explanation of the mission they were to carry out in the coming hours — to destroy the Cuban Revolutionary Air Force's planes on the ground — the pilots of the B-26 light bomber squadron were isolated for security purposes. The task didn't seem difficult, far less impossible, because of the condition of Cuba's remaining fighter planes.

The CIA had drawn up and provided detailed intelligence information. It was the result of the technical spy surveillance carried out by U-2 planes and by agents who had illegally entered Cuba. "Gar" read the report to the pilots who would take part in the operation:

The Air Force is completely disorganized and has very little operational capacity. Since the drastic purge that Castro carried out in June 1959, the Air Force has been left without trained pilots and maintenance and communications specialists. The Air Force doesn't have organized squadrons or conventional units or flights. Rather, it depends on individual flights, which are controlled and dispatched from the general headquarters in Havana. Most of the planes are obsolete and inoperative, due to inadequate maintenance and a lack of spare parts. The few planes that are operational are considered capable of taking off, but are not

---

67 General George (Reid) Doster.
68 Ferrer, *Operation Puma*, 138.

entirely combat ready. The Air Force's combat effectiveness is nearly nonexistent; it has a limited emergency warning capability for opposing sea and air units and could engage in pursuit operations against lightly armed invaders, but in terms limited to the transportation of troops and matériel, strafing and visual patrols.[69]

The report was quite accurate: little operational capacity, a scarcity of trained pilots and mechanics, a lack of squadrons, obsolete planes and no spare parts. Unquestionably, the Agency had good informants with access to the Cuban Air Force, in addition to the deserters who had gone to the United States not long before.

The few planes which could fly weren't really capable of confronting the enemy. The CIA analysts, accustomed to assessing the strength of enemy forces, had left out only one thing: the fighting spirit of the few revolutionary pilots. That omission, the result of carelessness or of inability to measure the subjective factor, was to prove of key importance. The human factor was extremely important — often decisive — in the war. This was shown during the 70 missions which the 10 Revolutionary Armed Forces pilots (only 16 percent as many as in Brigade 2506's air force), some of whom had had very little instruction, carried out during the three days of the fighting.

Unquestionably, Brigade 2506's air force was superior to Cuba's. It had three times as many fighter planes, not including its two- and four-engine transport planes, all in perfect condition, with a supply of spare parts, armaments of several kinds and plenty of ammunition. It also had six times as many pilots, without even considering the extremely important aspect of training. That disadvantageous situation for Cuba's Revolutionary Armed Forces would be exacerbated by the bombings of Saturday, April 15, which destroyed three of Cuba's fighter planes on the ground.

In the briefing that morning, General Doster emphasized two other very important aspects: the surprise factor, which they should make the most of, and the fact that they would be flying planes that had been painted to look just like those of the Cuban Air Force. This would ensure the surprise factor up to the moment of opening fire. The pilots of the B-26 squadron were delighted. They would be committing a criminal act which clearly violated the rules of warfare set down in the Geneva Convention — and therefore, if captured, they could be executed as spies — but it would ensure their success.

Such procedures were nothing new to the military men of the CIA and of the U.S. Armed Forces. During World War II, in the Battle of

---

[69] The plan for Operation Pluto.

the Ardennes, they had captured scores of Germans who wore U.S. Army uniforms and spoke English perfectly. They had been infiltrated in the rear guard of the U.S. troops to cause as much destruction as possible to both lives and property. All, without exception, were shot. Moreover, it wasn't quite 20 years since Japan's surprise attack on Pearl Harbor, which was an affront to the U.S. Government and the people of the United States.

The day after Cuba's airports were bombed, Fidel Castro spoke at the burial of the victims, saying:

> The people of the United States considered the attack on Pearl Harbor to have been a crime and a treacherous, cowardly act. Our people have the right to consider yesterday's imperialist attack a doubly criminal, doubly cunning, doubly treacherous thing.[70]

The Brigade's air superiority in planes, pilots and other resources compensated for the difficulties involved in operating from a distant base — Happy Valley, the code name for the Brigade's air base at Puerto Cabeza, Nicaragua, on the Caribbean coast, about 580 miles (around two hours and 50 minutes' flying time in a B-26) from the landing area. Though flying from a distant base, the B-26s could carry out their missions with a full load of machine guns, bombs and rockets and remain over Cuban territory for an hour or more. To lengthen the time they could stay over the combat area, the space in the tail normally used by tail gunners was filled with extra fuel. For emergencies they could "unofficially" use the landing strip on Grand Cayman, British territory which also offered some additional facilities, such as a radio beacon at the halfway point on their way to Cuba.

Two days later, at 2:00 a.m. on April 15, eight B-26 bombers — half of the squadron — took off from Happy Valley. They would bombard Cuban military installations with the devastating power of 20,800 pounds of TNT, 64 five-inch missiles and 23,040 bullets of .50 caliber. All that to destroy just over a dozen fighter planes.

When the planes drew near the island, they split off in three directions. The "Puma" squadron, consisting of three planes, was to attack the airfield at Ciudad Libertad, in the eastern part of Havana, where U-2 photos had shown a lot of vehicles loaded with bombs and armaments, including munitions for the four-muzzle antiaircraft guns popularly known as "four-mouths." The "Linda" squadron, also consisting of three bombers, headed for the air base at San Antonio de los Baños, which had five B-26s, three T-33s and three Sea Furies,

---

[70] Fidel Castro, April 16, 1961, speech at 12th and 23rd Streets, Vedado, Havana.

several of which weren't in flying condition. The "Gorilla" formation would attack Santiago de Cuba's Antonio Maceo Airport, near the eastern tip of the island. Intelligence reported that it had one T-33, one B-26, two Sea Furies and the only PBY (hydrofoil) in Cuba.

The attacks took place simultaneously a few minutes before 6:00 a.m. on April 15. At Ciudad Libertad, antiaircraft guns hit the *Puma II*, piloted by Daniel Fernández Mon, with Gastón Pérez as navigator, and it withdrew with smoke coming out of its left engine. When it reached the coast, it exploded in a ball of fire and fell into the sea. The right engine of *Puma I* was hit, but the plane managed to get away from the combat area and go straight to the Boca Chica Naval and Air Station at Key West, Florida, where it made an emergency landing half an hour later. At San Antonio de los Baños, the *Linda III* was hit, had difficulties with its fuel supply and had to land on Grand Cayman.

Without waiting for the first reports on the results of the mission to come in, David A. Phillips ordered Radio Swan to broadcast news of the bombings. Its tone, as always with that station, was boastful.

In spite of the utter surprise — because of the unexpectedness of the attack and the insignia painted on the attacking B-26s — the antiaircraft gun at San Antonio began shooting at the first B-26 as soon as it released its first missiles. The members of the antiaircraft gun crew had been keeping the enemy formation in their sights ever since they first noted its maneuvers, but they had thought the planes had come from Santiago de Cuba.

Even though some pilots slept at home and others in barracks some distance away from the airfield, two of them managed to get their fighter planes into the air.

At Ciudad Libertad, the ground fire was so heavy that some of the enemy pilots fired their machine guns near the base. Scores of people who lived near the airfield witnessed the combat, and 53 of them were wounded and seven killed, including militia Eduardo García Delgado, who, knowing that he was dying, wrote "Fidel" on a door with his own blood.

The surprise factor was greatest at the Santiago de Cuba airport, where only one antiaircraft gun could go into action. The other heavy machine guns had been taken apart for cleaning. That mistake wouldn't be committed ever again.

The damage to the military installations was relatively small, and none of the airfields lost its operational capacity. In fact, the Brigade's pilots didn't destroy any Sea Fury pursuit planes. In his book, Ferrer mentioned "a Sea Fury which was in the hangar at MOA Bay Mining

Company."[71] He couldn't have seen it, because there wasn't any such plane. Likewise, two, not three, B-26s were destroyed. Several historians have noted that the reports the pilots made on their return to Happy Valley were exaggerated.

As for the planes which took part in the three days of fighting after the April 15 attack, the Revolutionary Air Force had 10 fighter planes: three T-33s, three Sea Furies and four B-26s. However, they were never all functioning at once. It had other planes, but only 10 were in flying condition. The April 15 attacks had wiped out 27 percent of Cuba's fighter planes. The enemy would have to destroy the remaining 73 percent to get control of the skies.

Much has been written and argued about President Kennedy's suspension of the air attacks which some say had been scheduled for the dawn of D-1 Day. Others claim these air attacks were to have taken place on D Day itself and still others assert they were to have been made on both D-1 and D Days. As many things have been omitted in these versions of the history of the Bay of Pigs invasion, it is worth dwelling on this point.

First, some reflections on the eight B-26 bombers which took part in the attack on April 15. It has been claimed that:

> The Brigade members' small air force wasn't allowed to use all its air power against Castro's airports in the surprise attack of April 15.[72]

If we describe the Brigade's air force as "small," how can we describe the Cuban Air Force on the morning of April 15? The Brigade's squadron of B-26 bombers consisted of at least 16 planes in perfect condition. Some writers have said there were 17, and a U.S. instructor said in his memoirs that there were 23.

The original version of the April 15 operation called for attacks on two other airports, as well — the San Julián Air Base, in Pinar del Río Province, and the military camp at Managua, City of Havana Province — but they were ruled out at the last minute when it was found that there weren't any fighter planes at either of them. If they had been included in the operation, it would have meant that at least six more planes would have participated, so only two at most would have remained at the base. It is clear that the U.S. officers who prepared the operation and had planned to attack five airfields considered that the

[71] Ferrer, *Operation Puma.*
[72] Enrique Ros, *Girón: La verdadera historia.*

mission would be carried out successfully with that number of planes for each target.

In addition, a formation of three B-26s in the air could confuse the Cuban artillerymen, who might suppose that the planes belonged to the Revolutionary Air Force — which is what happened. This resulted in their beginning to fire only after the attack had begun. A formation of five or six planes would have alerted the base right from the start, because everyone knew that the Revolutionary Air Force couldn't put so many planes in the air. The surprise factor would have been considerably reduced.

Diocles Bello Rosabal, the operator in the control tower at San Antonio de los Baños, was reading a *Bohemia* magazine when he first saw the planes. He dismissed them as unimportant and went on reading, sounding the combat alarm only after the attack had already begun. As he said later, "If I had seen any more planes, I would have leaped out of my seat."[73]

That difference in time would have allowed Bourzac and Fernández, the two pilots who got a Sea Fury and a T-33 into the air, to have done so a few minutes earlier, before the attackers had already turned tail.

Moreover, if all of the Brigade's 16 planes had taken part in the attacks on the three airports, that would have meant running the risk of eliminating or considerably reducing the air protection they could give the battalions which were about to land. It should be kept in mind that, in order to provide air protection for the Brigade, the Tactical Air Force had to send two planes to the combat area every hour, which returned nearly seven hours later. Therefore, it was absolutely necessary to have as many planes as possible.

Unquestionably, the most debatable aspect was the suspension of the other bombings. The total destruction of the Revolutionary Air Force's planes was of key importance to the CIA. General Lyman L. Lemnitzer, head of the Joint Chiefs of Staff, noted in a memo on the operations that, if even a single Cuban fighter plane escaped destruction and blocked the runway, the operation could be seriously affected.[74]

In Point 9 of that memo, General Lemnitzer noted that if they lost the surprise factor the air mission might fail, because a single plane

---

[73] Testimony of Diocles Bello Rosabal.

[74] Memorandum JCSM-146-61 (Point 3), dated March 14, 1961. Taken from Enrique Ros, *Girón*.

armed with .50-caliber machine guns could sink all or most of the invading force.[75]

Long before April 15, Fidel Castro had been preparing to protect Cuba's planes.

> In March, the Commander in Chief visited the San Antonio base and called all the pilots and technicians together on the runway. There, he ordered us to keep our few planes scattered and to take good care of them, because it was obvious that we would have to use them in combat.[76]

That dispersal of the fighter planes, one of the measures that was taken to protect the airfields, was largely responsible for keeping the damage done to Cuba's fighting capacity on April 15 to a minimum. If a second air attack had been made at dawn on April 17 — that famous bombardment whose cancellation, according to many U.S. and Cuban-American writers, caused the Brigade's failure — the Cuban Air Force would have given the Brigade's Tactical Air Force more of a drubbing than it would have received.

On the morning of April 15, Commander Fidel Castro went to Ciudad Libertad and San Antonio de los Baños to see what damage had been done. He had witnessed the dawn attack at Ciudad Libertad from Point One, staff headquarters for the troops that were defending the capital.

> I was there at staff headquarters, waiting for news, when I saw a B-26 fly by, quite close, at 6:00 a.m. A few minutes later, I felt the explosions of the bombs and the antiaircraft guns' fire. I looked up and saw that it really was a military attack on Ciudad Libertad, at the artillery school and the runways. Another B-26 followed it immediately.[77]

On arriving at San Antonio de los Baños that morning, Fidel chatted with the pilots. He asked Captain Enrique Carreras Rolás, "What did the pilots do? Did they hide?" The captain replied that two "homeland or death" planes had taken off, explaining that "homeland or death" planes were those that could barely make it off the ground.[78] Fidel agreed with Carreras that the pilots slept too far from the planes and

[75] Ibid.

[76] *Verde Olivo*, 1976. Testimony of Enrique Carreras Rolás.

[77] Fidel Castro, appearance on Cuban radio and television, April 23, 1961.

[78] *Verde Olivo*, 1976. Testimony of Enrique Carreras Rolás.

that each pilot and mechanic should take up residence under the plane's wings.

That same day, April 15, two new batteries of quadruple 12.5-mm antiaircraft guns arrived at the San Antonio base, each of them consisting of six units of four heavy machine guns. In total, it received reinforcements of 48 new heavy antiaircraft machine guns.

Another two batteries of the same kind arrived at Ciudad Libertad. That night, yet another battery, with 37-mm guns, was added to the San Antonio base's defenses. In short, Cuba was ready for a second attack.

Above all, we were thinking of the possibility of a dogfight, and we kept scanning the sky, searching for the first enemy plane, to give the alarm so our planes could take off as quickly as possible. The comrades who were with me urged me to stop worrying and go to sleep. They told me, "Captain, go to sleep. You should rest. You'll probably have to go into action tomorrow." But I was too tense to sleep. I thought that, if the enemy planes came, I would lose time waking up, climbing into the cockpit and starting the engine. We put my Sea Fury close to the head of runway 05, with a T-33 nearby. We did this so that, if there were another air attack, I could take off in the T-33 with its two .50-caliber M-3 machine guns, to intercept and fight the enemy in the air. If there were a landing, I would take off in the Sea Fury, which carried more missiles and bombs and was designed for attacking ships. We put Lieutenant Gustavo Bourzac's Sea Fury on runway 11 and Captain Silva Tablada's B-26 bomber between the heads of the two runways.[79]

But that wasn't all. Several hours before dawn on April 17, Fidel Castro had learned of the landing at the Zapata Swamp.

I sent men out to check, to ratify the report, because reports came in of ships at several places, but then, with the first men wounded in the fighting, reliable reports came in that an invading force was directing heavy fire against Girón Beach and Larga Beach in the Zapata Swamp with bazookas, recoilless cannon, .50-caliber machine guns and guns on ships.[80]

It was 3:30 a.m. on April 17. Enrique Carreras was asleep under a wing of his Sea Fury 542. He was awakened and told that Fidel had called,

---

[79] Enrique Carreras Rolás, *Por el dominio del aire*, 104.
[80] Fidel Castro, April 23, 1961, radio and television appearance.

ordering two Sea Furies and a B-26 to shell the ships at the Bay of Pigs as soon as it got light. Soon afterwards, they woke Bourzac, who was sleeping under the wing of his Sea Fury 580. At the other end of one of the runways, Jacques Lagás was awakened. He had his cot under the aluminum bulk of B-26 number 937. The artilleryman and the mechanic were sleeping inside the plane. Other pilots stayed under the wings of their fighter planes. They could take off in a matter of minutes, and they would do so on hearing the alarm or the first shots of antiaircraft artillery.

At 4:45 a.m., Fidel called the air base again. His instructions were taken down in shorthand at Point One:

> Fidel orders Silva [the pilot Silva Tablada], at the San Antonio de los Baños air base, to carry out a mission with two Sea Furies, one B-26 and a jet; this last should be ready to defend the base... Three ships of enemy forces are at Perdiz Point... Take off at 0520.[81] Attack the ships first, then return to Havana to report. Jet ready to defend the base... Silva, go to the end of the Bay of Pigs; everything on the beach is the enemy's.

At 5:20 a.m., Silva Tablada's B-26 took off and headed for the Bay of Pigs, while two other Sea Fury pursuit planes took off, one on runway 05 and the other on runway 11. The first mission assigned to them was to defend the airport until dawn.

This was the situation that Brigade 2506's B-26s would have encountered if the second dawn air attack had been authorized: all of the antiaircraft batteries reinforced with 48 heavy 12.5-mm machine guns and one 37-mm battery; two Sea Fury pursuit planes, which had much greater speed and maneuverability in the air than the heavy B-26s and whose guns, machine guns and missiles were ready to open fire; and five pilots under the wings of their fighter planes, ready to take off.

But there was more. President Kennedy did authorize a second air attack, at night, against the San Antonio de los Baños base, where the U-2 planes had reported that all the fighter planes of the Revolutionary Air Force had been dispersed. Night was a better time for the attack because, during the day, the Brigade's fleet would have encountered Cuban planes in the air. The Cuban planes couldn't fly at night, because Cuba didn't have any radar.

The authors of some books on the invasion that were published in the United States strove to minimize the importance of the second

---

81 The author's emphasis.

bombing of the Cuban air base. Others touched on it only superficially, so their readers couldn't be aware of its real meaning. Still others presented fantastic reasons to explain its failure. And yet others, the least scrupulous, simply ignored it, as if it had never taken place.

JFK realized that the news from the front portented disaster unless the FAR was knocked out. He gave the go-ahead for an air-to-ground strike. Intelligence reports indicated that the dangerous T-33s were now based at San Antonio de los Baños, much closer to the front than Santiago. Six B-26s from Happy Valley arrived over San Antonio at dawn on Tuesday. But the field was obscured by a heavy cloud cover and ground haze. The planes did not have enough fuel to circle until the cover broke. They returned to Happy Valley.[82]

In *The Invisible Government*, David Wise and Thomas B. Ross wrote:

Exactly three B-26s took off from Happy Valley at 8:00 p.m. Monday, April 17. Their target was the San Antonio de los Banos airfield. The strike was led by Joaquin Varela, despite the fact that he and his co-pilot, Tomas Afont, had flown that morning. Varela was unable to find San Antonio in the dark. Under orders to hit only military targets, he dropped no bombs and returned to Happy Valley. The second plane, piloted by Ignacio Rojas and Esteban Bovo Caras, developed engine trouble and turned back before reaching the target. So did the third plane, piloted by Miguel A. Carro and Eduardo Barea Guinea. Two hours later, at 10:00 p.m., two more B-26s took off from Happy Valley. Their crews also had flown earlier that day. Gonzalo Herrera and Angel Lopez were in one bomber. Mario Alvarez Cortina and Salvador Miralles were in the other. They had no more success than the first three planes. Five B-26s had gone out Monday night. All returned, but they inflicted no damage on their targets.[83]

Eduardo Ferrer was one of the Brigade 2506 pilots. He wrote the following about the second attack on the San Antonio de los Baños base:

Just after midnight of April 17 two flights of two B-26's took off. Joaquín "Pupy" Varela and Ignacio Rojas captained the aircraft of

[82] Warren Hinckle and William Turner, *The Fish Is Red*.
[83] David Wise and Thomas Ross, *The Invisible Government*, 63.

the first formation, with Tomás Afont and Esteban Bovo-Carás, as navigators. The commanders of the second flight were Gonzalo Herrera and Mario Cortina, with Angel López and Salvador Miralles as navigators. Bad weather had moved in and a blackout had been imposed in the area surrounding San Antonio. This resulted in the crews being unable to locate the target, and the mission was aborted.[84]

Clearly, the time chosen was correct. The Cuban pilots were at the base. One of them recalled the attack as follows:

"We were in the dining hall," Bourzac said. "I remember that the first thing they brought was a steak that didn't fit on two dishes. It was bigger than a sheet. "The guy who's hungriest should begin," Carreras said. "Me," I replied, serving myself. "Be quiet, everybody; be quiet. Don't you hear?" "What's the matter with you, Prendes?" Carreras asked. "Be quiet, you guys," Prendes replied.

It was the sound of engines, and none of them was in the air. Immediately, they heard the air raid alarm. Del Pino took up the story:

We couldn't hear our antiaircraft artillery guns. When those of us who hadn't remained in the building couldn't find the switches for turning off the lights, we began to shoot them out. It was like something out of a western. One light stayed on, in spite of the shooting. Everybody was under the tables.[85]

I thought the base was under a night attack by mercenary planes. I thought I heard missiles exploding on the flat cement roof, not knowing it was a .50-caliber antiaircraft gun up there whose shots were giving me a splitting headache.[86]

I heard the air raid alarm and my comrades saying, "A plane!" The antiaircraft artillery unit immediately began shooting with its machine guns and its new 37-mm guns... The sky was filled with thousands of tracer bullets of different calibers. There were several minutes of heavy gunfire, in the midst of which nearly everybody sought protection in the trenches.

---

[84] Ferrer, *Operation Puma*, 205.
[85] Quintín Pino Machado, *La Batalla de Girón*. Testimony of Enrique Carreras, Alvaro Prendes, Rafael del Pino and Gustavo Bourzac.
[86] Alvaro Prendes, *En el punto rojo de mi kolimador*, 120.

When we couldn't hear the planes any more, our antiaircraft batteries stopped firing, the people calmed down, and everybody started talking about what had happened.[87]

There wasn't any "bad weather," "heavy cloud cover," "ground haze" or "blackout" that made it impossible to find the base — which some of the attacking pilots were very familiar with as they had served at it and probably why they had been selected for the mission. The real reason for their turning tail was the barrage that covered the sky over San Antonio de los Baños. Several people who lived in San Antonio remember that some of the attacking planes dropped bombs on the area around it, one of which landed on a poultry farm.

The second air attack, which didn't have the advantage of the surprise factor, could only be carried out at a high cost to the attacking planes and had very poor results.

In fact the first strike, designed to be the key, turned out later to have been remarkably ineffective; and there is no reason to believe that Castro's air force, having survived the first and dispersed into hiding, would have been knocked out by the second.[88]

As may be seen, the U.S. authors cited different causes for the failure of the operation in which five planes participated, nearly a third of the B-26 squadron. They agreed on only three things: a second bombing was authorized, it was carried out and it was a complete failure.

Some people have stated that the D-2 bombings (on April 15) were a mistake, since they warned the Cuban leadership. Those who believe this say that the air bases should have been subjected to a surprise attack at dawn on the day of the landing.

However, it wasn't the bombings of April 15 which alerted the Cuban Government to the imminence of the invasion. If anything, they simply confirmed suspicions in this regard. Even if the first air strike against Cuba's airfields had taken place at dawn on D Day, the attacking planes would have found the Cuban Air Force in a state of maximum combat alert since 3:30 a.m. That's only to be expected in war.

Even so, I believe that carrying out the first air raid two days before the landing was a mistake. But neither that nor the postponement of the second attack, which had been scheduled for dawn of D Day, to

---

[87] Enrique Carreras Rolás, *Por el dominio del aire*, 120.
[88] Theodore C. Sorensen, *Kennedy, the Man, the President*, 301.

that same night, nor the absence of air cover by jets of the U.S. Air Force caused the Brigade's defeat.

To repeatedly claim that the Brigade members were told they would have clear skies doesn't mesh with the invaders' instructions and equipment. None of the CIA and Pentagon experts, professionals in the art of warfare, could have made any such assurance. This doesn't rule out the possibility that some official, in his eagerness to encourage the Brigade chiefs, may have assured them that they would have control of the sky. But the fact remains that no such assurance appears in any document, instruction, order or memorandum that was issued. Appendix E of the plan for Operation Pluto, which lists all the actions to be taken by the Brigade, several copies of which were given to the Attack Brigade's staff, states the following:

Appendix E (Tactical Air Support) of the Plan for Operation Pluto

1. Situation
a. *Enemy forces* (see Appendix A)
b. *Friendly forces*. When the landing strip in the area which is the goal of the Tactical Air Force has been taken, it will begin attacks for the purpose of destroying or neutralizing the enemy's air, naval and land forces.[89]

If it was certain that no Cuban plane would take to the air against the invaders, there would have been no need to include that order in the plan of operations to be carried out after the landing.

This aspect of the plan of operations wasn't carried out. We will see why later on.

Another of the many arguments used to explain the ultimate defeat was that, since Castro's planes hadn't been destroyed, the Brigade was defenseless. That isn't strictly true. The escort ships *Blagar* and *Barbara J.* were heavily armed and should have defended the Brigade against air attacks. In fact, they did so on the morning of the landing.

We got there and were surprised to see a convoy consisting of four freighters, landing craft, LCU and LCVP attack craft, an LSD ship and smaller launches taking personnel to the coast. There were also two LCI escort ships, which opened heavy fire against our squadron as soon as they caught sight of us, using their revolving turrets with double cannon mounted on the sides of the ships and six .50-caliber machine guns... I kept climbing, followed by

---

[89] Plan for Operation Pluto, 26. The author's emphasis.

thousands of tracer bullets. One of them hit me; the plane shivered, the engine began to fail and smoke began pouring out of it...

Prendes had always demonstrated great proficiency, mastery and skill in jet planes. As soon as he reached the area, he got his bearings and located the ships several miles from the coast. Close to them, he attacked the last in the formation with his missiles, damaging an LCT, which started to drift. Recovering from their surprise, the enemy opened antiaircraft fire against the jet in its second attack and managed to hit it during its rapid climb.[90]

The plane dove, and this time I saw the lines of fire from the enemy tracer bullets coming up toward me. They seemed to come straight at me and then, through an optical illusion, to swerve away violently at the last minute — the more violently, the closer they passed. I also saw explosions at my height, which indicated that cannon were shooting, too... Then I felt the impact, a sharp blow that made the whole plane shudder.[91]

At that moment, Bourzac felt an explosion, and the Sea Fury began to falter. The pilot saw blue and red flames coming out of the fuselage... While returning to the base, he was urged to bail out. Bourzac thought, "What could I fly later? Not even a broomstick." And, risking his life, he decided to save the plane. His landing was the most dramatic one made in that period... A crowd of men rushed toward the plane. The mechanics quickly gave their verdict on examining the Sea Fury: a cannon ball had carried away a section of the fuselage.[92]

Six of the eight Cuban planes that had been in flying condition were hit on the morning of April 17. Alvaro Prendes, Alberto Fernández, Gustavo Bourzac and Enrique Carreras made one emergency landing each that morning on returning to the base. Luis Silva Tablada, flying a B-26, and Carlos Ulloa, in a Sea Fury pursuit plane, were shot down by the antiaircraft fire from the *Barbara J.* and *Blagar* escort ships.

The effectiveness of the Brigade's antiaircraft fire was noteworthy. The Brigade was far from defenseless. But the operation's specialists hadn't foreseen the reaction by the Cuban pilots, who, even at the risk of their lives, brought their damaged planes back to the base and took off again shortly afterwards, heading back to the combat area.

[90] Enrique Carreras Rolás, *Por el dominio del aire*, 113-5.
[91] Alvaro Prendes, *En el punto rojo de mi kolimador*, 105-6.
[92] Ibid, 113.

In contrast, after the merchant ship *Río Escondido* was sunk and the *Houston* damaged, the Brigade's escort ships set out for the open sea at full throttle. The official (but little-publicized) testimony of Commander José Pérez San Román, military chief of Attack Brigade 2506, should bury any doubts which might remain about the escort ships' precipitate flight:

> Number one: the U.S. officer, captain of the flagship *Blagar*, was forced to withdraw by the enemy air attack after two of the ships in the tiny fleet were sunk.
>
> That officer made that withdrawal against my orders to hold his position and fight. (It is a military principle that the commander of the support forces takes orders from the commander of the supported forces.) His reply to my orders was, "A higher authority has ordered the contrary," and the ships headed south, never to return. Because of our fleet's withdrawal, the Brigade lost the support of the 75-mm recoilless cannon and .50-caliber machine guns which were mounted on all the ships. Moreover, the fleet took thousands of tons of supplies, weapons, basic communications equipment, hospital equipment, drugs and other indispensable medical supplies with it. And, as if that weren't enough, it also took the fuel for the planes, bombs of all kinds and munitions for the guns of our B-26s, which would have given us the capacity foreseen in the plan for operating our planes from the beachhead instead of having to do so from Nicaragua.[93]

That valuable material for the planes was aboard the merchant vessel *Caribe*. Its flight postponed, but didn't cancel, the start of operations from the Girón Beach airport. The CIA knew that Cuba's planes couldn't fly in the dark, and, on the night of April 17, Girón Beach was calm. The fighting was going on dozens of kilometers away. Why didn't the ships, particularly the *Caribe*, return in the dark to complete their unloading? They would have had close to 12 hours, from shortly after 6:00 p.m. to nearly 6:00 a.m., in which to do it, which was more than sufficient for coming in close to the beach, unloading and departing once again.

Another thing they might have done was use the Girón Beach airport immediately. They occupied it as soon as they got on shore. With one or two flights of the C-54 transport planes when it got dark on the 17th, they could have brought enough cargo to Girón Beach to keep some B-26s in the air, operating from the landing strip at the

---

[93] José Pérez San Román, *Respuesta*, 29.

beachhead. If they had done that, their B-26s could have given cover and air support to the Brigade for more hours and, since they wouldn't have had to carry extra gasoline, could have had tail gunners, with whom they could have shot down the Cuban fighter planes. The work of adapting the bombers could have been done during the night and dawn of April 18, before there was any fighting near Girón Beach. The squadron could have taken off that morning, but none of that was done. It was a military mistake.

The only Brigade plane which landed at the Girón Beach airport did so at dawn on Wednesday, April 19, when the invading forces were already practically surrounded. It brought supplies of munitions.

Some researchers say that the landing strip at Girón Beach wasn't operational when the landing took place and that that was why it wasn't used. Nothing could be farther from the truth.

Again, Commander José Pérez San Román's testimony is eloquent:

> [A]nother criticism of the CIA is its incorrect information on the target area, information which came from its intelligence archives and was given to me and to my subordinate officers in the Brigade. It was so incorrect that it included U-2 photos showing that the Girón Beach airstrip wasn't finished yet, was still under construction. That forced us to carry dozens of gasoline-powered saws for cutting down the trees along the highway, so it could be used for landing our B-26s and C-46s... When we got there, we found that the airport had been completed, even to the last detail of its control tower. The highway didn't have any trees that could prevent the landing of small and medium-sized planes.[94]

If Castro's planes had been destroyed, if the U.S. Government hadn't left the exiles to their fate, if they had had greater participation in the planning, if the attack had been made at Trinidad, if the underground had been alerted, if a diversionary landing had been made at Baracoa, if air cover had been provided, if the Brigade had been better equipped, if there had been direct intervention...

The exiles thought that, if any of those things had happened, it would have ensured their success. They refused to accept the real reason for their defeat, which was demonstrated by how the fighting developed and can be summed up as follows: the Cuban people were at the peak of their patriotism and revolutionary fervor, and their support for the Revolution and its leader, Fidel Castro, had reached heights never before attained in the hemisphere.

---

[94] Ibid, 32.

Heading for the southern coast

It was 2:45 p.m. when Battalion 2 was ordered to set out. At a walking pace, staying in formation, the men began to descend the small elevation that separated them from the esplanade in front of the Brigade's headquarters. That was where they had held a parade in front of Idígoras Fuentes, the Guatemalan Head of State, and where they had practiced their victorious entry. José Ramón Pérez Peña turned his head and said a silent good-bye to the barracks which had served as his refuge since his arrival at camp in September 1960, seven months before.

It was April 12, 1961, and Attack Brigade 2506 was getting ready to leave for somewhere in the island of Cuba. In front of the installation which housed the staff offices, Colonel Jack Hawkins, military chief of the Brigade, was closely watching the men who drew close to the truck. In spite of his rank, Hawkins wouldn't participate in the invasion. He would direct activities from Happy Valley (Puerto Cabezas). José Pérez San Román, whom he himself had taught carefully, would head the Brigade at the beachhead. In November 1960, when the strategy for confronting Fidel Castro had been changed, Colonel Valeriano Vallejo, the expert in guerrilla warfare, had been replaced. Hawkins organized the men in combat battalions, companies, platoons and squads and had trained them for a conventional type of confrontation.

Each squad consisted of nine men, with two of them — numbers five and six — armed with Browning automatic rifles. During the fighting, the squad would subdivide into two firing groups (from two through five and from six through nine). Number one, the chief, would place himself in the middle. Each soldier carried 160 rounds, in addition to a knife or bayonet, and the chief would carry a Garand rifle, adjusted for sniping. The fourth squad of each company would also carry two .30-caliber machine guns for reinforcing the area of greatest danger. That structure would provide a barrage of fire far superior to that of the militia batallions' squads.

The chief of José Ramón's squad was Edgar Buttari, whose father had been a minister in the Prío Administration and owned a fortune.

Company E, like all the rest, had two bazookas, two .30-caliber machine guns, a 57-mm recoilless cannon and an 81-mm mortar.

Infantry Battalion 2, to which José Ramón belonged, consisted of five companies, with 166 men.

In an orderly manner, the men began to get into the trucks. Beside them, standing in an informal group, the paratroopers, who would be the last to leave the camp, were saying good-bye to old friends. José Ramón shook hands with Julio Bolet, a student at the University of Miami; Manuel Menéndez Pou, son of the President of Aspuru Cia, S.A. (nationalized); and Irán, who had run for alderman. Now, they were members of the Paratroop Battalion. José Ramón asked about Néstor Pino, a former officer in the Cuban Army, and was told that he was now second in command of the company. "Have you seen Arturito?" he asked, and his friends repeated what he already knew. Arturo Menéndez Rodíl had gone AWOL a month before, after getting a letter from his girlfriend. He had intended to cross the Mexican border and then go back to Miami. He was declared a deserter and was captured by the Guatemalan authorities a week later, 10 kilometers from the Mexican border. He was taken to Petén, a prison in the middle of the jungle, from which it was very difficult to escape. After he had been there for a month, a U.S. officer gave him a choice: stay in the prison until everything was all over, or return to camp. He chose the second option. He was then put in Battalion 5, which had just been set up with the new men who had joined in the most recent, hasty recruiting in Miami. Two weeks later, he asked to be transferred to the Armored Battalion, saying that Battalion 5 was mainly composed of soldiers and policemen of the Batista dictatorship. The recruits had dubbed it "Henchmanland."

While José Ramón was getting into the truck, there was a slight earthquake, coming from the Santiaguito Volcano. The soldiers began to sing the national anthem. They were determined to free Cuba from Fidel Castro, but they also had another purpose, which would require the overthrow of the Cuban leader. A hundred of the invaders had owned enormous tracts of land, which had been expropriated and given to those who worked it. Another 67 had owned tens of thousands of rental housing units; the Revolution had turned them over to those who lived in them. Two hundred and fourteen of the invaders were members of wealthy families that had controlled business, banking and industry; 194 had been members of the Armed Forces which supported and kept the dictator Fulgencio Batista in power; and another 112 had been engaged in businesses which the Revolution had done away with: prostitution, gambling and drugs.

The military convoy took the only passable road, which skirted the cliffs, but the men weren't aware of the danger. They had crossed them several times, climbing hills and wading rivers on long training hikes. Soon afterwards, the unmistakable sound of an improvised conga could be heard; the men were slapping out the rhythm on the wooden crates. No question about it, they were Cubans.

The paratroopers were the elite. When the battalion was created in November 1960, the men who had been selected were sent to the Halcón Base, on La Suiza Farm, around 15 kilometers downhill from the Trax Base. In December, they were moved again, this time to the "Garrapatenango" Base, some 40 kilometers from the Trax Base, near the town of Quetzaltenango. They did their jumps there. Those transfers were made because the main base, Trax, was located in the mountains, making large-scale operations impossible. It had been selected because it was a good spot for training guerrillas, not a conventional force.

The "Garrapatenango" Base, on San José de Buenavista Farm, wasn't guarded very carefully, and the recruits' unauthorized visits to the nearby town alarmed the U.S. chiefs. This led Pérez San Román, the Cuban chief, to call the Brigade members together and tell them that the U.S. Government would take punitive measures against those who were picked up outside the base. Among other things, those measures would consist of expelling them from the United States and cutting off economic support to their relatives.

At the beginning of February, the men from all the battalions — except for the tank drivers, who had left for Fort Benning, Georgia, Louisiana, and Virginia and who would complete their training a month later, in March 1961 — were at "Garrapatenango." They were given two days' rest at Sipacate, a beach on Guatemala's Pacific coast, where they were taken in open trucks, in full view of the inhabitants. That was a month prior to April 13, when they bade a last farewell to the Trax Base.

The trucks took nearly three hours to get to Retalhuleu, site of the Brigade's air base. Two armed Guatemalan soldiers told the convoy to halt. After identifying themselves, the Brigade members drove on into the military area, stopping in front of a hangar. Hugo Sueiro, the chief of the battalion, ordered the men to get out of the trucks. He gave them instructions for the next step, and then the men scattered throughout the base. They were surprised that they couldn't see any fighter planes — only some C-47 troop transports. José Ramón commented that they must be close to the island of Cuba. He was right.

Two weeks earlier, on April 1, General Reid Doster, the U.S. chief of the Rayo Air Base, had notified Manuel Villafaña that, within 24 hours, all of the pilots and planes would be transferred from the training base to the base from which they would fly toward Cuba. The pilots understood that they would be moved somewhere closer to the island. The next day, April 2, the B-26, C-46 and C-54 squadrons flew from the Rayo Base and were lost from sight. When they took off, the pilots still didn't know where they were going. The commanding officer of each flight had been given a sealed envelope which contained the maps and flight plan for reaching the new air base. They were ordered not to open the envelopes until they were in the air. Several hours later, the planes began landing at Puerto Cabezas. The pilots were informed that the base would be called Happy Valley.

At 8:10 p.m., the members of the battalion were ordered to return to their area. Shortly afterwards, one after another, they boarded the three planes. They were transports without any markings, with paper glued over the windows. Nobody except the pilots knew where they were going. On board, the men began making conjectures. Some thought the invasion would take place from the Guantánamo Naval Base; others thought it would be in Pinar del Río; somebody else thought they would be split up, to land at several points. Gradually, the voices were stilled, and most of the men slept. Several hours after having taken off, the crew members told them they were about to land.

It was 2:00 a.m. and cold at the Puerto Cabezas air base, on the Atlantic coast of Nicaragua, from where the ships and B-26 bombers would set out for Cuba. There was a lot of movement at the base, with trucks coming and going, while the Nicaraguan guards, using reflectors, guarded the landing strip and the accesses to the base. A few minutes after getting out of the planes, the members of the battalion were surprised to be ordered to board the trucks. Soon afterwards, they were being taken through the town of Puerto Cabezas. The soldiers saw that most of the houses were small, two-story frame affairs, evidence of extreme poverty. There wasn't a soul to be seen in the dirt streets. The inhabitants had retired early and now found it difficult to sleep, because of the noisy vehicles, but nobody dared to go outside in the streets. The more curious peered through their windows. Somoza's soldiers had seized the town.

Fifteen minutes later, the trucks halted in front of the train station. Inside the building and around it, other Nicaraguan soldiers, armed with rifles, stood guard. While getting into an old railroad car whose windows were covered, José Ramón commented that, if anybody had considered deserting at the last minute, he should give up the idea. A rumor was going around that they were in Nicaragua, where Anastasio Somoza held absolute sway.

For José Ramón, Somoza was the same as Batista, but he knew that very few members of the Brigade would care if Somoza, Stroessner or Trujillo was involved. The only important thing was to overthrow Castro.

José Ramón and the other members of his company made themselves as comfortable as possible in their railroad car. They were told not to smoke or show a light of any kind. Slowly, the train started to move. A little less than 30 minutes later, it stopped next to a dock that stuck out into the sea. They had arrived at the port, at the Caribbean. Farther out, at the entrance to the Gulf, this same water touched the beaches along Cuba's southern coast.

The men in the battalion walked down the dock to the last ship. Two cranes were loading heavy crates into its holds. They contained rifles, explosives, radio equipment, medicine, food, drinking water and hats with mosquito nets. These last would have told the men a lot about the characteristics of the terrain chosen for their landing, so the crates containing them had been tightly sealed. The CIA had ordered thousands of these protective devices to be made in the utmost secrecy.

José Ramón walked to the bow. He wanted to see the name of the ship that would take them to Cuba. "*Houston*. It must be American," he commented to his companions. But José Ramón was mistaken. The *Houston* was owned by Eduardo García and his sons. The ships of García Lines, S.A. plied between Havana and U.S. and Central American ports, and the firm had leased the CIA the five merchant vessels which would transport the troops. Two of them, the *Río Escondido* and the *Houston*, wouldn't return from the adventure. Both would be sunk off the coast near the Bay of Pigs.

Four .50-caliber machine guns had been placed on board: one at the bow, another at the stern and one each on the port and starboard sides of the ship. Obviously, they were to be used in case of attack by enemy planes and for strafing the coast.

José Ramón's squad was ordered to stay on the dock. He leaned his knapsack against one of the piles, closed his jacket — the temperature had dropped — and stretched out on the dock. Almost immediately, he was asleep. Shortly after 3:00 a.m., the men were ordered to get on board.

When Edgar Buttari managed to get all his men on the ship, the scene on deck impressed him. The men of the two battalions —

numbers 2 and 5 — covered nearly all the space: the fore and aft holds, the lifeboats, even under the stairs. Buttari ordered his men to sack out by the starboard rail.

Dawn of April 13 didn't catch the men on board sleeping. The intensive activity on the docks and on the ships had made it nearly impossible to sleep. Moreover, a glance was sufficient to tell them that their merchant vessel wasn't adequate for a military operation such as the one they were about to embark on. They were crowded together on deck, unprotected from the sun and dew; the space was insufficient for the nearly 400 men; and what few cabins there were had been reserved for the highest-ranking officers of the Brigade, who would also be the only ones apart from the crew members who would receive cooked meals on board. The rest would have to resign themselves to cold rations in cardboard boxes, canned food, sugar, salt, chocolate and preserves. Moreover, there was another problem that might mean tragedy: barrels of gasoline were stored in the bow holds and nearly everywhere on deck. The men had to make their way around 45,000 gallons of high-octane gasoline.

During the morning and afternoon of April 13, all of the Brigade members were moved from the Trax Base to the port of embarkation. The men were concentrated on the dock, which extended into the sea for almost a mile. Nicaraguan soldiers closed off the landward end to keep the Brigade members from going to the hamlet of Puerto Cabezas, around 500 meters away. Despite the ban, some wore camouflage uniforms and managed to get past their guards and reach the bars in the town. Those who had money picked up teenaged girls who were just getting started in prostitution.

José Ramón walked along the dock when someone told him that some Americans had arrived at the air base and were meeting with the battalion's staff.

Seated on rustic wooden benches, the members of the Brigade's staff and the heads of the battalions and companies listened to the invasion plan. Colonel Jack Hawkins told them that the invasion would begin that afternoon at 5:00 p.m., with the Brigade's departure from the dock. It was called Operation Pluto and would consist in having a force land at three points around the Bay of Pigs, in southern Las Villas Province: Blue (Girón) Beach; Red (Larga) Beach; and Green Beach (at Caleta Buena Inlet, 10 kilometers west of Girón Beach). Girón Beach would be the center of the operation, and headquarters would be set up there. Larga Beach would be the infantry outpost, 30 kilometers to the northwest. The paratroopers would be dropped at Horquitas, near Yaguaramas; at Jocuma, near the Covadonga Sugar

Mill; and on the road between the Australia Sugar Mill and Larga Beach. He added that the Brigade's task would be to attack, occupy and defend those places and to hold them for at least 72 hours.

Those attending the meeting observed that, every so often, one of the visitors amended what Hawkins had said, and it became clear in the course of the briefing that the individual was the highest-ranking person there. He was addressed as "Mr. Dick." Later, those details made investigators think he must have been the CIA's Richard Bissell.

José Ramón had just cleaned his M-1 carbine and was gazing out to sea. The *Río Escondido* and *Lake Charles* merchant vessels were close by. Soon afterwards, he went down to the dock again and began to walk slowly among the men. Suddenly, he discovered a group of men, some in civilian clothes and others in uniform, but all wearing dark glasses and toting pistols or submachine guns. One of them wore a white suit and cloth hat. It was Luis Somoza, head of the Nicaraguan Army. The group halted when the man dressed in white, holding an M-1 in his hand, was in front of José Ramón. Other members of the Brigade surrounded him, and Somoza gave a short speech. He wished the invaders luck, assuring them that they would be victorious, as they were well equipped.

The men applauded. Heading back to the *Houston*, one former member of the Rebel Army commented disgustedly, "After having fought against one dictator, I'll be damned if I applaud this one." Friction between the former army men and those who had fought against Batista and were now members of the Brigade had been evident right from the beginning of their training. Some tried to avoid it.

Finally, at 5:00 p.m. on April 13, the first ship weighed anchor. It was the *Atlantic*. The *Caribe*, *Lake Charles* and *Río Escondido* were next. The *Houston* cast off at dusk, followed by the *Barbara J.* and the *Blagar*. This last carried the top-ranking officers of the Attack Brigade. The five merchant vessels and two gunboats had cast off with 1,242 men on board; in their holds, they carried thousands of tons of war matériel. Some of the men spent the night worrying because they hadn't seen any U.S. warships. As Pérez San Román later told Haynes Johnson, those who were trained in Guatemala took part in the invasion only because Americans would be there. As he put it, they didn't believe in him, the other officers or even themselves; they believed only in the Americans.[95] That worry was relieved at dawn when, euphoric, the men on the *Houston* spied a U.S. Navy destroyer. It had shut down its engines and was clearly waiting for the *Houston* to

---

[95] Haynes Johnson, *The Bay of Pigs.*

draw closer. With binoculars, José Ramón made out its markings; it was destroyer 701. Its presence raised the troops' morale, and the day's rations tasted better than what they had eaten the night before.

At 9:00 a.m. on April 14, the heads of the companies were called to a meeting. Three hours later, they returned to their combat units and mingled with the men. In that informal way, in the middle of the ocean, where no agents of Fidel Castro could possibly pass on the information, they revealed the secret which the CIA had guarded so jealously: the place selected for the invasion of Cuba — the Bay of Pigs, in the Zapata Swamp, on the southern coast of Cuba.

"In the swamp?" Buttari, the squad leader, asked.

"We won't have any problems," the field officer commanding Company E replied. "The area is practically deserted, and there are no military forces in the region. Girón, one of the landing points, is a beach where they're building a tourist center and has a landing strip. One company will take the airport and help the corps of engineers to make it operational as soon as possible. From three to five days after our landing, when the beachhead has been consolidated, a plane will bring in the members of the Cuban Revolutionary Council, our provisional government, from Miami. And then the Americans."

Some of the men smiled. "Will we have to go into the swamp?"

"No, not at all," the officer stated. "We'll land on one of the three beaches that cover around 40 kilometers of solid ground along the coast. I repeat: it's high, solid ground. It's the militia who will have to slog through the swamp if they want to get close to us, and it won't be easy for them, because our paratroopers will seize the two roads that run through the swamp from the nearest towns to the coast."

"Then they'll be the first ones to go into combat?" José Ramón asked.

"That's what's planned, but the U.S. chiefs say that everything will go so smoothly — and that we won't stop until we get to Havana. They expect a lot of people to join us."

"What's our mission?"

"Our battalion will be the first to land at Larga Beach. Battalion 5 will follow us. Our Company E will move to the left, to a railway junction with a line going north. We'll advance four kilometers to a hamlet called Pálpite, where we'll wait for the platoon of paratroopers. Another platoon of ours will advance along the right flank to a hamlet called Soplillar, which we'll also occupy."

By late afternoon, the men on deck were trying to protect themselves as best they could from the sun. The artillerymen at the four .50-caliber machine guns kept busy, some of them going over their guns and others scanning the sky. Soon after, night began to fall. Most of those in the two battalions were already up by 5:30 a.m. on Saturday, April 15. It was cold. They could see destroyer 701 around three miles to starboard, going in the same direction. Evidently, it was part of the U.S. naval escort that would accompany the five ships and two gunboats. Some of those on board took out transistor radios and tuned in to Radio Swan. The news on that day's first morning bulletin gave details on a supposed crisis for the regime. Radio Swan reported that Che Guevara had been ousted in a purge and that, during an argument with Fidel, Raúl, Martínez Sánchez and Núñez Jiménez in the Prime Minister's office, Martínez Sánchez had shot and wounded him. Radio Swan challenged the regime to present Che in public.

Those who were listening to the broadcast quickly told those who didn't have radios what they had heard, and their spirits soared. Nobody questioned the veracity of the report. The station had been broadcasting news bulletins for nearly a year. Reports such as this led the men to leap to the conclusion that the regime was crumbling and that one decisive blow would topple it – a blow which they would provide. In fact, Che Guevara was then in Pinar del Río Province, for he had been placed in charge of its defense. Fidel Castro was at Point One, the Revolutionary Armed Forces' and Militia's command post.

That report wasn't the most electrifying of the morning, however. An hour later, a news flash announced that planes of Castro's Air Force had bombed the airports at Camp Columbia and San Antonio de los Baños and Santiago de Cuba's Antonio Maceo International Airport. Radio Swan repeated the new flash several times, adding that there had been many dead and wounded and that the military bases had been practically destroyed. The men on the *Houston*, like those on the other ships, shouted with joy.

At mid-morning, José Ramón tuned in to Radio Swan again. The bulletins on the bombing of the Cuban airports were repeated, with the addition that, after strafing Camp Columbia, one of the Revolutionary Air Force planes had been forced to land at Miami's airport. It was a B-26 bearing the number 933, and there were many bullet holes in its fuselage. The report repeated that pilots of Castro's Air Force had carried out the raid against the airports and announced that the pilot who had deserted would make important statements in the coming hours. That afternoon, an immigration official presented the press a statement by the supposed deserter:

I am one of the 12 B-26 pilots who remained in Castro's Air Force after Pedro Luis Díaz Lanz's defection and the purges which followed it. For months, three of my comrades and I have been planning how to escape from Castro's Cuba... Yesterday morning, I was assigned to a routine patrol of a section of Pinar del Río and around the Isle of Pines, starting from my base at San Antonio de los Baños. I told my friends from Camp Libertad about this, and they agreed that we had to act.[96]

The details held together so well and the announcers were so emphatic that many of those on board commented that it might be true. Others refused to believe it. They had seen the B-26s painted with Cuban insignia on the landing strip at Happy Valley and now understood why. Someone suggested that they tune in to Cuban stations. All were broadcasting the Cuban Government's denunciations of the bombings and warning the people that new attacks might be coming.

At noon, after handing out the meal rations, the officers of the battalion were called to attend a meeting in the ship's mess hall. Each officer wore a 10-gallon hat to distinguish him from the troops. Those hats proved to be a pain in the neck, however, and some of the officers dispensed with them as soon as the fighting began. Needless to say, the officers weren't in the front lines.

They seated themselves around a rectangular table in the mess hall. Holding a copy of the plan of operations, Hugo Sueiro, who commanded Battalion 2, and Erneido Oliva, second in command of the Brigade, began to explain exactly what the Brigade's and the battalion's missions would be. Sueiro spread out a map and some enlarged aerial photos, and the heads of the companies and squads studied in detail what they would have to do after landing.

The photos showed everything extremely clearly: the two roads that traversed the swamp, the channels, even the thatched-roof huts. The map wouldn't remain in the invaders' hands for long, however:

At Larga Beach, I found a map belonging to Erneido Oliva. It was plastic coated and had been brought up to date with aerial photos. It included the road between Larga and Girón Beaches, which my map didn't have; my map was old.[97]

The invasion chief reiterated that prisoners shouldn't be mistreated and that they should be brought to headquarters immediately after

---

[96] Statement by Mario Zúñiga, invader.
[97] Testimony of José Ramón Fernández, then head of the Militia School.

capture, for questioning. He also insisted that women shouldn't be sexually abused and that payment in cash or with a document signed by the head of the battalion should be given for all food that was seized.

All motor vehicles in running condition would be requisitioned. Good treatment of the civilian population was very important for gaining supporters. "What will be done with the prisoners?" somebody in the room asked. "That's up to G-2 and the people at Operation 40," Sueiro hastily replied. No more questions were asked. In fact, the men in the room knew very little about the mysterious Operation 40. They had heard of it in early March, when 63 men arrived at the Trax Base and were assigned to a barracks that was quite some distance from the rest of the troops. Vicente León León, a former Army colonel who had been an aide of President Carlos Prío, was their commander. The recruits soon learned that those men had been in charge of investigating everyone who had gone to the Front's offices in Miami and signed up.

The leader of this team, Juaquín Sanjenís, had remained in Miami. He would fly directly to the liberated territory and take over civilian intelligence. He had visited the Trax Base for slightly over a month, and, while he was there, more than 20 had been assigned to the G-2 section which would be in charge of interrogating prisoners during the fighting. The rest would make the trip aboard the *Atlantic*, the last ship in the convoy, and would be the last to disembark, once the beachhead was consolidated. Twenty-seven of them were divided into nine three-man teams. They would do reconnaissance ahead of the lines of fire, to ascertain the location of the revolutionary forces, what arms and how many combatants they had, what their morale was like, what supplies they had and which access routes they were using.

In carrying out their missions, the members of the teams would wear civilian clothes or militia uniforms, and they would have radio equipment for keeping in touch with the rear guard. Twelve other members of Operation 40 would interrogate civilians to obtain information about the cities near the battlefield; descriptions of the revolutionary leaders, both military and civilian; and data on the location of army barracks, police stations, the electric and telephone companies and banks.

Finally, 20 other men, forming 10 teams, would be in charge of getting workers in the cities controlled by the Brigade back to work. They would seize the public archives and those of the Cuban Security bodies and would take charge of the pro-regime military and civilian prisoners, killing those who were most committed to the government

— after getting them to pass on all the information they had. Torture would not be ruled out in interrogations.

This last group never landed. On the morning of April 17, following the attacks by Revolutionary Air Force planes, the *Atlantic* weighed anchor and headed for the high seas. The captain made that decision without consultation but promised to return at nightfall, which he never did. The ship didn't stop until it reached New Orleans.

The members of Operation 40 who were taken prisoner managed to conceal their real mission. Only one invader, a member of the Brigade's command, provided nearly complete information about the composition of the team and what mission they had been assigned.[98] The only details he ommitted were the third-degree interrogations and the killing of prisoners.

When the meeting was nearly over, the head of the battalion again stated emphatically that civilians should be well treated, adding that the ships contained around 10,000 rifles that would be given to those who joined the invaders.

At the end of the meeting, the battalion's S-4 (supplies) coordinator appeared with a case of cold beer. Beer had also been given to the troops. One of the men in the room commented, "We'll drink the next one in Havana," and the others laughed confidently.

At lunchtime, the men began to protest again about the cold, precooked food. Some of them claimed that the officers had hot meals from the ship's galley. There were so many complaints that Erneido Oliva and Luis Morse, captain of the *Houston*, had to give orders for the cook to provide a hot meal for everybody the next day.

The officers kept telling the men not to smoke, but there was no way of stopping them.

When it got dark, a shot rang out, and confusion reigned for a moment. It turned out to be an accident: a member of Battalion 2 who was cleaning his rifle had touched the trigger by mistake. The bullet wounded him in the leg, and he was quickly taken to the mess hall for treatment. Again, the men were urged to be careful when cleaning their weapons, but some of the invaders suspected that the man had shot himself on purpose. In spite of their confidence that they would have U.S. support and be victorious and that the collapse of the regime was imminent, the proximity of Cuba, which nearly all of them had left in the previous two years, added to the extreme tension.

---

[98] José Raúl Varona González, head of G-2 in Brigade 2506, gave an extensive description of Operation 40.

That wasn't the first accident on board. During a drill, one of the gunners had fired a burst from a .50-caliber artillery piece, killing one invader instantly and wounding another.

When things returned to normal on board the *Houston*, it was pitch dark, and the men stretched out to sleep. Shortly before dawn, José Ramón suddenly awoke; the ship had cut its engines, and the men on deck looked in surprise at the sea. A powerful light blinded them. A few minutes went by, and then the source of the light went around the stern of the ship; the light was then turned off, and everything was dark again. The *Houston* resumed its advance, and the men started conjecturing, but very few got it right. One of the submarines escorting the invading fleet had surfaced so as to take off the injured man.

At dawn on Sunday, April 16, the men on board the *Houston* clustered around their transistor radios, tuning to Radio Swan. That morning, they heard reports of important victories scored by the anti-Castro insurgents in the Escambray Mountains, the bombs that had gone off in Havana during the preceding days, other acts of sabotage all over the island, new uprisings in Oriente and Pinar del Río Provinces and the large number of people killed in the bombings of the day before. The radio station kept calling on the Cuban people to rise up against Fidel Castro's regime and announced that the time of liberation was near.

One invader commented, "If we wait a little, we can go ashore in Havana instead of the swamp," but he didn't impress those who heard him. Very few on board questioned the truth of the news broadcasts, but some of them wished they could hear that another invading force was landing somewhere else, far from the swamp; then they would feel better.

In fact, the CIA *had* organized a diversionary landing operation in Oriente Province to confuse Fidel Castro. A battalion was supposed to be fighting near Baracoa right then, but an invasion of Oriente was an extremely dangerous undertaking: the province was defended by a considerable force of militia and soldiers of the Rebel Army, all eager to confront the enemy.

Major Raúl Castro, Minister of the Revolutionary Armed Forces, had been in Oriente since early April. He had also been appointed military chief of the province. With his staff officers, he was once more going over the details of the plan for the defense of that large eastern territory. The most vulnerable places were the coastline between Nicaro and Pilón and the area around the Guantánamo Naval Base. Major Eddy Suñol was in charge of defending the former, and several units reinforced with artillery pieces and antiaircraft guns were assigned to him. Baracoa was another possible point of disembarkation, and it was reinforced with three battalions. A group of battalions at Mangos de Baraguá, under the command of Captain Senén Casas, could move quickly either north or south. On analyzing the operational situation that had existed in Oriente Province in those days, Fidel Castro said:

> On the evening of April 14, Raúl [Castro] was in Oriente. They had the troops distributed and the regions organized — even some planes at Santiago de Cuba's airport... Then they called me here in Havana and told me that a group of ships could be seen near Baracoa, which meant a possible landing... The forces in Baracoa took measures to repel a landing... No soldiers were mobilized from west to east for that operation, because there were plenty of men in Oriente, in those mountain areas — armed and organized farmers. Any force that landed there would have failed to achieve its objective. Of course, a landing would have caught our attention and interest, but it wouldn't have had any military consequences, because there were sufficient means in Oriente to defeat an invasion.[99]

The group of ships near Baracoa to which Fidel Castro referred was supposed to be used in the CIA diversionary operation, code name Marte. As one of the participants in that operation stated:

> I set about training to be part of the invasion forces which Nino Díaz commanded... We had trained at the camp north of Lake Pontchartrain up to the second half of April 1961, when we took ship for Cuba. We left from the Algiers Naval Base, on the Mississippi River, in New Orleans. There were around 160 of us. Our ship was the *Santa Ana*, flying the Costa Rican flag.[100]

On April 14, the same afternoon on which the Attack Brigade weighed anchor from Puerto Cabezas, the *Santa Ana*, with 168 men on board, waited for nightfall to land the battalion on a beach near Imías, a few dozen kilometers from the Guantánamo Naval Base. The greatest danger they would have to face would be posed by the Cuban troops around the U.S. naval base, though they wouldn't be able to go immediately to the landing area, because they couldn't leave the

---

[99] Quintín Pino Machado, *La Batalla de Playa Girón*.
[100] Statement by Enrique Fernández Ruiz de la Torre ("Kiki"). Archives of the Cuban Ministry of the Interior.

territory around the base unprotected. The most important mission of the battalion of invaders on board the *Santa Ana* would be to go into combat as soon as they landed and make enough noise to force Fidel Castro to move forces toward that province. Then, two days later, when the real invasion took place at the Bay of Pigs, he would be caught with his pants down.

At midnight, the *Santa Ana* approached the coast until it was just four miles offshore. A speedboat was lowered and headed quickly and silently for the coast.

> We wore olive green uniforms just like those used by the Cuban Army… We drew close to Mocambo Beach, very close to Imías. I spent the night of April 13 on a reconnaissance patrol.[101]

Then there began an exchange of messages between the CIA officer in charge of the operation, who was on board; Higinio Díaz Ane, the head of the battalion; and the scouts. Over and over again, the scouts signaled that they could see many lights along the coast, which they presumed meant military forces. "Curly," the U.S. officer, insisted on finding a good place. A little later, the scouts came back and confirmed that military forces were there. The head of the battalion said that, in that case, the landing would have to be suspended. "Curly" kept insisting on a landing (although he didn't have to go ashore). After an argument, they decided to put off the attempt until the next night. The scouts were right. The presence of the *Santa Ana* and of the vessel that was hovering just off the coast hadn't gone unnoticed.

> Raúl told [Major Eddy Suñol] to bring an antiaircraft battery[102] up near the coast and to use it in case of a landing. I remember clearly that Raúl told Suñol not to fire until the mercenaries had landed. He repeated that two or three times.[103]

The bombings of the airports at dawn of the next day didn't completely calm the fears of the invaders on board the *Santa Ana*, but they did raise their morale. None of them really doubted that they would be victorious in the coming days, and they were eager to get started. That night, the scouts headed silently for the coast once again.

---

[101] Ibid.

[102] It was an antiaircraft battery of multiple machine guns popularly known as "four-mouths." The battery had six of them, for a total of 24 guns.

[103] Testimony of Rebel Army Captain Luis Más Martín.

The second night, the intermediary launch that was taking us to shore struck a reef, and the propeller was bent. Another speedboat had to come and get us. In the midst of that situation, we heard the sound of trucks and jeeps.[104]

"They're waiting for us," one of the battalion's officers commented to Nino Díaz, who refused to go along with the CIA officer's efforts to get them to land. Finally, the ship headed out to the open sea.[105]

Meanwhile, at midnight on that Sunday, April 16, the *Houston* advanced slowly up the Bay of Pigs. There was absolute silence on board, apart from the sound of the merchant vessel's engines and the slap of the waves. All lights had been turned off except for one small one on the bridge, where the radio-telegraph operator was sending messages.

---

[104] Statement by Enrique Fernández Ruiz de la Torre ("Kiki"). Archives of the Cuban Ministry of the Interior.

[105] There has been conjecture about the true purpose of this operation, which the CIA had so carefully prepared. Division General Fabián Escalante Font, former Director of the National Security Affairs Study Center (now the State Security Historical Research Center [CIHSE]), told the author, "The troop's real mission may have been to attack the naval base from Cuban territory, simulating an attack by revolutionary forces — after the fighting had begun in the Zapata Swamp — in reprisal for the invasion. This would have ensured direct intervention by the United States, which was on Dulles's and Bissell's agendas. That's why Imías, an area relatively close to the U.S. Naval Base, was selected instead of Baracoa, which would have been better for simulating another invasion. It's also why Nino Díaz's men wore olive green uniforms, not camouflage outfits, and why they were trained not in Guatemala, as the Brigade members were, but in the United States, in the utmost secrecy. And, for that same reason, the CIA officer remained on board the ship and kept insisting up to the last moment that the men should land. Moreover, just a month after the invasion failed, the CIA drew up a plan for attacking the base from Cuban territory, combining that attack with an assassination attempt against Fidel and Raúl Castro on July 26. Cuban State Security crushed the plan and arrested the agents who were involved in it. It seems to me that that plan for the attack on the base wasn't drawn up in May 1961 but was the same one that Nino Díaz's men were to have carried out."

The inevitable battle

Shortly after 1:00 a.m. on April 17, the ladders were put out. José Ramón checked his equipment for the last time. The ropes fastening the eight boats with outboard motors were untied, and the fore and aft cranes hoisted the first boats and set them on the calm water. The ship rolled slowly, and a gentle breeze eased the tension. The artillery crews for the four antiaircraft guns were at their combat positions, scanning the sky and the coast. The crews for the 75-mm guns on the escort ship *Barbara J.* were just as alert.

A short while later, the first men of Battalion 2 went down the ship's ladders to the boats. José Ramón settled himself in the bow and looked toward shore, clutching his M-3 submachine gun. The darkness was impenetrable, but, far away, a mile shoreward, he could see a green light. It was the signal placed by the frogmen. José Ramón thought that they would take the beach without any fighting. It looked deserted. He was right. There were no defense combat units on Larga Beach.

During the first week of April, Fidel Castro and some other officers of the Rebel Army had toured the projects under construction on the Zapata Peninsula. While at Girón Beach, walking on the concrete jetty, he had said, "This is an ideal place for the landing."[106] Fidel gave instructions for a battalion to be transferred from Cienfuegos to the Australia Sugar Mill, 30 kilometers from Larga Beach and 70 kilometers from Girón Beach. That unit would be in charge of defending the coast between Larga Beach and Rosario Cove, a point between Larga and Girón Beaches. A few days later, he ordered another battalion to be posted at Girón Beach. Due to organizational and communications problems, that order wasn't carried out.

Reminiscing about that time, Fidel Castro said:

---

[106] Testimony of Abraham Maciques, then director of the Zapata Peninsula development plan.

A few days earlier, I had ordered a battalion to be sent to the place where the landing took place, but everything was just beginning back then; we didn't have a staff as yet.

Therefore, on the night of the landing, Girón Beach was defended by only half a dozen charcoal makers, militia who were on duty. They were armed with Czech M-52 semiautomatic rifles, with 60 rounds each. Mariano Mustelier, the head of the militia, had a Czech submachine gun with 90 rounds.

The only defenses at Larga Beach, the other point of disembarkation, where the first boat from the *Houston* was about to land, were five men from a Battalion 339 squad commanded by militia José Ramón González Suco, who were at an observation post.

The battalion arrived at the Australia Sugar Mill on April 8 or 10. On April 13, if I'm not mistaken, four men from my squad and I were sent to Larga Beach. I was chosen because I knew how to work the Motorola shortwave radio that was there. I had been there in January, working on the tourist installations, and, at the construction chief's orders, had requested sand, cement and some other materials over the radio, which belonged to the Ministry of Construction.

That beach was like paradise. When I took charge of the radio equipment, the radio operator, who was going home on a pass with the rest of the workers, warned me not to keep it turned on all the time, because the voltage was defective. We turned it on every 30 minutes to communicate with the battalion and report. The only arms we had — which were the only ones around — were five Czech submachine guns with 90 rounds each and a BZ bipod machine gun with 200 rounds for a cartridge belt or clip. We liked it better with the belt; it looked like something out of a movie... That Sunday afternoon, a company came from the battalion. Its members had been cutting burned-over sugarcane, and all the men were covered with soot. They had a swim at the beach and then went back to the Australia Sugar Mill. If they had stayed, those people wouldn't have landed. At least, we would have been able to hold out until the rest of the battalion arrived. But they left. They had only come to swim at the beach...

Quintana had the BZ. He was from the Canary Islands and incredibly strong but not very smart. I asked him if he knew how to use it. He said he did, but he started to play around with it, and a few shots went off. Then I used the shortwave radio to ask the head of the battalion to send somebody to teach us how to use the thing. "The Chinaman" came and gave us instructions...

Shortly after midnight, the man on guard at the beach saw something and notified me. I had been told that a Navy boat would be coming to the cove a little farther to the right. The night was very dark, and you couldn't see anything. Then I heard the sound of a motor. I told my men that I would tell the boat to halt and that they should stay behind with the BZ. A few minutes later, I saw it and, perfectly clearly, a man with his foot on the bow. He had a rifle slung over his shoulder. I slipped off the safety of my submachine gun, shouted "Halt!" and shot once into the air. They replied with a burst from an M-3. Imagine: when I shot back with my Czech submachine gun, which was of much smaller caliber, it seemed like I was shooting with a toy. The BZ opened fire but immediately jammed. After the battle, I found out that the BZs' cartridge belts are shit. They're more effective with clips. But the boys wanted it to look like the movies.[107]

The five militia couldn't put up any resistance, but they did manage to report to the battalion's headquarters that they were being attacked. Then they took refuge in one of the buildings that was under construction, where they were taken prisoner the next morning.

Early on the morning of April 17, José Ramón González sent a message that they could see lights and movement at sea. Néstor Ortiz, the radio-telegraph operator on duty, gave the message to Captain Cordero, head of the battalion. Soon afterwards, he received another message from José Ramón:

A boat is landing and shooting at the beach. They're right on top of us. We're going to destroy this radio and head for the trench.

The message left no room for doubts, and Cordero ordered the battalion to form ranks.

My son Jesús was head of the squad of the third platoon in Company 3, which Cordero ordered to head for Larga Beach. There wasn't any transportation for the rest of the troops. We had advanced around 20 kilometers when the driver of the truck, who was a civilian, one of the ones who hauled sugar, chickened out. He told us the truck was running out of gas and couldn't get us there. At one point, he stopped the truck. Then Jesús told him,

---

[107] Testimony of José Ramón González Suco, Cuban militia.

"Look, if you can't go on, my dad knows how to drive trucks, and he'll take us to the beach." Then the man went on. When we got to a curve quite close to the beach, we got out of the truck and took up positions.[108]

The platoon crouched down. "Count the men, Solís." "Twenty-seven; 28, counting you." I told the men with the three BZs to take out the cartridge belts and put in the clips. We had 200 rounds for each BZ and 80 for each rifle — which was shit, compared to what the enemy had. Lastly, I told the men to hold their fire until I started shooting. We began to advance along the road in the middle of the night. We had only gone a short distance when one of the men said to me quietly, "Lieutenant" — I wasn't a lieutenant; the man seemed nervous — "some men are coming over there." When I set up the BZ, its legs made a noise. Then we heard one of the guys who was coming: "Halt! Who are you?" "The 339th, from Cienfuegos," I replied. "And you?" "Company E of the 2nd Battalion." "That doesn't exist in Cuba." Then a mercenary on the other flank shouted, "We're from the Army of Liberation. We didn't come to fight against you. Surrender!" "Fire!" I shouted.

There was a hell of a lot of shooting. Some time later, they stopped shooting, and we did, too. There was a great silence. I heard them clearly when one of them said to another, "Hey, my ears are buzzing like a telephone." "And I'm thirsty." I heard them say that one of them was wounded, and they took him away. Then they came back to shoot, this time with heavy machine guns — and we, with what we had. We had fallen back to the other side of the ditch, and we returned their fire from there, but they had a terrible advantage. Our Czech rifles weren't automatic. If they rushed us, I knew they would wipe us out, but they didn't dare. We heard their passwords: "Eagle, eagle," and the other one answered, "Black eagle." "If you don't say the password fast, I'll shoot." You could tell they were nervous. Another one spoke, it seemed, over a radio unit, saying, "Mr. Officer" — they spoke formally among themselves — "since I've been here, nobody's sent us any water, ammunition or relief. If you don't send me relief, I'm going to withdraw." At least he could ask. We didn't have any communications equipment or water, and our ammunition was running out.[109]

---

[108] Testimony of Angel Villafuerte Ayala, Cuban militia.
[109] Testimony of Luis Clemente Carralero ("Oriente"), Cuban militia.

Jesús Villafuerte Ayala had ordered his men to spread out, with several meters between them. He had taken the position in the middle, together with the BZ operator. His father had run, and, when it got lighter, Jesús found that he was next to him. Knowing that the old man wouldn't leave him, he didn't criticize him for having left his position. The BZ had run out of ammunition, and now the men were firing sporadically at the enemy lines, mainly to let them know that they were still there and hadn't withdrawn. But now, in the light of day, in the middle of that land which the bulldozers that were building the tourist installations had cleared of brush, the militia of the 339th Battalion were easy targets.

Edgar Buttari, head of the squad from the mercenaries' Company E — the squad that José Ramón Pérez Peña, the former clerk in the five and ten in Camagüey, belonged to — put his Garand on his shoulder and began to pick off the militia who were hugging the earth 80 meters away, next to the road.

> Jesús moved the men from one place to another, trying to offer smaller targets. While we were doing this, we heard the engine of a truck coming straight at the mercenaries' positions. The back didn't have any railings, and, from our position, we could see several women. At that moment, a cannon or bazooka opened fire against it. The truck was blown into the air.[110]

As Mario Abril subsequently told journalists David Wise and Thomas B. Ross, the mercenaries shouted "Eagle", but there was no reply. The truck kept coming closer, so all of them took their weapons and began firing, and it blew up — POW! It leaped into the air, enveloped in flames. Then they saw that the only people in the truck were three women and two little girls. He said he didn't know how that had happened, but that's what they found in the wreckage: the bodies of three women and two little girls.[111]

It is difficult if not impossible to imagine how the people in that truck could have heard that strange password, since the men of Company E were under cover several dozen meters away. With the motor running, the old truck made so much noise it was impossible to hear anybody. Moreover, there weren't any militia in the truck; it carried civilians only, who were perfectly visible.

---

[110] Testimony of Angel Villafuerte Ayala, Cuban militia.
[111] Wise and Ross, *The Invisible Government.*

At Girón Beach, 39 kilometers to the east, the priest Ismael de Lugo went over the words he was about to read over the Brigade's radio transmitter, addressed to the Cuban people:

The Reverend Father Ismael de Lugo, of the Capuchin order, head of the Ecclesiastic Services of the Attack Brigade, is addressing all Catholics in Cuba, on both his own behalf and that of his fellow priests. Attention! Attention! Cuban Catholics! The forces of liberation have landed on Cuban beaches. We have come in the name of God, justice and democracy to reestablish the rights and freedoms that have been trampled underfoot and organized religion, which has been slandered. We come not in hatred but in love. We come to bring peace, even though, to obtain it, we must make war. The Attack Brigade consists of thousands of Cubans, all of whom are Christians and Catholics. Their morality is that of the Crusades. They come to reestablish the principles which the Master gave us in His Sermon on the Mount. Before landing, all have heard Mass and received the blessed Sacraments. They know what they are fighting for, and for whom they are fighting. They want to stop the suffering of the dark Lady of Charity of El Cobre, who, from her sanctuary, looks on so much ungodliness and communism.

At this time, we need the cooperation of all Cuban Catholics. We ask you to pray for our triumph, for divine protection for our soldiers and for civilians' cooperation in not leaving their homes. We pray to the God of the armies that the struggle may be brief, so that the least possible blood of our Cuban brothers may be shed. Our struggle is that of those who believe in God against the atheists, that of spiritual values against materialism and that of democracy against communism. Only a superior ideology can overthrow ideologies. Christian ideology is the only ideology that can overthrow communist ideology. That is why we have come, and that is what we are fighting for.

Cuban Catholics! Our military force is overwhelming and invincible, but greater yet is the strength of our morality and our faith in God and in His protection and help. Cuban Catholics! I send an embrace from the Army of Liberation to all your friends and relatives. Soon, may we be together. Have faith that we will be victorious, because God is on our side, and Our Lady of Charity cannot abandon her children. Catholics! Long live free, democratic and Catholic Cuba! Long live Christ the King! Long live our glorious Patron Saint! Her blessing on you. Father Ismael de Lugo, head of the Ecclesiastic Services of the Brigade.[112]

A few meters beyond where the truck was burning, Angel and Jesús Villafuerte sought cover in that open space. They couldn't see the men of Company E, but their enemies could see them. The invaders had seized a small hill that had several pits, because a gas station was being built there. The elevation gave them a clear view of the highway on both sides. The men in José Ramón Peña's squad kept on shooting down the remaining militia.

> After it got lighter, the bullets hit very close to us and had killed or wounded several men in the battalion. Then Jesús said, "Dad, I'm wounded." I slithered closer to him and touched him, but I couldn't see any wounds. Then I talked to him, and he didn't answer. He had collapsed. I turned him over; the bullet had hit him on the other side. I gave him a little water, and it ran down his face. He was dead. Then I stayed there, looking at him, not knowing what to do. I put his cap on him. I didn't want to believe it. A comrade told me, "Don't move; they're sniping at us."[113]

Shortly afterwards, Angel was slightly wounded and taken to the town of Jagüey Grande.

> After they treated me in the hospital, I went to the funeral parlor to look for my son's body, but it wasn't there. The people told me that, since he was from Cienfuegos, his body had been sent there. When I arrived in the city, I went straight to the Pujol Funeral Parlor, where I worked, but his body wasn't there, either. Then I went home. When my wife saw me without the boy, she was upset. I didn't have the courage to tell her the truth. I said he was wounded. Then I went to Aguada de Pasajeros, but his body wasn't there, either. I went all the way thumbing rides. Then I went back to Jagüey Grande. Jesús was at the funeral parlor. I called my boss, and he sent me the hearse. I put dry ice in the coffin, and we went to Cienfuegos. All the way, I kept thinking about how I was

---

[112] Ismael de Lugo's real name was Fermín Asla Polo. He was born in the Lugo region in Spain and had served in the Spanish Civil War on Franco's side. The above speech was found in his notebook.

[113] Testimony of Angel Villafuerte Ayala, Cuban militia.

going to tell my wife that they had killed our son. She died soon afterwards. She never recovered.[114]

The war ended there, at that moment, for Angel Villafuerte Ayala. Although he didn't know it, the resistance that he, his son and their comrades had put up since the early morning hours had defeated a part of the Attack Brigade's plan. They had kept Company E from advancing four kilometers northward to the town of Pálpite and then six kilometers eastward to the sugarmill community of Soplillar, and had therefore kept the enemy from seizing both towns near where the swamp began, at the end of the beachhead, where they were to have joined the paratroopers. The men in Battalion 2 stopped advancing almost as soon as the fighting with the militia of Battalion 339 began. Even though they had superior firepower and could have over- whelmed the militia, they didn't do it. They had been told that most of the militia would join them and were surprised when the militia fired instead of surrendering.

The clash with the few militia at Girón Beach hadn't turned out as expected, either. Mariano Mustelier, head of the militia there, was the first to spot a light at sea. That night, he was in a jeep, checking on the tourist area that was under construction. Valerio Rodríguez, a 13-year- old literacy teacher, was with him.

There was something strange about that red light that kept on blinking. Mariano thought it was a ship that was heading for Cienfuegos and had gone off course in the bay. He got in the jeep and headed east to get in front of the ship and signal it with the jeep's headlights. The literacy teacher, who had arrived in the swamp two months earlier and thought everything was a tremendous adventure, quickly jumped into the jeep.

About a hundred yards offshore, one of their six red beach marker lights suddenly started blinking.[115] Several of the men scrambled for it. Gray [Lynch] reached it first, covered it up and groped for the switch. It had been carefully taped on "off." The blinking, caused by a short, stopped... Fifty yards offshore, he heard a jeep coming... Gray never forgot the loud, long squeaking of the brakes. He raised his head for a look. At that moment the jeep swung around toward the sea, bathing the landing party in its headlights.

---

[114] Ibid.

[115] The position lights which Grayston Lynch's frogmen had placed could be seen only from the sea if they were functioning correctly.

At once, Gray started firing directly into them. They were the first shots at the Bay of Pigs.[116]

The jeep's headlights were smashed, and some fragments wounded Valerio Rodríguez in the eye. A strange paradox: the first shots fired in the invasion which sought to wipe out the Cuban Revolution had been fired by a U.S. officer, and the first person to be wounded was a literacy teacher who was there teaching the charcoal makers how to read and write.

Mariano Mustelier made an important decision. He sent one of the workers to the Covadonga Sugar Mill, 30 kilometers to the north, to warn the people there, and another to sound the alarm over the radio. Soon afterwards, members of Battalion 4 seized the radio.

We were in one of the cabañas making a census of those who could not read or write when we heard the shooting. I looked out the window and saw a ball of fire coming from the sea. A few minutes later, Valerio and some other literacy teachers came in. He was wounded in one eye. "It's a landing," they told us. We stayed in the cabaña, and some men with strange uniforms came in soon afterwards and took us prisoner. At dawn, they took us to the dining hall. They had taken a lot of charcoal makers prisoner — around 300 of them. They separated the men and women and began interrogating us. They did that in a little room next to the dining hall. "Where are you from?" they asked me. "Bolondrón." "What are you doing here?" "I'm teaching people how to read and write." "Is that why Fidel brought you here?" "No, no; Fidel didn't bring us; we came because we wanted to." They took notes of all my answers and suggested that I change sides. I said I wouldn't. "I'm a teacher; I like to teach; I don't like the army."[117]

By giving a reply just as indirect, Manuel Alvariño, the charcoal maker who had taken care of Fidel on May 25, 1959, and who loved telling the story of the pig's foot, also managed to get through the interrogation given him by the members of the Brigade's G-2.

They told me they would give me five pesos for every member of my family and that, if I joined their army, I could be anything from a soldier to a commander. "No, I don't like the army," I replied.

---

[116] Wyden, *Bay of Pigs: The Untold Story.*
[117] Testimony of Ana María Hernández Bravo, who was in charge of the literacy teachers at Girón Beach.

"We have the form you filled out to become a militia," they said, and they showed it to me. So I told them, "Yes, I'm a militia, but only to guard my work place."[118]

There were close to 400 prisoners in the half-built dining hall. Most of them lived in the area or were construction workers. Only six of them went over to join the Brigade: four foremen and construction workers, plus Antonio Blanco and his son, who owned a bar at Girón Beach.

At around 1:00 a.m., one of the mechanics from Girón Beach got to the Covadonga Sugar Mill with news of the landing. The telephone operator on duty in the sugar mill's office immediately sent the message on to the Rebel Army garrison in Cienfuegos, and it, in turn, sent it to the State Security headquarters in Las Villas Province. By this and other means, news of the landing reached Point One, in the capital, just three hours after the landing had begun.

The NCO on duty woke me at around 2:00 a.m., saying that the Commander in Chief was calling me on the shortwave radio... At first, I didn't understand what he was saying very well. I realized that Fidel was asking if I had heard about what had happened. I didn't know anything at all, and I was half asleep. Then he told me they were coming, but I still didn't really understand — *what* was coming? Then, finally, I understood that there had been a landing... Fidel told me to take a vehicle. I remember perfectly clearly that he told me, "Go to Matanzas as quickly as you can and go with the men at the School to fight the landing..."

Comrade Fidel had ordered the School of Militia Leaders at Matanzas to be set up to give courses to a group of workers, especially labor leaders who had been selected, to train them as officers to head the Revolutionary National Militia... Many of those militia officers are now colonels — and some of them, generals — in the Revolutionary Armed Forces... I remember that I got to Matanzas at dawn. It was still more dark than light. At the entrance to the School, they were requisitioning all the trucks that went by on the highway, filled with the most incredible products and fruits; one was loaded with chickens...

Everybody at the School was up, and I will never forget seeing the people coming out of the dining hall holding pitchers — they had just had breakfast... The School was in good condition, and morale was high. I think it was the best combat unit in Cuba at the time. No doubt about it... I left the School to get itself organized

---

[118] Testimony of Manuel Alvariño, charcoal maker.

and went ahead… I clearly remember the people I saw: a farmer with a cow, another clearing away underbrush along the side of the road, another going to work. They didn't know what was happening…[119]

Captain José Ramón Fernández didn't know the strength of the enemy that had landed. Many of the command cadres of Brigade 2506, against whom he would soon be fighting, had been students of his. Captain Fernández had graduated from the Cadets' Academy in 1947, at the top of his class. Five years later, he completed an advanced artillery course, which he later continued at the Artillery School at Fort Sill in Oklahoma City. He then worked as a teacher at the Cadets' Academy. On March 10, 1952, however — still in uniform — he began to conspire against dictator Fulgencio Batista. Four years later, on April 3, 1956, he was arrested. Tried for the crime of conspiracy for rebellion, he was decommisioned and was sentenced to four years in prison — a sentence which was cut short by the triumph of the Revolution on January 1, 1959. Eight days later, Fidel Castro appointed him head of the Cadets' Academy.

A first-aid station had already been set up in Jagüey Grande. The people were in good spirits, and there was a lot of movement, everybody with a very good attitude, in their militia uniforms. Everybody was mobilized… This was especially so at the Australia Sugar Mill. When I got to the mill, I saw the administrator and asked him how many militia he had. "Seven." I went to the phone and reported to the Commander in Chief. I think it was 8:00 in the morning. "How are things over there?" Fidel asked me. "I don't know; I just got here," I answered. Then a rumor started going around that paratroopers had landed on both sides of the mill. People began to gather near the water tank, to the east, asking for weapons — around 200 people.[120]

The first forces began to move toward Yaguaramas and the Covadonga Sugar Mill, to the northeast and north of Girón Beach. Fidel had instructed Major Juan Almeida, head of the Central Army, whose headquarters was in Santa Clara, to move Battalion 117 to the Covadonga Sugar Mill and place it under the command of Major Filiberto Olivera Moya. Almeida instructed Major René de los Santos to attack, moving from the town of Yaguaramas toward Girón Beach.

---

[119] Testimony of José Ramón Fernández.
[120] Ibid.

"What is my mission, chief?" René de los Santos asked. "Pick up the people and keep going until you hit the beach."[121]

Shortly afterwards, Fidel ordered that a force from Cienfuegos advance to Girón Beach, passing through Juraguá. The main lines of the offensive for surrounding the beachhead were established and being implemented before dawn of April 17.

To provide a clearer idea of the area where the battle took place, here are the distances between the main points.

Australia Sugar Mill—Pálpite	25 km.
Australia Sugar Mill—Larga Beach	29 km.
Larga Beach—Girón Beach	39 km.
Australia Sugar Mill—Girón Beach	68 km.
Covadonga Sugar Mill—Girón Beach	30 km.
Covadonga Sugar Mill—San Blas	15 km.
Yaguaramas—Girón Beach	44 km.
Yaguaramas—San Blas	29 km.

Meanwhile, 88 percent of Brigade 2506's men had landed by dawn of April 17. Battalions 3, 4 and 6 had landed at Girón Beach, as had the tank company. They had seized the airport, which, to the surprise and joy of the invaders — especially the Brigade's Staff — they found to be operational. Infantry Battalion 3 was moving to the east, toward Buena Bay and Juraguá. To the north, toward the Covadonga Sugar Mill and Yaguaramas, Company A of Paratroop Battalion 1 was holding the positions assigned to it. To the west, at Larga Beach, Infantry Battalion 2 had landed. Battalion 5 was still on board the *Houston*, because the presence of Revolutionary Air Force planes had made the captain of the ship decide to spend the night farther out to sea and then return to the bay in the morning. Now, it was going back to Larga Beach, after receiving a counterorder by radio from Happy Valley, apparently issued by Colonel Jack Hawkins, the U.S. military chief. That order would prove fatal for the battalion — which was composed of recruits who had arrived at the Trax Base in the last 60 days and who, therefore, hadn't been thoroughly trained — but not for the Brigade.

The squads of 75-mm recoilless guns and 12.7-mm machine guns were under the command of Erneido Oliva, second in command of the Brigade, who was directing operations at Larga Beach. One serious difficulty, at dawn on April 17, was that Company E of Battalion 2 at Larga Beach hadn't been able to advance and seize the hamlets of Pálpite and Soplillar, due to the resistance put up by a group of militia

---

121 Testimony of René de los Santos.

at the end of the beach. The greatest danger was posed by the Cuban planes, even though the naval force was active in its antiaircraft defense.

Shortly before 6:00 a.m., the squadron of six C-46s and one C-54 passed by, heading north, to drop the paratroopers. Those planes were escorted by four B-26 bombers.

We overflew the town of Girón, heading northeast along the San Blas road. I pushed the button activating the light in the rear cabin which would alert the paratroopers to get ready for their jump. About eight miles further down the road, I spotted a jeep with three passengers. As we passed over them, they stopped and began to fire rifles and pistols at us. A few of the bullets hit the plane but did little damage. I wanted to put as much distance between them and the jeep as possible, so I decided to drop the troops a couple of miles before the planned drop site. When we reached the spot, I pushed the button that lit the green light and rang the signal bell. In less than 15 seconds all 30 men were in the air. I banked eastward, allowing the PDO's, Alberto Pérez and Chiqui Ginebra, time to pick up the static lines and hook up the new ones for unloading the supplies which we then dropped without mishap. I descended to 50 feet and headed back down the road, planning to scare off the men in the jeep. We were surprised to see it overturned and smoking, its occupants apparently dead.[122]

Down below, on another road farther to the west, a truck was heading toward Jagüey Grande. Like Eduardo Ferrer, the pilots of the B-26 that was escorting the two transport planes had excellent visibility for seeing that the passengers who were hanging on to its railings were civilians.

The plane dropped the paratroopers onto a plain just before San Isidro. Then we saw another plane that was flying very low, almost scraping the road, behind us. My father told my mother, "Tap the driver and get him to stop." Then he pushed my brother and shouted, "Throw yourself on the floor, 'cause that plane is going to land on the road." I was sitting on a crate of cans of condensed milk, holding my six-month-old nephew. Then the plane began shooting. My mother fell, wounded in the stomach and one arm. A bullet hit my grandmother in the backbone; she was crippled for life. Bullets struck my brother in a leg and an arm. I crouched

---

[122] Ferrer, *Operation Puma*, 176-7.

down, and my mother opened her eyes. I asked her if she was wounded. She raised her arm and tried to touch me but then sank back. Then my father got me out of the truck. "If you don't get my mother down, I won't go; she's alive," I said. My father had put a sheet over her, and we couldn't see the wound at her waist. That's why I thought she was still alive. Then the wind lifted the sheet, and I saw the wound. Everything was hanging out. My father put me under a tree. My brother told us, "If I die, don't leave me like you did Mama." A little later, an officer in the town militia got us out by road, and then he sent us to Jagüey Grande. Mama had already been taken there. I wanted to see her, and they took me to the funeral parlor. I kept remembering how the wind had lifted the sheet and I saw that wound. I saw my mother's insides.[123]

The truck in which Nemecia's family was traveling was a '51 Ford, with wooden and rope sides. The doors were painted blue, with INRA (National Institute of the Agrarian Reform) in yellow letters. There wasn't any possibility of mistaking it for a military vehicle.

Due to a navigational error, one of the platoons of paratroop Company B was dropped quite far from its target, near the road between Pálpite and the Australia Sugar Mill.

They dropped us far from where we were supposed to land. I had a Garand and a .45 pistol. We landed around two or three kilometers from the Australia Sugar Mill. A group of around 27 of us got together in some woods, where we left almost all the weapons, fixed so they would explode if anybody touched them. When we left the cay, we ran into the guards on a farm, who wounded one of us. We scattered. When we were captured, we admitted to a lieutenant at the Australia Sugar Mill that we had left our weapons like booby traps, and the same guy who had set the traps deactivated them.[124]

The other platoon which was supposed to seize Pálpite noted a lot of movement in the sugar mill community and two vehicles going along the road and decided to wait in the nearby woods. The two trucks were transporting 30 civilians from Jagüey Grande, whom the head of the military post had sent to Larga Beach. A little farther ahead, they were intercepted by Abraham Maciques, director of the Zapata Peninsula development plan, who told them that the invaders had

---

[123] Testimony of Nemecia Rodríguez Montalvo.
[124] Statement by Galo Astor García, invader.

seized Larga Beach and that Fidel said they mustn't let them take Pálpite. It was decided that 10 men should stay in the sugar mill community.

We took up positions behind the charcoal ovens and the sacks. A plane came by nearly at dawn. At first, we thought it was ours, but then it shot off a rocket that blew Cotilo Morejón's stand to smithereens. The plane made three passes. We began calling to the people, and, since nobody answered, I said, "They've killed everybody here." Then we saw the paratroopers drop on Sicotes. That's where the group that was going to seize Pálpite was dropped. Then they dropped a big box. In all, we counted 24 paratroopers. They remained hidden over there.[125]

The company that was dropped near the Covadonga Sugar Mill had better luck. They immediately seized the hamlets and sugar mill communities along the road toward Girón Beach and posted an advance guard at a point very close to the Covadonga Sugar Mill, but they didn't venture to advance on it.

At around 6:00 a.m., the telephone rang — the long rings that mean a long-distance call — and I picked up the receiver.

"Look, because of what's happening there, we're going to establish a direct line with Point One. The password is 'Death to the invader,' and the response, 'We will win.'" Then I heard Fidel's unmistakable voice.

"What are you?"

"Me? The telephone operator, Commander."

"But what else, dammit?"

"A militia."

"Well, what's happening there?"

"They're invading at Girón Beach. It's people in messy-looking clothes. Fidel, we need you to send some weapons here, man."

"How many of you militia are there?"

"A hundred and eighty militia at the sugar mill, but without any weapons. We need weapons."

Just then, they told me some paratroopers were landing. I told Fidel, and I went out to check. I went out of the door of the office at the sugar mill and managed to see some of them still in the air. Somebody shouted that he had counted 24 of them. I went back to the telephone and lifted the receiver.

---

[125] Testimony of Julio Somoza, a resident of Jagüey Grande.

"Death to the invader." It was Fidel.

"We will win," I answered. "Twenty-four have been dropped."

"How far away?"

"Two kilometers."

"Let's see." It seemed that he was in front of a map. "How far from the Covadonga Sugar Mill, and where?"

"Have you been to the mill?"

"Yes."

"Going out of the mill by the road to Girón Beach, at a curve where there's a windmill — there, in the clearing there; that's where they landed."

"Do you know if they're advancing or falling back?"

"I don't know. It seems they aren't advancing, because some comrades took the few rifles we had here and spread out, and they're shooting sporadically. Fidel, why don't you send us some weapons?"

"How many weapons do you have there?"

"Eleven: eight M-52 rifles, two Springfield rifles and a Brazilian carbine."

"Goddammit! With those weapons, I wouldn't let them pass. Where are your balls?'"

"Hey, man, don't say that. How can you say that, if we're asking for weapons?"

"Listen, don't give me any more of that shit about needing weapons. Arm yourselves with machetes, sticks and stones, but don't let them take the sugar mill, dammit!"

Immediately, I told the people what Fidel had said. The comrades from the Integrated Revolutionary Organizations [ORI] didn't believe that I'd really been talking with Fidel, and they came to see me. "Hey, 'Chelé,' are you sure the guy you were talking to was Fidel?" I got mad. I picked up the receiver, and Fidel was on the line.

"Death to the invader."

"We will win. Hey, Fidel, the comrades from the organizations here don't believe it's you who's giving me instructions."

"Put them on."

I heard one of the guys from ORI say, "Yes, Commander; yes, Commander; yes, Commander," and he hung up. "It's Fidel; we have to arm ourselves with machetes, and they mustn't take the sugar mill." And he went out of there like a bat out of hell.

By around 9:00 a.m., the guys from the sugar mill had armed themselves with whatever they had. There was a lot of excitement, and the people were all worked up. Some of them went to Cienfuegos to get weapons and came back. The general population was asking for weapons. The 40 or so counterrevolutionaries in the town had been rounded up and taken to Rodas.

At around 12:30 or 1:00 p.m., several trucks went by, bringing militia. I picked up the telephone.

"Point One. Death to the invader."

"We will win. Fidel, those bastards' goose is cooked."

"Why? What happened now?"

"The troops are coming."[126]

Battalion 117 had been placed under the command of Major Filiberto Olivera Moya, head of the Covadonga Front, but not all of the battalion had come. The men who reached the Covadonga Sugar Mill were from two companies and an 85-mm mortar battery. Major Filiberto Olivera instructed his troops to dislodge the enemy from the Jocuma curve, around four kilometers from the sugar mill.

Along their left flank, two companies of the battalion were advancing from Yaguaramas toward San Blas.

At Girón Beach that morning, Manuel Alvariño, who had climbed on a chair in the dining hall where the prisoners were being held, reported to the charcoal makers on the air battle that was taking place in the skies over Girón Beach:

The little plane is going over the ship. The ship exploded, and the flame almost got the little plane, that's now going upside down, straight as a die. There's smoke coming out of one of the big planes.[127]

By the afternoon, their guards were less confident.

One of them came at 1:00 p.m. and told us to stand up, because he was going to count us and bring us some lunch, but they never brought anything. The windows shattered because of the bombs the planes dropped on the ships. Then they let us go. At the edge of Girón Beach, we were taken prisoner again. "We don't have orders to let anybody go." One guy went to get instructions and came back and said it was OK. "It's a pass, that's all. They'll be back at 6 in the morning. Our password is 'Eagle,' and you should answer,

---

126 Testimony of Gonzalo Rodríguez Mantilla ("Chelé"), a worker at the Covadonga Sugar Mill.
127 Testimony of Manuel Alvariño.

'Imperial.'" Some of the mercenaries didn't agree and said, "These guys are leaving now, and they won't come back tomorrow, except with the militia."[128]

At Larga Beach, Erneido Oliva decided to hold prisoner the close to 150 civilians and the half dozen militia from Battalion 339. Suco, the head of the squad from Battalion 339 that had been guarding the radio at Larga Beach, recalled:

One of the literacy teachers had his head on my shoulder, when a mercenary walked up to him and asked, "What kind of uniform is that?" "A literacy teacher's uniform." "Are you a Communist?" "I support Fidel," the boy, who wasn't even 15 yet, answered. And the mercenary replied, "You know that everybody who supports Fidel is a Communist." "Well, then, I'm a Communist." "Mother fucker!" the mercenary said, and he walked off.

Every so often, one of them would come in and say something. One of them told me that he was going to kill us — the militia — that night, because we had killed his brother. "Gnat," a construction worker who had quite a reputation because he was always drunk but very funny, answered him. (People said the mercenaries had taken him prisoner when he was lying on the sand, sleeping off too much to drink, and he spent nearly all day waking up and going back to sleep again.) Well, "Gnat" woke up at one of those times when the mercenary was telling us that, and, thinking it was directed at him, he told a charcoal maker, "Forget it, pal; the Commander will be here soon, and that will be the end of this." We all looked at one another. That mercenary was so mad, he looked like he wanted to kill "Gnat" right there.[129]

At the Australia Sugar Mill, after checking that there weren't any paratroopers nearby, Captain José Ramón Fernández was waiting impatiently for the battalion from the Matanzas School of Militia Leaders, when Battalion 225 arrived, composed of militia from the surrounding area.[130] They had very scanty military training and were armed with M-52 rifles with just 20 cartridges each. Fernández ordered their chief to seize Pálpite. The men in the battalion set out along the road but didn't reach the sugar mill community. They ran into some of

---

[128] Testimony of Pedro Flores, charcoal maker.
[129] Testimony of José Ramón Suco, Cuban militia.
[130] The numbers of the battalions from Matanzas Province started with 2; those from Las Villas Province, with 3; and those from Havana Province, with 1.

the men from Paratroop Company B, and they deployed on the road. Because of the importance of that road and the possibility that the invaders would dynamite the culverts to block the way, Captain Fernández later assigned them the mission of protecting the road. At around 9:00 a.m., the battalion from the Matanzas School arrived.

I told them not to get out of the trucks, and I climbed up on one of the cabins. I remember I told them that the mercenaries had landed, that those who wanted to destroy the Revolution were on Cuban soil, that Fidel had given us the mission of fighting against the landing, that they constituted a trained unit and that they had possibilities. I ordered them to advance toward Pálpite... It seems that one group of mercenary paratroopers had landed somewhat spread out. The unit from the Matanzas School of Militia Leaders took Pálpite... It was around noon. The map showed a tiny landing strip at Soplillar; I immediately ordered Company 5 to advance to Soplillar, take it and place obstacles on the landing strip... Then I called Fidel and told him we had taken Pálpite, and he said, "We've already won the war." He was right. The taking of Pálpite was decisive, because it gave us access to the beachhead; it gave us a beachhead within the enemy-held territory.[131]

The platoon under Tomás Cruz, head of Company B of the Brigade's paratroop battalion, remained hiding in the woods, watching the battalion from the Militia School head for Pálpite, around 10 kilometers farther south. The other platoon that had remained on the outskirts of the sugar mill community without seizing it, scattered when the Militia School battalion arrived.

At dawn, the planes shot at Carmelo Hernández's truck, that we were traveling in. The 13 of us in my family all headed for the woods. My wife and two children, who were 6 and 8 years old, were with me. We ran into three paratroopers. "Hey, where are you going?" they asked. "They told us to get out of the village," I replied. Then, after asking if there were any militia around, they let us go, perhaps because of the picture we painted. They were going toward Girón Beach. They looked like they were running away. "Those are bad people," I told my children, "but don't say so."
    We spent all day in the woods. We saw a plane coming, and we went out to cross the road. Then we saw a truck that was coming in

131 Testimony of José Ramón Fernández.

first gear — the driver didn't know how to get it into second. We thought it was somebody we knew, but we were wrong. They were five mercenaries, paratroopers. One of them was on the hood with a machine gun that had two legs. One of the mercenaries told me, "Give me your clothes." My dad looked at him and said, "All right, we'll give them to you." But another one, who seemed to be the chief, told the one who had asked me for my clothes, "What do you want his clothes for? Let them go." They asked us again if we had seen any militia. We went back into the woods. We set up camp and mixed some cans of milk with tide pool water. It's the best thing there is. I'll never forget it; I don't know if it was my hunger that made it so good. I mixed it thicker for the two kids.[132]

Shortly after 11:00 a.m. on Monday, April 17, Captain Fernández was ordered to advance and take Larga Beach. He quickly sent a messenger to Pálpite.

All messages were delivered personally, by car, jeep or motorcycle. We didn't have any radios, telephones or anything like that... I ordered Battalion 225, from Bolondrón, to neither advance nor retreat but to guard both sides of the road from the Australia Sugar Mill to Pálpite, including all the culverts, because that road was so important. Really, I thought the invaders were going to be more aggressive, and I imagined them as groups with dynamite charges blowing places up, trying to get to our rear guard, with all the possibilities they had. I was afraid they would blow up some of those culverts and make it impossible for vehicles to get through, at least for quite some time. All that time, no reinforcements came up, and no heavy weapons. I was at the command post at the Australia Sugar Mill, which had the telephone. There were maps on the wall, and it had a swinging door. People kept coming in and going out: one person would come bringing a report, and somebody else would bring in a warning... Fidel had told me to stay by the phone at the Australia Sugar Mill.[133]

The battalion from the School of Militia Leaders, consisting of slightly under 800 men, began its advance on Larga Beach, four kilometers to the south, on foot, in two columns, on both sides of the road. It was around 2:00 p.m. They were without any antiaircraft artillery protection, because the big guns hadn't yet arrived. Soon after their

---

132 Testimony of Oscar Hernández, charcoal maker.
133 Testimony of José Ramón Fernández.

advance began, two B-26s appeared over them. After making three passes, the planes withdrew.

Claudio Argüelles was one of the first militia to be killed in that attack. Two weeks earlier, the Telephone Workers' Union, to which he belonged, had chosen him to be part of a group that would visit the Soviet Union. Even though he was taking the militia leaders' course in Matanzas, he got permission to be away for two weeks. Claudio commanded a company, and his promotion was ensured.

His flight to Europe had been scheduled for dawn of April 17. When he learned of the invasion, he took off his suit and tie, put on his militia uniform and went to Matanzas. When he reached the school, the battalion had already left for the Australia Sugar Mill. He caught up with it on the road and took command of his company.

> We were going along the road when we saw two B-26s. There was a lot of patriotic feeling. Just imagine how happy the troops felt when we went through Jagüey Grande and saw the people in the street shouting and singing revolutionary songs. They urged us, "Give them hell! Beat the shit out of them!" We were going down the road just raring to get at them. Then the planes flew overhead, and we all waved at them. They had Cuban flags painted on their tails. The second time they came by, they opened fire on us. The road had some culverts, and we dived for them. We shot at the planes with our FALs and 7.92 machine guns when they came over. When the planes came — they made several passes — we threw ourselves into the culverts, and, when they had gone by, we came out and fired. That's where they killed Claudio Argüelles. A rocket made a direct hit. They also killed Félix Edén Aguada; he was 19 years old. When they left, we regrouped and kept on advancing. We still didn't have any antiaircraft artillery, and those planes could do whatever they wanted to, but we continued our advance.[134]

The presence of those planes in the area was reported to the air base at San Antonio de los Baños, and two T-33s that were flying toward Girón Beach were alerted. One of them shot down one of the B-26s, and a Sea Fury went after the other, but the second B-26 managed to escape, protected by a U.S. Navy jet.

A dozen men from the battalion were killed or wounded. It was clear that the advance would be very difficult without air protection, and the antiaircraft artillery was still on the way. The offensive was postponed.

Brigade member Eduardo Ferrer got carried away in his version of the air attack:

> The bombers made three runs over the convoy, dropping napalm, firing rockets and strafing with deadly accuracy. The Communist casualties exceeded 500 and the road lay strewn with bodies — a scene from the Apocalypse.[135]

According to the same author, another bombing put 900 men in Battalion 123 out of action. He was so unscrupulous that he said he had taken the figure from "a report published by the enemy."

José Pérez San Román, head of the Brigade, outdid him when he reported:

> According to U.S. Government intelligence sources, 1,800 of the communist troops were killed and between 3,000 and 4,000, wounded.[136]

They have been prolific, not only in seeking scapegoats for their failure, but also in imagining legions of militia wiped out, roads covered with bodies and apocalyptic scenes. It would seem that, over the years and with tons of paper and ink, the crushing defeat they were dealt will end up competing with the most spectacular episodes of Rambo.

Total losses for the revolutionary forces during the 66 hours of the battle were 156 dead and around 500 wounded.

After the air attack, Erneido Oliva, second in command of Brigade 2506, who was directing the offensive at Larga Beach, didn't have any doubts. The revolutionary forces had every intention of forcing him off the beach. He reported the situation to San Román, and Companies 2 and 3 of Battalion 4, three tanks, the mortar squad, several bazookas and two trucks mounted with heavy machine guns were sent to him. Oliva knew that he could put all of his artillery, the tanks, the bazookas and the recoilless guns on the road that came from the Australia Sugar Mill and Pálpite. The positions he occupied were excellent for defense. The enemy would have to advance along the narrow road, and, therefore, only the vanguard could enter into

---

[135] Ferrer, *Operation Puma*, 189.
[136] José Pérez San Román, *Respuesta*, 41.

combat. He was convinced that, once he wiped out the vanguard, the others would retreat. At least, that's what military logic indicated.

In those positions, the men in Company E of the Brigade were annoyed — among other reasons, because their commanding officers hadn't even come close to the line of fire.

The situation was just the opposite in the militia's battalions. The commanding officers on the four fronts had placed themselves in front of their men during the advance. Something else also made a decisive contribution to raising the revolutionaries' morale: Fidel Castro's arrival on the scene of the battle.

He got out of a car in front of a cafeteria in Jagüey Grande and drank a cup of coffee. The people said, "This won't last long, now that Fidel's come." Then he came here, to the sugar mill. While he was going around, he came up to me and I asked, "Major, how are things going?" And he told me, "Don't worry, pal; we'll finish them off in no time."[137]

Fidel arrived between 3:00 and 4:00 p.m. He began asking me about the situation... While he was doing that, Captain Alvarez Bravo arrived with the antiaircraft artillery: one or two batteries of 85-mm guns. And the tanks were coming behind them. We went around the sugar mill, looking the place over. There are people from the area, showing good revolutionary spirit. He gave the artillerymen instructions. I told him, "Well, Commander, I want to go with my men..."

There was good morale but not much order in Pálpite. The artillery arrived, and I began to discuss where to position the guns, on the other side of the hamlet. It had been laid waste. I'll never forget it: on the left side of the road, going from the Australia Sugar Mill toward Larga Beach, there was a house that had been burned. The only thing that was left was the framework of an iron bed...

I was seeing to the preparations for the offensive. It was nearly dark, and then Fidel and some others drove up. Every eight or nine or ten minutes, an enemy grenade would fall there... It wasn't heavy fire from batteries of artillery, but they were falling. I began discussing things with Fidel. After a while, he chose Major Borges, the dentist, to take Battalion 111, enter Soplillar and go to San

---

[137] Testimony of Dámaso Rodríguez Valdés, general secretary of the labor union at the Australia Sugar Mill.

Blas...[138] We decided to attack Larga Beach at midnight. Meanwhile, we decided to organize the artillery fire. Fidel stayed there around 40 minutes; I think it was less than an hour — we all put a lot of pressure on him to leave, for his safety.[139]

At dusk on Monday, April 17, Battalion 326 — composed of workers, students and farmers from the region — advanced along the coast from Cienfuegos toward Girón Beach, as carefully as possible for a combat unit. It was commanded by Captain Orlando Pupo, and Fidel had ordered it to move up to within a few kilometers of Girón Beach and halt there.

There were close to 400 men in the battalion. Almeida reinforced us with a squad of men from the Rebel Army armed with bazookas. We didn't have any mortars. Our convoy, which consisted of over 10 trucks, went from Cienfuegos to the railroad junction to Abreus. From there, we went down to the Constancia Sugar Mill, arriving at nightfall. We went on farther south, trying to reach the coast. We passed Las Charcas and Juraguá. From there, going along karren paths, we slowly approached Girón Beach from the east, a direction they didn't expect us to come from.[140]

By dusk of April 17, the revolutionary forces, both north of Larga Beach and at Girón Beach — without artillery, heavy weapons or aviation — had managed to push the paratroopers south out of their advanced positions, thus reducing the size of the beachhead. Near the Covadonga Sugar Mill, two companies from Battalion 117, supported by soldiers and civilians who decided to join the troops, forced the vanguard of the paratroopers' battalion out of their positions at the Jocuma curve. The invaders retreated to a point called Muñoz's Channel, where they dug in after being reinforced. From then on, to continue advancing, the militia would have to traverse six kilometers of narrow road with swamp on both sides — which meant that they wouldn't be able to leave it. Filiberto Olivera Moya harassed the Brigade's forces with mortar fire during the night, and, at dawn, he sent out a group of scouts.

---

[138] This meant traversing the swamp along the northern border of the beachhead from west to east, a distance of around 40 kilometers, skirting that area and coming out at the farthest point reached by the paratroopers' battalion, in San Blas.

[139] Testimony of José Ramón Fernández.

[140] Miguel Angel Sánchez, *Girón no fue sólo en abril*, 189. Testimony of Orlando Pupo, now a colonel.

On the Yaguaramas front, east of the Covadonga Sugar Mill, the paratroopers had retreated at midday. Captain Víctor Dreke, who had been driving toward the landing area since early in the morning, was now marching in the vanguard of the two companies from Battalion 117 that were advancing along the road toward San Blas. When night fell, he halted the advance. Soon afterwards, he received important reinforcements: Battalion 113. With the arrival of that force, for the first time since dawn, Major René de los Santos, who was in charge of that area of the fighting, had a strong enough force for advancing in such difficult circumstances.

An important battle would take place early that morning on the western flank, near the Australia Sugar Mill, Pálpite and Larga Beach.

At the Australia Sugar Mill, shortly after dawn, Fidel was told that another landing was taking place in the northwestern part of Havana Province. He doubted that the report was true, but, on being assured that it was, decided to go back to the capital. He wasn't happy about leaving the scene of the fighting, but he decided to confront the invading Brigade at that other point of debarkation.

Fidel Castro had displayed impressive energy ever since his first steps in the revolutionary struggle. On one occasion, Charles de Gaulle was faced with an uprising by a group of generals in Algiers who opposed his policy of negotiating with the Algerian FLN. On being informed that General Challé, the main conspirator, would be in Paris at any moment with his paratroopers, de Gaulle replied, "Yes, if he were Fidel Castro, he would be here already; but not Challé."[141]

In fact, there was no second landing. It was a CIA scam. Ships approached the coast and, with very sophisticated means — sounds and lights which included explosions of different calibers — simulated a full-scale landing. It didn't divert any of the forces that were already committed in the Zapata Swamp, but it did draw Fidel Castro away from the combat area.

At midnight, the battalion from the School of Militia Leaders formed ranks on the Pálpite road. The men would march on the enemy in the first echelon, followed by Column 1 of the Rebel Army.

Company 3, under the command of Lieutenant Díaz, was the first to advance. Captain Fernández himself told the troops in Pálpite, "Left, left, and straight ahead until you clash with the enemy; march!" We began to advance along the left side of the road. We had been told that Larga Beach and the enemy were four kilometers away. After a while, word was passed quietly back:

---

[141] Nicolai Molchanov, *General De Gaulle*, 346.

"Drop everything that reflects light or makes a noise." The mortar shells passed above us toward the enemy's positions. Later, we learned that nearly all of them fell into the sea.[142]

Battalion 2 of Brigade 2506 had an exceptionally advantageous situation. Its positions were in the form of an inverted pyramid, so it could open fire after the column of militia was inside its flank. Oliva concentrated five men with bazookas on the left flank of his position. From the angle where they were placed, they had a great advantage over any tank that might appear. The road was clear up to there. He placed the recoilless 75-mm guns on a hill of earth, with one of the tanks, well camouflaged, near them. He gave instructions to the mortar and heavy machine gun crews and placed the infantrymen so they would be ready to open fire. To reach his positions, the militia would have to advance along a narrow front — slightly over 200 meters across.

On the other side, the road from Pálpite to Larga Beach was so straight that, by adjusting the sights on their weapons, the Brigade's members would batter the revolutionary forces that were advancing along the road some one or two kilometers back, and the revolutionaries wouldn't be able to do anything about it, because their advance had to be made in a long column. Thus, if the fire didn't hit the vanguard, it would get those in the center or the rear guard. Which is what happened.

Captain Fernández had ordered the artillery to stop firing, and four tanks came out of the woods and, with their lights off, began to advance. Meanwhile, at the curve, Oliva ordered his men to open fire.

When they began shooting, we threw ourselves in the ditch. They had set up their .50-caliber machine guns nine inches from the ground. That's why many comrades were wounded in the back and buttocks. Others were killed by that low fire.[143]

Benito Garay had asked me that afternoon, "Héctor, do you think I'll be able to see my baby?" His wife was nine months pregnant. That night, while he was advancing toward Larga Beach, a bazooka shell hit him. When we got back to the School several days later, I saw the telegram that his wife had given birth to a little girl.[144]

---

[142] Testimony of Emérito Hernández, Cuban militia.
[143] Ibid.
[144] Testimony of Héctor Argilés.

When the tanks caught up with the vanguard, Lieutenant Díaz ordered his men to fall in behind them and continue their advance. They had already entered the narrow strip of land which led straight to the enemy trenches. Dozens of dead and wounded remained behind them.

Oliva ordered the 75-mm artillerymen to open fire on the tanks that were approaching.

Lieutenant Néstor López Cuba, who was commanding the tanks and was in the first one, saw the red lights of the projectiles coming from far away. He was in exactly the same place where, 24 hours earlier, the militia of Battalion 339 had gone into battle against Company E.

We were just entering that barren area when the tank began to turn to the right. I thought it was the sandy edge of the ditch and told the driver to put on more power, to get us out of the dip. But, the more we tried, the more we turned toward that side. I finally realized that they had hit one of the treads. I ordered a fragmentation shell to be loaded. We also had perforating shells, but I didn't see any of their tanks, so, to shoot at infantry, I asked for a fragmentation shell. We tried to put it in the muzzle, but it wouldn't go in.[145]

Not only had the tank been hit in the tread, but a bazooka shell had also entered the muzzle of its gun. If they had managed to put the shell in the muzzle, the tank would have been blown to bits.

Lieutenant Díaz advanced behind a tank and, when it was put out of action, continued to encourage his men, shouting, "Forward! I've never commanded troops with more guts than you guys." A little later, he was hit and died.[146]

In the midst of that darkness, with fire along our flanks, the men got confused and didn't know where the vanguard was, or the platoons, or anything. The officers lost contact with their men. Each one of us advanced with a small group around him, but those groups weren't units or anything like that. In that difficult situation, the worst one I can remember in a battle, they began to bombard us with white phosphorus. The little fires that broke out

---

[145] Miguel Angel Sánchez, *Girón no fue sólo en abril*. Testimony of Lieutenant Néstor López Cuba, now a major general.
[146] Testimony of Emérito Hernández.

in the woods lit up our positions and made us easy targets for the sniper hiding in ambush.[147]

Soon afterwards, two more tanks were put out of action, and orders were given to halt the offensive. The men began to return to Pálpite.

Captain Fernández sent an urgent message informing Fidel Castro that the offensive was halted and that he didn't know how many dead and wounded there were. Fidel immediately sent Fernández new instructions. Major Augusto Martínez Sánchez — who remained at the command post at the Australia Sugar Mill, in telephone communication with Point One, where Fidel spent the dawn of April 18 — drew up the order:

4:40 a.m.
From Augusto to Fernández

Fidel received your message and told me to give you the following instructions:

1. Position all of the antiaircraft batteries to protect our people.

2. Have the tanks maintain the attack and position the field artillery pieces [122-mm howitzers] again.

3. Make sure you install every single antiaircraft gun.

4. He recommends that you send a unit from either Battalion 180 or Battalion 144 to advance through Soplillar and out to Rosario Cove, to cut the road and thus split the enemy in two.

5. If necessary, the 10 tanks that are about to arrive from Jovellanos can be sent to you.

6. You can divide those 10 tanks into two groups, to advance along the road and from Buena Ventura.

7. If it is necessary to move the tanks during the day, powerful antiaircraft protection can be sent to you.

8. Lastly, Fidel says that Larga Beach has to be taken — no excuses.

Augusto[148]

Several aspects of that order stand out. Fidel Castro had just been informed that the offensive had been halted on that front. He immediately issued new instructions to renew it, this time calling for an encircling movement with several tanks driven through the woods

---

[147] Testimony of Harold Ferrer, now a brigadier general.
[148] Archives of the Cuban Ministry of the Revolutionary Armed Forces. Girón documents.

to the sugar mill community of Buena Ventura so they could then turn and attack the enemy positions from the left flank while, simultaneously, the attack was renewed along the road, and sending a battalion to cut off the invaders' retreat toward Girón Beach. Battalion 144 carried out that mission, but, when it reached its destination (Rosario Cove), near Larga Beach, on the road to Girón Beach, Battalion 2 and the reinforcements had already gone by. Battalion 144 had delayed in leaving Pálpite because the guide had gotten cold feet.

Fidel always criticized the fact that those troops escaped, but the battalion that was to carry out that mission spent about an hour in the trucks waiting for the guide, who had disappeared. Finally, it left for Rosario Cove without the guide, and it got there.[149]

The militia and soldiers in Pálpite thought that their withdrawal meant defeat, but they were wrong. They had exhibited so much courage in their advance that, even though the invaders held strong positions, they were still worried.

One of their tanks came back with some dead and wounded. The wounded had to be taken to Girón Beach, because there were no doctors. Those who had fought and were relieved spoke badly of the officers. At that point, they brought in one of our tank drivers, whom they had taken prisoner. One of the mercenaries' officers questioned him in front of us: "Were you driving a tank?" "Yes, sir." "And are more tanks coming?" "There's a battalion of 100 tanks on the way, and around 10,000 militia."[150]

The tank driver's information was false, but it added to other worries that filled Erneido Oliva's mind. At 5:00 on the morning of April 18, he reported to the head of the Brigade that his situation was desperate. An hour later, a messenger brought the reply: "Hold out as long as you can." In spite of the reinforcements and the good positions he occupied, Oliva didn't feel secure. He established contact with Montero Duque, the head of Battalion 5, who — after the ship which was bringing his troops had been attacked with rockets — had managed to swim ashore and regroup nearly all the men of his battalion. They were around five kilometers along the coast from Larga Beach, separated from it by the sugar mill community of Buena Ventura, which was defended by only a dozen militia from Battalion

---

149 Testimony of José Ramón Fernández.
150 Testimony of José Ramón Suco.

339 who had become separated from their troop and some charcoal makers who lived in the area. A boat belonging to the Cuban Revolutionary Navy was tied up at the small dock at Buena Ventura, a few hundred meters from Larga Beach. Its crew had dismantled the .50-caliber machine gun it carried and had placed it on land. During the early morning hours of the landing, they had used up the little ammunition it had. There wasn't any serious impediment that could stop that battalion, once it had been reorganized, from heading for Larga Beach.

Years later, one of the members of Battalion 5 wrote an article in which he stated that they marched toward Larga Beach in spite of the difficulties, but that a troop of militia had taken possession of Buena Ventura, which kept them from carrying out their mission.

> By around midday, we were very close to the town of Buena Ventura, and Montero immediately ordered us to halt and demanded that there be complete silence. He organized a patrol of five men under the command of Portuondo — a courageous, determined veteran from the Trax Base. The rest of the men — mainly those who were armed — took up positions, ready to confront the militia, who should be entrenched *up on the hill...* because we held a place lower down on that *hill*, with the sea to the right and the swamps to the left; but we couldn't hope for more; we had to get through, no matter what the cost...[151]

González Lalondry twisted history so much he even changed the terrain. The town of Buena Ventura and all the surrounding land lies at sea level, except for some bits that are *below* sea level.

At Larga Beach, Oliva didn't think twice. Another attack like that of the morning, and his men wouldn't hold out. The day before, between 40 and 50 of his men had been wounded, and around 15 had been killed.[152] Something that took place at that time showed the state of morale of the Larga Beach invaders. The man questioning Eric Fernández del Valle, an invader who was captured by militia, reported:

> Fernández claims that when the mercenary Oliva, second in command of the Brigade, had finished interrogating a wounded militia who had been taken prisoner, trying to obtain information

---

[151] Julio González Lalondry, *Sangre en Bahía de Cochinos*, 54 (Author's emphasis).
[152] According to a report which Oliva showed to Peter Wyden, author of *Bay of Pigs: The Untold Story*.

from him about the size of the Cuban forces that were fighting, and Oliva walked away, Pedro González, Oliva's aide, caught up with him. [Fernández doesn't know anything about González's background, but we have learned that he was a member of the Bureau of Investigation in Batista's police.] González asked Oliva for permission to finish off the wounded prisoner, alleging that he would slow them down. Oliva didn't object to the request, leaving Pedro González to decide for himself. González immediately went over to the wounded prisoner and shot him dead with his pistol. Eric Fernández declares that he witnessed all this and that he was so disgusted by it that he protested to Oliva, who tried to calm him down, saying that he had instructions to abandon his position. This made Pedro González so mad he threatened Fernández, saying he would kill him with his machine gun.

At around 6:00 a.m., there was movement. The trucks filled with mercenaries fled, wheels spinning in the sand. They were in a hurry to leave. That's when we heard planes. We didn't know whose they were, and the people brought a white sheet and put it on the ground, weighted down with stones. Shortly afterwards, we left with that same sheet, heading for the railway junction. A lot of people had been killed there.[153]

At around 7:00, the vanguard of Battalion 180, headed by Lieutenant Jacinto Vázquez de la Garza, its commanding officer (who was in the first graduating class of the Matanzas School of Militia Leaders), approached the railway junction, where the fighting had been very fierce early that morning.

I found a scene that could have come straight out of Dante: our dead and wounded. The mercenaries had everything they needed for holding out: a narrow road that didn't offer any cover for us but where they were very well protected on a slight curve in a hollow; burned thatched-roof huts; a truck which had also been burned; and, along with it, several dead, including a woman. Seeing that dead woman made me very indignant... There was a hole with a .50-caliber machine gun in it and several dead mercenaries behind it. Lieutenant Díaz, a teacher from the Matanzas School, lay dead a few meters from the parapet, and several other comrades from the school lay on the parapet itself... In spite of the narrowness of the

---

153 Testimony of José Ramón Suco. Eric Fernández del Valle rose to the rank of lieutenant colonel in the U.S. Army. Some U.S. investigators have mentioned Pedro González Fernández as having been linked to the plot against President Kennedy.

road and the .50-caliber machine gun, they had managed to get that far! ...Since then, I have often thought of the heroism displayed by the fighters from the second graduating class of the School of Militia Leaders. They made the mercenaries at Larga Beach lose all hope of winning the war.[154]

One of the arguments used in the United States to explain why Battalion 2 withdrew and the invaders were defeated is that they ran out of ammunition. It is clear that the Brigade ran into difficulties with matériél, mainly because of the flight of the *Caribe* and *Atlantic* and the sinking of the *Río Escondido*. Moreover, the *Houston* had been put out of action, but that didn't disable the Brigade. Battalion 2, at Larga Beach, was supplied and reinforced on Monday, April 17.

Captain Hugo Sueiro, head of the battalion, which came to have 370 men when the reinforcements from Captain Bacallao's Battalion 4 were added, repulsed one enemy attack and counterattack after another. These forces, supported at first by one tank and then by three, plus 60- and 81-mm mortars, wiped out Castro's Battalion 339... Two of the Brigade's B-26s fought in support of Sueiro and his courageous men, but were shot down after causing innumerable losses.[155]

In addition, the Brigade was supplied by air during the three days of the fighting.

In the afternoon, three C-54 transports were prepared to carry urgently needed supplies to the beaches at Girón... Approaching Girón Airport, we began the drop as scheduled. We later learned that half of the weapons had fallen into the sea. Fortunately, some had been recovered by members of the Brigade. The rest did land in the vicinity of the airfield... Captain Manuel Navarro took off in a C-46 immediately after Goodwin and Herrera... They were to land at Girón and deliver 8,500 pounds of ammunition. Just before sunrise, Navarro had completed his mission. After unloading the plane, he picked up the injured Matías Farías, who had been shot down two days earlier.[156]

---

[154] Quintín Pino Machado, *La batalla de Girón*. Testimony of Jacinto Vázquez de la Garza, head of Battalion 180.

[155] José Pérez San Román, *Respuesta*, 24.

[156] Eduardo Ferrer, *Operation Puma*, 209-14. Ferrer's description doesn't include the drops from the two other C-54s, which took off with the same mission.

Three days after the battle was over, Cuban State Security in Las Villas Province drew up a report on the weapons and ammunition seized from the invaders. Some of the figures are eloquent: 672 shells for 75-mm cannon, 183 for 81-mm mortars, 413 fragmentation hand grenades, 464 bazooka rockets, 416 shells for 60-mm mortars and 130,005 bullets for .30-caliber guns.[157]

After taking possession of the beach, Captain Fernández sent an urgent note to the Australia Sugar Mill:

> Major Augusto:
>
> 1. The enemy withdrew from Larga Beach, which our troops are occupying. The enemy moved toward Girón Beach.
> 2. I am moving antiaircraft and field artillery to Larga Beach, preparing to attack Girón Beach.
> 3. I hope to be able to attack during the day...

At the first light of dawn, the revolutionary troops began to advance toward the Covadonga Sugar Mill. It was the most dangerous stretch of the road, for there was nothing but swamp on both sides. This gave the battalion of paratroopers, who had been reinforced with field artillery, an added advantage. They began to bombard the road with mortars. As Arteaga, a Cuban militia, recalled:

> I had the bazooka, my U.S. bazooka, plus an M-3 that I had picked up on the way... I carried all that stuff: a knapsack, the bazooka and the M-3. I looked like a circus act, walking down the road... Then I heard a mortar shell whistle by on my left. The damn thing whistled by on my left, and then another went by on my right. I turned and saw the devastation. The mortar shell had fallen in the middle of a group. Three men were on the ground. I knew all three. Enrique was one. There was a hole right through him from the waist down. When I saw him like that, I said, "Enrique, what happened to you?" "Dammit, they've ruined me." The other two were even more seriously wounded.[158]

The advance didn't halt, and mortar shells from the revolutionary troops also fell on the defenses of the battalion of paratroopers. Nestor Pino, second in command of Company A, who was on the front line, radioed Alejandro del Valle, his chief, asking for support from heavier

---

[157] Archives of the Cuban Revolutionary Armed Forces. Girón collection.
[158] Quintín Pino Machado, *La batalla de Girón*, 119-20.

weapons to hold back the advance. San Román received the report at around 11:00 a.m. Shortly afterwards, Battalion 3, which was on the right flank of the Brigade (east of Girón Beach), received orders to move toward San Blas and place itself under the command of the head of the paratroopers. This unit's positions were occupied by several smaller units from Battalion 4 and a tank, all from the reserves.

Members of Battalion 6, supported by several tanks, were placed between Girón Beach and Larga Beach. Battalion 2 was moved to the reserves.

From the truck on which he was leaving Larga Beach, José Ramón Pérez Peña had seen the group of farmers with a piece of white cloth who were walking in search of militia. When he reached Girón Beach, he asked if there were any farmers there. He was told that they had been released on the afternoon of the day before, with orders to present themselves at 6:00 the following morning. "Where are they?"

"None of them came back," was the reply. "We have only five communist teachers in a cabaña."

Ana María Hernández, who was in charge of the literacy teachers at the beach, and Valerio Rodríguez, Patria Silva, Yoyi and Gerardo, the literacy teachers, were in the cabaña, guarded by Antonio Blanco, the son of the owner of the bar at Girón Beach. Antonio and his father had joined the invaders. Tony was wearing a camouflage outfit. The Brigade members could recognize him through the window, which may be why he avoided talking with the prisoners.

There were a substantial number of mercenaries around the cabaña. We could hear the sound of cannon in the distance, and our captors looked nervous. They put a tank in front of our cabaña, and it scared us. "Let's write our names and where we're from, so we can be identified if they kill us," Patria Silva proposed. Each one of us wrote that information on a piece of paper, and we put the papers in our pockets. I did it, too.[159]

East of Girón Beach, near Buena Bay, the charcoal maker Manuel Alvariño and one of his sons heard voices. They scouted and saw it was militia.

I told Captain Pupo about the weapons I had seen at Girón Beach when I was a prisoner of the mercenaries, but I didn't know what they were called. I told him, "Look, there are bulldozers with five

---

wheels on each side, without tires — with treads like tractors — and each one has a big tube with a club on the end."

"Those are tanks," he told me.

"Some of them have knapsacks on their shoulders with long tails."

"They're for communications. I wish I had one," the captain said.

"There are other tubes that are in two pieces that they put together and put on their shoulders."

"Those are bazookas."

Then we went along the path to my farm. My family was there.[160]

When Pupo came to the house, he told me, "Take this pound of coffee beans and make coffee for the troops." But I put in detergent instead of sugar. It made a lot of foam. When the captain saw it, he said, "What have you done?" and I burst into tears. He hugged me, but I kept on crying. Then he told me, "Don't cry. You've done very well, considering your age and what you've been through. We'll strain it, and then, when the foam's gone, we'll drink it."[161]

A little later, Battalion 326 resumed its advance toward Girón Beach. Fidel had instructed Captain Pupo to remain around four kilometers from Girón Beach and to dig in without making any noise. Fidel was sure that, once defeated, the invaders would try to retreat in that direction, thinking there wouldn't be any troops there.

That Tuesday morning, part of the Brigade's staff managed to meet at the command post. Manuel Artime, Erneido Oliva and Ramón J. Ferrer (chief of staff) were there. San Román presided. They had exchanged information about the situation on the battle fronts and Oliva had reported on the advance of revolutionary forces from Larga Beach. Oliva suggested that all the forces meet at Girón Beach, force their way eastward along the coastal road toward Cienfuegos and then head for the Escambray Mountains.

As San Román later recalled:

I told Oliva that it was a very long way and that it was natural that they would attack us from Cienfuegos, a city which was too large and important for it not to have a strong enemy concentration

---

160 Testimony of Manuel Alvariño.
161 Testimony of Xiomara Alvariño, daughter of a charcoal maker.

there... I was sure we would get support soon. I was convinced of that...[162]

Two weeks later, sitting on the floor of my cell, Fidel Castro and I discussed that point of tactics. Smiling, he told me that my decision had been correct, but added, "I was ready to knock the stuffing out of you."[163]

On the Larga Beach side of Girón Beach, the invaders who occupied the defenses understood that if something didn't happen pretty soon, they would be going into combat. During the early morning hours, vehicles had gone by carrying their dead and wounded, and, at dawn, the invaders had seen the arrival of a caravan with close to 400 men, tanks, mortars, cannon and armored trucks, which had withdrawn from Larga Beach. They remained alert all day, never taking their eyes from the road. When dusk began to fall, they started to get nervous, for they knew that the militia's strongest attack had taken place at night.

Twenty kilometers away, a dozen Leyland city buses were moving quickly toward Girón Beach. The commanding officers, under Captain Fernández, knew that there weren't any enemy troops along that stretch of road. They themselves had proved that an hour earlier. The orders they had were to advance around 20 kilometers, which was approximately the length of the highway that had just been explored, and then stop the buses and continue forward on foot until they made contact with the enemy.

Inside the buses, the militia of Battalion 123 gripped their FAL rifles while looking at the woods or the sea. The battalion was composed of men of all ages and professions — except the military: masons, carpenters, schoolteachers, sales clerks, shopkeepers, dock workers, bank and office employees, telephone company workers, musicians, artists, writers, witch doctors, surveyors, doctors, architects, house painters and others. They were from the capital. Very few liked military life. Each had donned a uniform and carried a weapon for the same reasons that had led 300,000 other Cubans to join the Revolutionary National Militia.

Perhaps because of their lack of combat skills, they didn't pay much attention to the formation of three planes painted with the colors of the Cuban flag which came overhead. Suddenly, a hail of missiles and .50-caliber bullets began to fall on the buses. The drivers stepped on the brakes while, horrified, watching the windshields shatter into

---

[162] Johnson, *The Bay of Pigs,* 142. Testimony of José Pérez San Román.
[163] José Pérez San Román, *Respuesta,* 51.

pieces and bullets pierce the buses. Inside, the trapped militia struggled to get out.

Captain José Ramón Fernández described the scene as follows:

> I was told that our planes were going to attack the mercenaries at Girón Beach. I decided to send the buses so the infantry could advance more quickly. It was impossible by foot: it's 39 kilometers between Larga and Girón Beaches. It would have taken at least eight or nine hours to cover the distance, walking — if the men didn't encounter the enemy and kept up a good pace... When my officers saw the planes, they ordered the bus drivers to continue, because they knew our planes were going to attack Girón Beach at 3:00 and believed them to be our planes.[164]

Once again, a gross violation of the rules of war wrought havoc in the ranks of the Cuban fighters.

> We got out of the buses as best we could, some heading for the coast and others, for the woods... They surprised us in the middle of the road, without any weapons with which to shoot at them. The artillery was behind us.[165]

After their second pass, the B-26s began to drop napalm.

> I didn't know anything about napalm... We thought it was an expansion bomb, and what I had read had made me think we should throw ourselves as close as possible to minimize the effect. But it was a napalm bomb, and it enveloped us in flames. I covered my face with my rifle and hands... The napalm didn't go out. Those who were burning threw themselves into the water or writhed on the ground, but the napalm didn't go out; when a little breeze blew up, the flames were rekindled.[166]

The squadron of planes that attacked the buses had taken off from Happy Valley at 2:00 p.m. and was composed of six B-26s. Near the Bay of Pigs, three of them headed for San Blas, north of Girón Beach, to support the forces that were fighting there. The other three turned to the left, over the road to Larga Beach. Two of the pilots were U.S. citizens — Billy Goodwin ("Seig Simpson") and another trainer, who

---

[164] Testimony of José Ramón Fernández.
[165] Testimony of Humberto Valdés, Cuban militia.
[166] Ibid.

went by the name of "Doug". Each plane had taken off with a full load of missiles and machine-gun bullets. They had also been supplied with 6,000 pounds of napalm bombs. When the U.S. pilots returned to their base, they told of the success of their mission. They felt euphoric. Some of them believed that they were repeating scenes from the Korean War. The next morning, four other U.S. pilots would fly toward the Bay of Pigs. None of them returned.

There was a lot of commotion in the town of Jagüey Grande. Battalion 123 had lost nearly 100 men — dead, wounded and those hurt in the napalm attack.

As Caridad González, who lived in the town, recalled:

> It was a very difficult time; they didn't want to lie down, because of their burns. We spread an unguent on all their burns. Later, they were taken to Colón, Jovellanos and Matanzas. The women went with them, to care for those who had transfusions.[167]

Carmen Cavadilla admitted, "I cried because I thought they were losing and the mercenaries would soon be in Jagüey."[168]

Bambi Martínez Díaz was another of the many townspeople who helped the wounded.

> They brought in a mercenary who was wounded in the hand. He was the son of García Serra. He had a medal of Our Lady of Cobre. When I took him some juice, I asked him, "How can you, a man who believes in a saint, come to kill your brothers?" "Nobody told me it would be like this. I came because of this saint." "No, you came to kill." That man hugged me. If he is still alive and is honest, he'll remember that day.[169]

That invader couldn't believe his eyes. Nobody welcomed him in the town, but, even so, they treated his injuries. The town of Jagüey Grande didn't have the facilities for handling so many wounded and evacuees, but its residents had been doing their best ever since dawn of the landing day.

At 6:30 a.m. on April 17, a truck with a loudspeaker drove through the town asking for volunteer blood donors, because the first of the wounded had already come in. It also asked for supplies with which to improvise new hospital wards, since the only ward the town had, with

---

[167] Testimony of Caridad González, a resident of Jagüey Grande.
[168] Testimony of Carmen Cavadilla, a resident of Jagüey Grande.
[169] Testimony of Bambi Martínez Díaz, a resident of Jagüey Grande.

just 10 beds, wasn't large enough. The people's response left no doubt about their massive support for the Revolution. They brought mattresses, sheets, pillowcases and beds to the truck. The operation was repeated several times during the first day of the fighting; by the morning of the second day, the people of Jagüey Grande had set up eight hospitals, with around 600 beds.

When the bloody bedding began to pile up, a woman from the town picked up a bundle and took it home. Carmen Cavadilla recalled:

I called on my neighbors. We took two rails from the railroad and six big cans and set them up as washtubs. We needed wood for boiling the bedding, so José Luis, my youngest son, who was 8, and some of his friends went and brought us wood. We spent five days boiling, washing and ironing nonstop, but the wounded always had enough clean bedding.

Close to 1,000 swamp dwellers, who had been evacuated from the area of the fighting, began to crowd the town hall. They had been wounded, had lost a friend or relative or had lost their homes or belongings. Somebody from the town said, "I'll take one family home with me." That was all it took for others to do the same. It is estimated that around 800 of the close to 1,000 evacuees were taken to private homes. The rest were put up in public buildings, including the church, which opened its doors.

Eleven community kitchens were organized spontaneously. Practically all of the families gave some of their food for the fighters and the wounded.

As Captain Fernández recalled:

After the attack by the enemy planes, I reorganized Battalion 123 on the spot and ordered its members to advance. By the next morning, they got to around five kilometers from Girón Beach; I then ordered them to turn north, go into the woods and form columns of platoons — there were around 30 platoons — to hold back the mercenaries whom I knew were going to flee. I didn't have any doubts about that. That battalion recovered very quickly from the blow dealt it by the planes. After the attack, I continued advancing and reached Perdiz Point[170] without making contact with the enemy... The police battalion arrived... The offensive for the next day was organized.

---

[170] Eleven kilometers from Girón Beach. Author's note.

2100 hours
Major Augusto

1. I am thinking of advancing until we make contact with the enemy at Girón Beach. I think our lines can get to within two or three kilometers of Girón Beach.
2. I am putting 122-mm guns and the mortars in position. I beg you send me two more 120-mm mortar batteries now, so I can use them. With all that, I'll fire on the enemy during the night.
3. I am planning to attack with artillery, infantry and tanks and advance with the infantry on Girón Beach at dawn.
4. In view of experience, I am thinking of the need for a crane to move tanks that are hit. Urgently request tank treads from Managua.

Fernández[171]

At the Covadonga Sugar Mill-San Blas-Girón Beach headquarters on the afternoon of that day, Tuesday, April 18, Néstor Pino, a former officer in Batista's army and now head of one of the companies of paratroopers, asked Alejandro del Valle, head of the battalion, for heavy arms support to contain the advance of the revolutionary forces. One reinforcement in heavy machine guns and 81-mm mortars was sent to La Ceiba, near San Blas, a sugar mill community which was still held by the Brigade. The fighting there was very heavy.
Major Félix Duque recalled the fighting there as follows:

At a curve in the road that we identified as La Ceiba, we found a pocket of resistance which had much more firepower than the one at Muñoz's Channel... There, we suffered heavier losses than we had been dealt before... We made three attempts to take San Blas, two of which failed.[172]

At midday on Tuesday, April 18, Major Pedro Miret arrived at the Covadonga Sugar Mill at the head of several batteries of 122-mm guns.

He asked me, "Do you have an aspirin?" I gave him one and made him something to drink. "Hey, where can we find a room for using some maps?"... Then one of the men who had come with Miret took off his shoes and climbed on the desk with a drawing triangle

---

[171] Testimony of José Ramón Fernández.
[172] Elio Carré, *Girón, una estocada a fondo*. Testimony of Félix Duque.

and made measurements and drew lines and talked to the other man who had come with him.

"Pedrito, what are those guys doing?"

"They're taking the points of reference for emplacing a weapon that's never been used here before: 122-mm guns."

Then Major Filiberto Olivera arrived, and Pedrito asked him, "Filiberto, when can you withdraw the infantry?"

I said, "Shit, they're going to withdraw!" When Filiberto left, I asked Miret, "Pedrito, why are you going to withdraw the troops?"

"Look, you're a militia, but you haven't ever studied war tactics. We have the infantry right on top of the enemy, and we're going to fire with a powerful weapon — the 122-mm guns — and we might hit some of our own troops with it."

"Ah, I understand now!"[173]

During the night, the batteries of guns fired on the Brigade's positions at Bermeja, Helechal, Cayo Ramona and San Blas.

By the end of Tuesday, April 18, the second day of the fighting, the Brigade's beachhead had been considerably reduced. To the west, after having occupied Larga Beach, the revolutionary troops had advanced southeastward 30 kilometers in spite of the air attack and were at Perdiz Point, 11 kilometers from Girón Beach. The invaders' Battalion 5 had become permanently separated from the rest of the Brigade, and its members remained in hiding at Cazones Point, near where the *Houston* had run aground. Nearly all of them surrendered without putting up any resistance.

To the north, the battalion of paratroopers had retreated to San Blas, where it was attacked with 122-mm guns. The revolutionary forces had crossed the swampy areas near Yaguaramas and the Covadonga Sugar Mill and were preparing to attack San Blas, 15 kilometers from Girón Beach.

To the east, along the coastal road, on the Brigade's right flank, a battalion of militia lay in wait for the Brigade to retreat or be put to rout.

Everything was ready for winding up the battle the next day, within 72 hours of the landing. For the first time, the militia and soldiers of the Rebel Army would have equipment similar to that of the Brigade — tanks, mortars, cannon, heavy machine guns and antiaircraft artillery — on the two main battle fronts: from Larga Beach to Girón Beach and from the Covadonga Sugar Mill to Yaguaramas, San Blas and Girón Beach. However, the revolutionary forces didn't

---

173 Testimony of Gonzalo Rodríguez Mantilla ("Chelé").

yet have one very important thing in the war: means of communication. Their warnings, orders, reports and requests continued to be sent personally, using any vehicle that was available.

At dawn on April 19, the revolutionary forces began advancing on the battle fronts. Major Félix Duque headed the troops at the Covadonga Sugar Mill, and heavy howitzer fire soon began to fall on them. As Víctor Casaus described it:

> They were giving us heavy punishment. I was flat on the ground close to "The Galician" [José Ramón Fernández], whom I had known from Civic Square. We were together, and the enemy was beating the hell out of us; we couldn't even stick our heads up. Mortar shells kept whistling past, above us.[174]

Battalion 3, supported by two tanks, began a counteroffensive to stop the militia troops' advance and halted it for a few moments. After a short attack by the 122-mm guns, the militia continued their advance, and the members of Battalion 3 took to their heels. Alejandro del Valle removed Noelio Montero, the head of that battalion, and replaced him with Roberto San Román. As one of the invaders recalled it, "We began an offensive that was stopped dead."[175]

Major Filiberto Olivera Moya, who headed some of the troops that were pushing back the invaders, said, "We advanced on San Blas under the mortar fire. One company and then another passed us. We occupied Kilometer 14 and kept on going toward San Blas."[176]

South of the Covadonga Sugar Mill, on the road linking the town of San Blas with Yaguaramas, a strong offensive was prepared with eight tanks and a company in trucks, with the infantry behind them. That force, which was under the command of Captain Emilio Aragonés, was three kilometers from San Blas. The invaders weren't expecting to be attacked from that direction. The offensive was set for 9:00 a.m.

The first and only battle between the contending forces on the coastal road took place soon after that. Protected by a tank, a company belonging to the Brigade's Battalion 3 made contact with an advance guard of 20 of Pupo's men, who fired at the tank with a bazooka, hitting a tread. The company that was advancing behind the tank halted and withdrew after an exchange of shots.

As Orlando Pupo described it:

---

[174] Víctor Casaus, *Girón en la memoria*.
[175] Statement by Julio Mario Alonso Fernández, invader.
[176] Testimony of Major Filiberto Olivera Moya.

I was going to order them to shoot at it again with the bazooka. It would be an easy thing to do, because, since its infantry protection had been withdrawn, we could surround it. But no, the tank was there, immobilized, not giving any signs of life... My comrades ran along the left side, by the sea; climbed on top of the tank; opened the hatch; and, pointing inside with their guns, shouted, "Surrender! You haven't got a chance!" Nobody replied. No, it wasn't a tank with a phantom crew; it had an escape hatch in the floor, and the crew had fled through it without our noticing.[177]

The advance along the road from Larga Beach to Girón Beach was also begun at dawn of that day. Captain Fernández placed the light combat company of Battalion 116, which had reached Perdiz Point the night before, in the front echelon as part of the battalion from the Revolutionary National Police. That company would have the mission of scouting and making contact with the invading forces that were defending the western side of Girón Beach. It was divided into two groups, each headed by a police battalion officer who had been in the Rebel Army. One of those groups, headed by Captain Sandino, went along the left side of the road, close to the woods, and the other, headed by Captain Carbó, went along the right side, close to the sea.

Captain Fernández had positioned the field artillery and opened fire on Girón Beach, but the terrain — which didn't offer any possibilities for digging in and over which the men had to advance on karren or along the edge of the woods — meant that the advance would take a high toll in lives.

Major General Samuel Rodiles recalled that part of the fighting:

When we were in position on the left side of the road, Comrade Sandino began advancing on the other side. During the advance, some sad news reached us: in advancing along the right side, the militia, who didn't have very much experience in combat, didn't notice that they were level with a stone trench that the mercenaries held between the road and the sea. The mercenaries killed several of the militia there; they let them come close and then fired almost point-blank at them... Later, we saw how they had killed so many of our men on that curve: they had a tank and some artillery pieces there. They caused us heavy losses along that stretch of road around 500 or 600 meters long, because we couldn't dig any

177 Miguel Angel Sánchez, *Girón no fue sólo en abril*, 225. Testimony of Orlando Pupo.

trenches there; we didn't have anywhere to take refuge. In all, I think we had around 32 dead and 100 wounded.[178]

That situation lasted for several anguishing hours, but the light company of Battalion 116 and the vanguard of the police battalion neither retreated nor called off the offensive.

I halted the cars and tanks, and we advanced on foot. We found ourselves in the middle of a hail of bullets. We sought protection in the ditch. We advanced toward a tank that was close to us. We saw the fire that was crossing from the coast, with other fire crossing, too, but from the left side of the road, where the only thing we could see was the woods. Unquestionably, they had prepared a good defense. It went from the coast along the road to Girón Beach, which splits in two there, with one of the smaller roads bypassing Girón Beach and hooking up with the road to San Blas. The coastal road was the one that entered the town. Major Samuel was fighting there, by the sea.[179]

José San Román, head of the Brigade, had sent Erneido Oliva to take command of that area and reinforced him with Battalion 2 and another tank. That is why the squads headed by Captain Carbó, which had advanced close to the sea, had been subjected to deadly fire when they emerged at the place where the road divided. They were battered from both the center and the left flank. To increase their difficulties, only the vanguard group was able to return the enemy's fire, for the others were back around a curve.

When the invaders became aware that another force was advancing in the woods, they turned part of their flank in that direction. A tank took up position at the edge of the trees. At that moment, several T-34 tanks appeared, and fierce fighting broke out. On seeing the tanks, Captain Carbó ordered his men to fall in and advance behind them.

Facing heavy fire, they sought protection behind the tanks. As Major General Samuel Rodiles Plana recalled the fighting:

Carbó was a few meters behind me, giving orders to the comrades and exhorting them with great energy, walking from one side to the other, constantly risking his life. Some comrades who were

---

[178] Elio Carré, *Girón, una estocada a fondo*, 177. Testimony of Major General Samuel Rodiles.
[179] Testimony of Major General Efigenio Ameijeiras.

there told me that several times they warned him to be more careful, that he shouldn't get so worked up, both because he could be wounded and because he was the only captain there at the time. Sure enough, a few minutes later, while crossing the road from the side of the tank to a sea grape tree that was on a little hill, he was wounded in the left shoulder — but he went on exhorting the comrades and firing his FAL. He was very unlucky: after a few minutes of doing this, he was shot in the forehead and fell mortally wounded. Even then, he didn't let go of his FAL. He died facing the enemy and holding his FAL in his right hand. He was the most outstanding of our comrades, the most determined — just as he had been in the Sierra Maestra Mountains.[180]

A shell went through the heavy armor of the tank which the policemen and militia of Battalion 116 were using as protection. Three crew members got out with their overalls on fire. One of them, the driver, had brought the tank from Managua, a distance of close to 300 kilometers, driving it along the road. It hadn't been possible to find adequate means for transporting the tanks. When they got to the fighting area, another tank operator realized how tired his comrade was and offered to relieve him. "Since I've come this far, I'll go on to the fighting," he answered. Shortly afterwards, he died on the outskirts of Girón Beach.

The second T-34 to reach the curve was also hit. As one of the tank operators described it:

It felt as if a shell had exploded right inside our heads. I was thrown backwards and smashed against the compartment that divides the tank into two sections. A ball of red light kept going around in my head.[181]

Erneido Oliva had concentrated the fire of six bazookas on the curve, where the road that led to Girón Beach split off. He also placed three trucks with heavy machine guns there and ordered Julio Díaz, the man in charge of the mortar group, to direct fire on the shore road.

The mortar shell came by and hit a stone. The explosion was so great that it killed five comrades from the police who were next to

---

[180] Elio Carré, *Girón, una estocada a fondo*, 182. Testimony of Major General Samuel Rodiles Plana.
[181] Miguel Angel Sánchez, *Girón no fue sólo en abril*. Testimony of Roldán Anglada, tank operator.

me, shoulder to shoulder with me. I lay quiet, very quiet. I thought I'd been blown apart; I had the taste of gunpowder and blood in my mouth... Then I saw another comrade from the police with a huge wound in the back of his arm.[182]

Oliva adopted those measures because he knew that, if he didn't halt the revolutionary forces' advance, they would break through the front and reach the tourist center, the last position which the Brigade held. For that reason, too, he ordered the head of Company G of Battalion 2 to advance and push back the policemen and militia who were advancing close to the sea. One of the tanks advanced in support of the company.

Major General Rodiles described what happened next:

Lieutenant Sosa was the only comrade who had an antitank grenade. We were in the open. The tank came forward and took up a position around 30 meters from us, between the sea grape trees and a small hill. They didn't see us, but we certainly saw the upper part of the turret and the tank's antenna. Then Lieutenant Sosa was given the order.[183]

The explosion shook the ground without hitting the tank, but it scared the living daylights out of its crew members — who must have thought that other shots would follow. They turned the tank around and fled. In fact, the police didn't have any more grenades. Their greatest support came from the shells of the 122-mm guns and the self-propelled SAU-100s, which were pounding away at the Brigade's positions.

Lieutenant Roberto Milián had driven the jeep up to a few meters of the line of fire. The vehicle was hit many times, but, miraculously, we were uninjured. On seeing the vehicle, the enemy had tried to put it out of commission. Milián climbed a tree and, from there, watched the field artillery's fire, which he had been directing since dawn under Captain Fernández's orders. After each shot, he climbed down out of the tree and corrected the aim, using the jeep's radio.[184]

[182] Ibid. Testimony of Jorge Travieso.
[183] Ibid. Testimony of Major General Samuel Rodiles Plana.
[184] *Playa Girón: derrota del imperialismo*, Vol. 1, 224. Testimony of Orlando Pérez Díaz.

The decision to keep on advancing, taking advantage of the tank's withdrawal and that of Company G, was what turned the tide in favor of the revolutionary forces. As Major General Rodiles recalled:

Soon afterwards, we wrested another trench from the enemy. We found some dead militia there, some inside the stone trenches and others on the road close by the trenches.[185]

At midday, Captain Fernández received a communiqué from the command post at the Australia Sugar Mill:

Fernández:

Re: Am sending you a 120-mm mortar battery under the command of Lieutenant Eduardo Rodríguez, who is to place himself under your orders. Am sending you two copies of Staff communiqués.

They sent a company from Battalion 120 to Buena Ventura, where it's said they've captured two prisoners and there are around 30 more.

We took San Blas.

The other comrades will take Girón Beach if you don't hurry.

One of our helicopters is going to the Australia Sugar Mill and Yaguaramas, arriving soon.

Note: I don't have any ammunition for 122-mm howitzers, but I've asked for some.

San Blas had fallen at around 11:00 a.m. on April 19. The offensive begun along the Yaguaramas road just three kilometers from the sugar mill community had been impetuous. The forces from Yaguaramas were joined there by those that were advancing from the Covadonga Sugar Mill.

The third battalion of the Attack Brigade was falling back to Girón Beach, and Alejandro del Valle was setting up his defenses when something totally unexpected happened. A jeep with a Rebel Army major in it came to a stop in front of them. The major was calm.

As they were forming their position, the paratroopers were astonished to see a jeep driven by a captain in Castro's militia come racing straight into their lines. Sitting beside the captain was Major Félix Duque, one of the top enemy commanders. The major had

---

[185] Elio Carré, *Girón, una estocada a fondo*. Testimony of Major General Samuel Rodiles Plana.

been in charge of the troops at Yaguaramas, and in the mistaken belief that the forces coming from Covadonga already had taken San Blas and moved south, he took a short cut — straight into the lap of the Brigade... A Brigade soldier called out, "Let's hang these Communists." The captain was frightened but Major Duque spoke up boldly: "Men, you don't know what's coming toward you. I have 5,000 men and 14 tanks. You'd better surrender. You know you're going to lose this war."[186]

In fact, the vanguard of the forces Duque commanded were advancing from San Blas, led by Captain Víctor Dreke.

> Our vanguard had orders not to halt. When we reached a big curve in the road, I ordered the men to halt. I didn't see any strange movement, and gave the order to resume march. We had advanced around 20 steps when heavy fire was opened against us.[187]

Dreke was wounded and was taken back while the militia returned the fire. Two tanks advanced along the road, and a third, in a nearby pasture.

One of the tanks was put out of commission when hit by an explosive shell, and another was also hit during the confusion that took place inside it. The driver asked the gunner through his communications equipment to shoot, but the gunner didn't hear him. They had pushed the wrong buttons, and the driver's voice could be heard clearly outside the tank, as if he were speaking over a loudspeaker.

As one of the tank operators defending Cuba described it:

> The gunner couldn't hear him, but I heard him again, from my tank, when the driver addressed the gunner: "Just look, you bastard: they've hit me because you didn't fire..." In fact, back then, we had almost no experience in using tanks. We had received them just a short while before and were taking courses when the attack occurred.[188]

The columns of militia continued to advance on both flanks, in spite of the enemy's fire. From a ditch, a fighter threw a grenade that blew up

[186] Johnson, *The Bay of Pigs*, 158.
[187] Miguel Angel Sánchez, *Girón no fue sólo en abril*, 235. Testimony of Captain Víctor Dreke.
[188] Elio Carré, *Girón, una estocada a fondo*, 190. Testimony of Ramón Martínez, tank operator.

a nest of machine gunners on the other side, and, a few minutes later, one of the tanks that Battalion 3 had for defending that point blew up.

Step by step, the paratroopers, the members of the Third Battalion and the two Brigade tanks were beaten back... By 2:00 p.m., Castro's tanks had formed a solid line and were firing straight into the Brigade position.[189]

Roberto Pérez San Román, head of the heavy weapons battalion, who had replaced the head of Battalion 3 whom Alejandro del Valle had removed, recalled that battle years later: "They hit so many men we knew we had to leave. Some men had already left and we only had about 40 men left. So we decided to retreat."[190]

At around 5:00 p.m., the tanks and troops of militia and of the Rebel Army took possession of a small sugar mill community called Helechal, around six kilometers from Girón Beach. It was late afternoon. At midnight of that day, it would be 72 hours since Brigade 2506 had landed. The Cuban Government considered it a challenge to completely defeat the invaders before the 72 hours were up. And, just before it got dark, Commander Fidel Castro arrived at that point so close to Girón Beach.

After talking with the officers there and learning details about the troops' advance, Fidel climbed on a tank and addressed the troops. Captain Angel Fernández Vila recalled that he said:

The enemy is trying to escape and pretend to the world that we staged the attack. We mustn't let any of them escape. Forward! We mustn't stop until we get to the beach. If the first man falls, the second will get there; if the second man falls, the third will get there — to the beach, right now! The tanks shouldn't stop until their treads are wet, in the water at the shore, because every minute that those mercenaries are on our soil is an insult to our homeland.

A fighter from Column One in the Sierra Maestra recalled that moment as follows:

[Fidel] said that the first tank would go as fast as it could, shooting as it went, and then the second and the third, etc., would go after it, also shooting. If they disabled the first one, the second and the

---

189 Johnson, *The Bay of Pigs,* 159.
190 Ibid.

others would keep on advancing and shooting until they reached Girón Beach. And we, the infantry, would go in after the last tank, making a line of fire. He assigned a major to each tank — to set an example, I think — and he went to get in the third one. Then everybody jumped up, saying, "Not you, Fidel; you can't go!" "Of course I'm going; I'm the one in charge here!" "No, Fidel; not you!"

As Lieutenant Joel Pardo, who was in his tank and had been fighting since dawn, recalled it:

> While they were arguing, I said, "Well, Commander, I'm leaving." I did that to gain time, so that, if he decided to go, I would already have advanced a good distance, reached the beach or made contact with the enemy.

Maciques remembered the end of that argument between Fidel and the troops as follows:

> Fidel's answer impressed all of us. Fidel told us energetically that he was the head of the Revolution and that, as head of the Revolution, he had the right — the *right* — to fight and to go to Girón Beach, just like the rest of the comrades... Everybody shut up; they just shut up.

And Fidel left in the tank.

He didn't know that, two hours earlier, José Pérez San Román, the head of the Brigade, had destroyed the radio and, together with 40 other invaders, was heading east through the woods near the coast, toward the troops of Battalions 326 and 329, under the command of Captain Orlando Pupo and Major Raúl Menéndez Tomassevich, who had reinforced that front in the preceding hours to keep the invaders from getting away.

To the west, the policemen and militia burst onto Girón Beach after a Revolutionary Air Force attack in which two B-26s, two Sea Furies and two T-33s participated. It was the culmination of three days of nonstop missions, in which nine B-26s had been shot down and two ships and three landing craft had been sunk. The planes had also provided air cover for the revolutionary troops on the march.

Major General Efigenio Ameijeiras described the scene:

> At 5:30 p.m., we all entered Girón Beach. At the second curve, in the ditch behind a small hill of sand, we could see a tank that had

been destroyed and the body of a dead mercenary lying on top of it. Farther ahead, there was another tank that had been destroyed, and, still farther on, a commando truck which had a platform with a .50-caliber machine gun that had been put out of commission. Somebody's leg lay in the ditch. The rest of him might be still alive nearby. It was impossible to see all of the weapons that had been left behind on different parts of the beach and in the town, especially cannon, mortars and bazookas. There were three tanks and several trucks with .50-caliber machine guns mounted on them. The faces of the people who entered Girón Beach — policemen, civilians, militia and members of the Rebel Army — all expressed overwhelming, tremendous joy.[191]

Captain Fernández also entered Girón Beach, on top of an armored car. Far out to sea, the silhouettes of two U.S. destroyers were fast disappearing. Two hours earlier, they had come within range of Captain Fernández's guns.

"Let's shoot at the ships, Captain," the militia suggested. I called the chiefs and everybody else together right there, under a tree. "Don't shoot at the ships; shoot at the boats."[192] And that's what they did… According to some testimony I read, the captain of one of the destroyers recalled that a shell went by just overhead, and another fell short. In artillery terms, that's called "forking." If you fire one long shot and then a short one, the next one hits the center of the ship. The captain said that the first lieutenant of the destroyer asked him to shoot at the land. He refused and ordered the ship to withdraw. It is true that the ships fled as fast as they could. That's how the incident of the ships ended. It was wise, because nobody knows how the situation would have evolved if we had fired a couple of cannon shots at the ships and they had responded.[193]

The militia, policemen and Rebel Army soldiers began to search the tourist cabañas and took around 20 prisoners, some of them wounded, who were immediately sent to the medical posts. Soon, they found the group of literacy teachers, who told them what had happened to them.

Later on, Ana María Hernández described that day as follows:

---

[191] *Bohemia*, July 1989. Testimony of Major General Efigenio Ameijeiras.
[192] The reference is to the boats in which the mercenaries were fleeing. Author's note.
[193] Testimony of José Ramón Fernández.

At dawn on Wednesday, April 19, it seemed that the world was coming to an end. At around 10:00 a.m., we were taken out of the cabaña and told to go to the breakwater. Two mercenaries stood guard over us. In the afternoon, we saw we were between two lines of fire, and then came the bombardment by our planes. We hid in the water, in a hole in the rocks, and at around 5:00 p.m. the two mercenaries told us they were going to see what was going on. They dropped their weapons and took off running. There was a great silence. We left, too. We saw Mariano Mustelier, and he told us they had left. Then we took a white sheet out of a cabaña and went in front of the club. One of my eyes was very inflamed, and it was hard for me to see. Then some policemen came, and we told them who we were, but they asked for identification. Patria Silva burst out crying. "How can you ask us for identification?" I asked the policemen. The policemen took us with them. They carried me, because I felt very bad. Valerio, the 14-year-old literacy teacher, had a fit and started shouting that the planes were coming. He was very sick. And Patria was crying because the policemen had confused us with the others. She hadn't cried at all during the three days we were held prisoner.[194]

Close to 1,200 of the defeated invaders hid in the woods and tried to get away. They went to the farmers' houses and took their clothes, trying to get through the encirclement. As Bernarda Hernández Rodríguez, a charcoal maker's daughter, recalled:

When we went back after the battle, the house was riddled with machine-gun bullets. We found pistols under the mattresses, and the wardrobe was nearly empty; they had taken our clothes.[195]

The people who lived in the swamp helped the Cuban military forces to round up the mercenaries. The invaders who were captured and put on trial were finally exchanged for baby food and medicine, which was desperately needed because of the U.S. blockade of Cuba.

---

[194] Testimony of Ana María Hernández Bravo.
[195] Testimony of Barnarda Hernández Rodríguez, daughter of a charcoal maker.

Interview sources

Alejo ("the Moor"), charcoal maker
Julio Mario Alonso Fernández, invader
Manuel Alvariño, charcoal maker
Xiomara Alvariño, daughter of a charcoal maker
Efigenio Ameijeiras, head of the Revolutionary National Police, now a
     division general
Mercedes Arce
Héctor Argilés, militia, Matanzas School of Militia Leaders
Carlos Arocha, a major general at the time of his death
Galo Astor García, invader
Octavio Barroso Gómez
Israel Behar, Ministry of the Interior, now a lieutenant colonel (R.)
Diocles Bello Rosabal
Juan José Bermúdez, former agent for Department of State Security
Alberto Julio Bolet Suárez, invader
Víctor Caballero, charcoal maker
Luis Clemente Carralero ("Oriente"), militia, Battalion 339
Carmen Cavadilla, resident of Jagüey Grande
Demetrio Clavelo Solís, insurgent
Lieutenant Víctor Cortés, Rebel Army
René de los Santos, Rebel Army
María Días Ojeda, Ministry of the Interior, now a colonel
José Luis Domínguez, Ministry of the Interior, now a colonel
Fabián Escalante Font, Ministry of the Interior, now a division general
José Ramón Fernández, head of the Militia School, now President of the
     Cuban Olympic Committee
Enrique Fernández Ruiz de la Torre ("Kiki")
Harold Ferrer, Rebel Army, now a brigadier general
Pedro Flores, charcoal maker
Héctor Gallo, Ministry of the Interior, now a major (R.)
Oscar Gámez, Ministry of the Interior, now a colonel
Irán Gómez Rodríguez, invader
Caridad González, resident of Jagüey Grande
Reynold González, National Coordinator of the People's Revolutionary
     Movement (MRP)
José Ramón González Suco, militia, Battalion 339
Ramón Grau Alsina, nephew of former Cuban President Ramón Grau San
     Martín

Juan Manuel Guillot Castellanos, National Military Coordinator of the Movement of Revolutionary Recovery (MRR)

Emérito Hernández, militia

Oscar Hernández, charcoal maker

Ana María Hernández Bravo, head of the literacy teachers at Girón Beach

Barnarda Hernández Rodríguez, daughter of a charcoal maker

Carlos Hernández Vega, invader

Elio Jorge, farmer

Rosalín Labrada Oliva ("Chavela"), former agent of Department of State Security

Captain Antonio Llibre Artigas, Rebel Army, now retired

Abraham Maciques, director of the Zapata Peninsula development plan, now Director of the International Conference Center, Havana, Cuba

Nora Martín, resident of Jagüey Grande

Bambi Martínez Díaz, resident of Jagüey Grande

Captain Luis Más Martín, Rebel Army

Manuel Menéndez Pou, invader

Federico Mora, Ministry of the Interior, now a colonel (R.)

Mario Morales, Ministry of the Interior, now a lieutenant colonel (R.)

Julián Oliva, insurgent

Filiberto Olivera Moya, Revolutionary Armed Forces, now a division general

Pablo Organvidez Parada, FBI agent and invader

Miguel Angel Orozco Crespo, member of an infiltration team

Amparo Ortiz, daughter of a charcoal maker

Reineirio Perdomo, former agent of Department of State Security

Benigno Pérez Vivanco, member of an infiltration team

José Reboso Febles, insurgent

Manuel H. Reyes García, member of an infiltration team

Gonzalo Rodríguez Mantilla ("Chelé"), worker at the Covadonga Sugar Mill

Nemecia Rodríguez Montalvo, daughter of a charcoal maker

Roberto Rodríguez Rodríguez, Revolutionary Armed Forces, now a lieutenant colonel (R.)

Dámaso Rodríguez Valdés, general secretary of the labor union at the Australia Sugar Mill

Julio Somoza, resident of Jagüey Grande

José Ramón Suco, militia, Battalion 339

Lieutenant Addis Torres, Rebel Army

Humberto Valdés, militia

José Raúl Varona González, head of G-2 in Brigade 2506

José Veiga Peña, Ministry of the Interior, now a lieutenant colonel (R.)

Angel Villafuerte Ayala, militia, Battalion 339

Mario Zúñiga, invader

THE SECRET WAR
CIA covert operations against Cuba, 1959-62
By Fabián Escalante
The secret war that the CIA lost. For the first time, the former head of Cuban State Security speaks out about the confrontation with U.S. spy agencies and details the CIA's operations in 1959-62, the largest-scale covert operation ever launched against another nation.
ISBN 1-875284-86-9

CIA TARGETS FIDEL
The secret assassination report
Only recently declassified and published for the first time, this secret report was prepared for the CIA on its own plots to assassinate Cuba's Fidel Castro. Included is an exclusive commentary by Division General Fabián Escalante, the former head of Cuba's counterintelligence body.
ISBN 1-875284-90-7

ZR RIFLE
The plot to kill Kennedy and Castro
By Claudia Furiati
Thirty years after the death of President Kennedy, Cuba has opened its secret files on the assassination, showing how and why the CIA, along with anti-Castro exiles and the Mafia, planned the conspiracy.
"Adds new pieces to the puzzle and gives us a clearer picture of what really happened." — Oliver Stone
ISBN 1-875284-85-0

IN THE EYE OF THE STORM
Castro, Khrushchev, Kennedy and the Missile Crisis
By Carlos Lechuga
For the first time, Cuba's view of the most serious crisis of the Cold War is told by one of the leading participants.
ISBN 1-875284-87-7

GUANTANAMO
Bay of Discord: The story of the U.S. military base in Cuba
By Roger Ricardo
This book provides a detailed history of the U.S. base on Cuban soil that has remained from the beginning of the century to the present day. It documents how the base has been used for continued violations of Cuban territory and why it remains a sticking point in U.S.–Cuba relations.
ISBN 1-875284-56-7

40 years of the Cuban Revolution
A new series from Ocean Press

FIDEL CASTRO READER
Edited by Mirta Muñiz and Pedro Alvarez Tabío
The voice of one of the 20th century's most controversial political figures — as well as one of the world's greatest orators — is captured in this new selection of Castro's key speeches over the past four decades.
ISBN 1-876175-11-7

PSYWAR ON CUBA
The Declassified History of U.S. Anti-Castro Propaganda
Edited by Jon Elliston
Newly declassified CIA and U.S. Government documents are reproduced here, with extensive commentary providing the history of Washington's 40-year campaign of psychological warfare and propaganda to destabilize Cuba and undermine its revolution.
ISBN 1-876175-09-5

CUBAN REVOLUTION READER
A Documentary History
Edited by Julio García Luis
An outstanding anthology documenting the past four decades of Cuban history. This Reader presents a comprehensive overview of the key moments in the Cuban Revolution, with most materials published in English for the first time. An unprecedented documentary history of the Cuban Revolution in the years 1959-98.
ISBN 1-876175-10-9

JOSE MARTI READER
Writings on the Americas
Edited by Deborah Shnookal and Mirta Muñiz
This Reader presents an outstanding new anthology of the writings, letters and poetry of José Martí—one of the most brilliant and impassioned Latin American intellectuals of the 19th century.
ISBN 1-875284-12-5

CUBA AND THE UNITED STATES
A Chronological History
By Jane Franklin
Based on exceptionally wide research, this updated and expanded chronology relates day by day, year by year, the developments involving the two neighboring countries from the 1959 Cuban revolution through 1995.
ISBN 1-875284-92-3

Che Guevara titles from Ocean Press

CHE GUEVARA READER
Writings on Guerrilla Strategy, Politics and Revolution
Edited by David Deutschmann
Three decades after the death of the legendary Latin American figure, this book presents the most comprehensive selection of Guevara's writings ever to be published in English.
ISBN 1-875284-93-1

CHE IN AFRICA
Che Guevara's Congo diary
By William Gálvez
Che Guevara disappeared from Cuba in 1965 to lead a guerrilla mission to Africa in support of liberation movements. Considerable speculation has always surrounded Guevara's departure from Cuba and why he went to fight in Africa. *Che in Africa* is the previously untold story of Che Guevara's "lost year" in Africa.
ISBN 1-876175-08-7

CHE GUEVARA AND THE FBI
U.S. political police dossier on the Latin American revolutionary
Edited by Michael Ratner and Michael Steven Smith
Thirty years after the death of Che Guevara, a Freedom of Information case has succeeded in obtaining the FBI and CIA files on Che Guevara.
ISBN 1-875284-76-1

CHE — A MEMOIR BY FIDEL CASTRO
Preface by Jesús Montané
Edited by David Deutschmann
For the first time Fidel Castro writes with candor and affection of his relationship with Ernesto Che Guevara, documenting his extraordinary bond with Cuba from the revolution's early days to the final guerrilla expeditions to Africa and Bolivia.
ISBN 1-875284-15-X

Ocean Press, GPO Box 3279, Melbourne 3001, Australia
● Fax: 61-3-9372 1765 ● E-mail: ocean_press@msn.com.au

Ocean Press, PO Box 834, Hoboken, NJ 07030, USA
● Fax: 1-201-617 0203